"I'm thrilled that the historical and importa ~~Harry Burleigh is finally being told! That h~~ a member and celebrated soloist at the very church I attend here in New York City makes it all the more extraordinary. Hats off to Craig von Buseck for his tremendous research and work!"

—**Eric Metaxas**, *New York Times* bestselling author of *Bonhoeffer: Pastor, Martyr, Prophet, Spy* and *Amazing Grace: William Wilberforce and the Heroic Campaign to End Slavery*

"Mr. von Buseck's book, *Nobody Knows*, reads like a good novel, and yet he balances this colorful historical narrative with reliable scholarship. His subject of choice is the great African American legend, singer and songsmith Harry T. Burleigh. Mr. Von Buseck's language is warm and accessible. I love being taken by surprise, particularly when being introduced with such clarity to a historical figure of my own country, a pioneering spirit, one of those rare musical types that gave the soul of this nation its voice. *Nobody Knows* is delightfully readable."

—**David Teems**, author of *Majestie: The King Behind the King James Bible* and *Tyndale: The Man Who Gave God an English Voice*

"This is an important book for people interested in American music, the Episcopal Church, and African American cultural life. Harry Burleigh was a star—he brought light to a vast number of people—his art was shared in Jewish and Christian communities, in New York City, Martha's Vineyard, and so many places. He was a man of deep feeling and ability who shared his gifts in all directions."

—**Rev. Tom Pike**, former rector of St. George's Episcopal Church in New York City

"We welcome Craig von Buseck's new book on Harry T. Burleigh, the great African American musician. *Nobody Knows* adds a rich chapter to the record of great American composers and musicians."

—**Vinson Synan**, Dean Emeritus, Regent University School of Divinity; author of *The Century of the Holy Spirit*

"*Nobody Knows* is an important tribute to a master of the American spiritual. An inspirational story, this work is an important read, as it sheds light on a key composer whose contributions to the history of American music are otherwise neglected."

—**Afa S. Dworkin**, executive director of the Sphinx Organization; member of President Obama's National Arts Policy Committee

Nobody Knows

The Forgotten Story of One of the Most
Influential Figures in American Music

Craig von Buseck

BakerBooks

a division of Baker Publishing Group
Grand Rapids, Michigan

© 2014 by Craig von Buseck

Published by Baker Books
a division of Baker Publishing Group
P.O. Box 6287, Grand Rapids, MI 49516-6287
www.bakerbooks.com

Paperback edition published 2014
ISBN 978-0-8010-1691-2

Printed in the United States of America

Library of Congress Cataloging-in-Publication Data
Von Buseck, Craig.
    Nobody knows : the forgotten story of one of the most influential figures in
  American music / Craig von Buseck.
       pages cm
    Includes bibliographical references.
    ISBN 978-0-8010-1609-7 (cloth)
    1. Burleigh, H. T. (Harry Thacker), 1866–1949. I. Title.
  ML410.B97V66 2013
  780.92—dc23
  [B]   2013030021

Scripture used in this book, whether quoted or paraphrased by the characters, is taken from the King James Version of the Bible.

14   15   16   17   18   19   20   7   6   5   4   3   2   1

I dedicate this book to my children, Aaron, Margo, and especially David, who asked at the age of six, "Daddy, how long is Harry T. Burleigh going to live with us?" Harry's finally moving out, guys, but I know he will always be in our hearts. Thank you for your never-ending love and encouragement. With much love.

Contents

Harry T. Burleigh

Family Tree

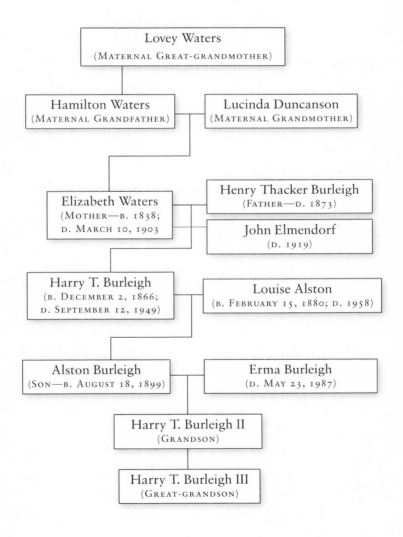

Lovey Waters
(MATERNAL GREAT-GRANDMOTHER)

Hamilton Waters
(MATERNAL GRANDFATHER)

Lucinda Duncanson
(MATERNAL GRANDMOTHER)

Elizabeth Waters
(MOTHER—B. 1838;
D. MARCH 10, 1903)

Henry Thacker Burleigh
(FATHER—D. 1873)

John Elmendorf
(D. 1919)

Harry T. Burleigh
(B. DECEMBER 2, 1866;
D. SEPTEMBER 12, 1949)

Louise Alston
(B. FEBRUARY 15, 1880; D. 1958)

Alston Burleigh
(SON—B. AUGUST 18, 1899)

Erma Burleigh
(D. MAY 23, 1987)

Harry T. Burleigh II
(GRANDSON)

Harry T. Burleigh III
(GREAT-GRANDSON)

Harry T. Burleigh Timeline

1832 (March 5) The final manumission is entered into the Somerset County, Maryland, deed book, titled "Bill of Sale," for the purchase of Hamilton Waters and his mother, Lovey.

1835 (April 13) Hamilton Waters secures a "Certificate of Freedom," allowing him and his mother to travel without fear of slave catchers.

1835–1838 Hamilton Waters marries Lucinda Duncanson (exact date unknown).

1838 Elizabeth Waters is born near Lansing, Michigan.

1838–1841 Hamilton, Lucinda, Lovey, and Elizabeth move to Erie, Pennsylvania (exact date unknown). Lovey dies in Erie (exact date unknown).

1841 Louise Waters is born in Erie, Pennsylvania.

1855 (July 11) Elizabeth Waters graduates with a bachelor's degree from Avery College in Pittsburgh.

1864 Elizabeth Waters marries Henry Thacker Burleigh.

1864 (November 14) Reginald Burleigh is born.

1866 (May) The National Conservatory of Music is founded in New York City.

1866   (December 2) Harry T. Burleigh is born in Erie, Pennsylvania.

1867   Lucinda Duncanson Waters, Burleigh's grandmother, dies.

1869   (May 24) Harry T. Burleigh and his brother Reginald are baptized at St. Paul's Episcopal Church in Erie, Pennsylvania.

1873   (February 27) Henry Burleigh dies of a heart attack while in Chicago.

1875   (April) Elizabeth Waters Burleigh marries John Elmendorf.

1877   (February 6) Hamilton Waters dies.

1891   Harry T. Burleigh wins a scholarship to cover tuition at the National Conservatory of Music in New York City.

1891   (Fall) Harry T. Burleigh begins classes as a student at the National Conservatory of Music in New York City.

1892   (Fall) Antonin Dvorak becomes director of the National Conservatory of Music in New York City.

1893   (December 16) Antonin Dvorak's Symphony no. 9 in E Minor, "From the New World," is completed and premiered in New York City.

1894   Harry T. Burleigh is chosen by J. P. Morgan, Rector William Rainsford, and choirmaster William Chester to be the baritone soloist at the prestigious St. George's Episcopal Church in New York City.

1895   (April 27) Antonin Dvorak resigns from the National Conservatory and returns to Prague.

1896   Burleigh graduates from the National Conservatory of Music.

1898   Harry T. Burleigh marries Louise Alston.

1898   G. Schirmer publishes Burleigh's first songs, "If You Knew," "Life," and "A Birthday Song."

1899   (August 18) Harry and Louise Burleigh welcome a son, Alston Waters Burleigh.

1900   Harry T. Burleigh begins a twenty-five-year career as soloist at Temple Emanu-El in New York City.

1901 Burleigh publishes his earliest arrangements of spirituals for solo voice and piano in *Plantation Melodies, Old and New*.

1903 Harry has his first commercial success as a songwriter with the publication of his song "Jean."

1903 Harry T. Burleigh begins to tour with Booker T. Washington to raise funds for the Tuskegee Institute.

1903 (March 10) Elizabeth Elmendorf dies.

1908 (July 3) Harry T. Burleigh sings before King Edward of England.

1911 Burleigh is hired as an editor at Ricordi and Company music publishers.

1913 (March 31) Burleigh's friend and supporter J. P. Morgan dies. Harry sings at the funeral.

1914 (February) Burleigh is one of 170 composers who become charter members of the American Society of Composers, Authors, and Publishers (ASCAP).

1915 Louise Alston Burleigh leaves Harry to pursue her career.

1915 Harry's original song "The Young Warrior" becomes the marching song for the Italian Army in World War I.

1916 Burleigh publishes his first solo arrangement of "Deep River," which becomes known as his masterpiece.

1917 (May 17) The National Association for the Advancement of Colored People (NAACP) gives Burleigh the Spingarn Award, acknowledging him for bringing spirituals to the attention of distinguished audiences nationwide and in Europe.

1917 Atlanta University confers an honorary Master of Arts degree upon Harry T. Burleigh.

1917 Burleigh publishes his popular "Little Mother of Mine."

1919 John Elmendorf dies.

1919 Harry T. Burleigh records "Go Down, Moses."

1920 (June 11) Howard University confers an honorary Doctor of Music degree upon Harry T. Burleigh.

1934 (May 10) Burleigh is the featured speaker at the Juilliard Student Club program titled, "The Negro in Music."

1940 Harry T. Burleigh's final spiritual, "In Christ There Is No East or West," is published.

1944 (February 4) St. George's Episcopal Church honors Harry T. Burleigh for fifty years of service as baritone soloist.

1946 Harry T. Burleigh retires from St. George's Episcopal Church after serving as baritone soloist for fifty-two years.

1949 (September 12) Harry T. Burleigh dies in Stamford, Connecticut.

1

The Gospel Train

The Lakeshore Limited was only partially filled with passengers as the short, handsome black man climbed aboard and shuffled down the aisle, searching for a seat next to a north-facing window so that he could watch his beloved Lake Erie as the train skirted the hills of northern Pennsylvania. As Harry Thacker Burleigh stowed his one small suitcase above the seat, the large metal beast shuddered and lurched forward from the wooden railway station, steam belching from the engine and wheels screeching as iron scraped against iron. The locomotive slowly picked up speed as block after block of Harry's childhood home of Erie, Pennsylvania, passed by his window. Once beyond the city, the train began weaving its way through the thick foliage that grew around the tracks, forming walls of green like a long, leafy tunnel. As the train picked up speed, Harry's heart began to race. After nearly a decade of paying his dues at weddings, funerals, church services, and even saloons and steamboats, he was finally on his way to New York City for his chance to become a professional musician.

The train emerged from the woods onto an open hillside overlooking the Great Lake as the late summer sun reflected off the surface of the water like a magnificent chandelier. Harry squinted and smiled as the golden rays bathed his face. The great freshwater sea had been a source of play, inspiration, and even provision for him. Now it faded into the distance as the train turned and made its way eastward through mile after mile of Concord grape vineyards and crossed the border into New York State.

It was only a month earlier that Harry's mother, Elizabeth, had stopped for a break from her job as a servant at the prestigious Russell mansion in Erie to browse through one of her employer's music magazines. Mrs. Russell, a leading socialite in Erie, was the wife of a wealthy industrialist and a passionate lover of music. She often invited the great musicians who traveled on the railroad from New York to Chicago to stop and entertain leading citizens in her home. Mrs. Russell was a loyal patron of the arts and subscribed to many of the leading music journals of the day, which she would pass on to friends and employees after she had finished reading them from cover to cover. Toward the back of one of these magazines, Elizabeth came across an advertisement that caught her attention:

> The National Conservatory of Music in New York City, offering scholarships to prospective students, is interested primarily in young Negroes and Native Americans.

"Oh, my Jesus," she said out loud. "This is for Harry." Elizabeth excused herself and made a beeline to the Koehler Piano Company, where her son worked as a clerk.

After years of unsuccessfully pursuing the music profession—and now at twenty-six years of age—Harry had surrendered to the reality of making a living outside of the music world. He had impeccable handwriting, so he had settled instead for the stenography profession. *At least I can be near music by working at a piano store*, he had decided when he answered the employment advertisement for Koehler Piano Company.

On that fateful day, Harry was alarmed when he saw his mother burst through the large glass doors of the piano showroom. Elizabeth had never visited him at work before. He rushed to meet her. "What is it, Mama? Is everything all right?"

"Yes, of course, dear," she smiled at the startled salesmen and customers, then pulled her son to the corner of the store near the display window. In a low voice, just above a whisper, Elizabeth handed him the magazine and said excitedly, "I just saw this advertisement and I knew you would want to see it."

The two sat down on a piano bench as Harry read the notice. When he finished he looked up at his mother and said excitedly, "Mama, this could be it."

"I know, sweetheart, I know," Elizabeth responded with glee.

"But how can I afford a trip to New York? I don't have much money saved. I would need a new suit, and luggage, and a train ticket."

"I don't know how, honey, but I know my God. And if this is what he wants for you, he will make a way." The two embraced with glistening eyes. Elizabeth kissed her son on the cheek and then slipped out the door to return to the Russell mansion. Harry stood and slowly walked to his small oak stenographer's desk at the back of the store. He barely accomplished any work the rest of the day as his mind raced at the thought of this new and glorious opportunity.

When the people of Erie who had heard Harry sing learned of the possible scholarship, donations began pouring in. A leading businessman, Isador Sobel, gave Harry a sizable gift from his personal account and encouraged others to donate as well. He had become acquainted with Harry through hearing the young man sing in the Jewish Temple choir. Sobel was not only moved by Burleigh's voice, but he was also amazed that a black Christian man would work so hard to be a part of a Jewish choir. Money flowed in from other friends and admirers, and soon Harry had enough for the trip.

When the day of his departure arrived, Elizabeth and her husband, Harry's stepfather John Elmendorf, accompanied the young singer to the clapboard railroad station. As John grabbed the small suitcase from the buggy, Harry and his mother walked arm in arm to the platform. Burleigh wore his best black suit, complete with vest and tie. It was faded and slightly tattered, but in good enough condition for the journey. As they approached the train, Harry stopped and looked into his mother's eyes. She was his inspiration, and the most graceful, kind, and talented woman he had ever known. Though prejudice had hindered her from realizing her dream of teaching the foreign languages she loved, Elizabeth believed her toil and expectations would be fulfilled through her children.

Elizabeth handed Harry a letter of recommendation written by Mrs. Russell. Before taking the job at the piano company, Harry had worked for years for Mrs. Russell, alongside his mother, learning everything he could from the traveling musicians.

"Mrs. Russell told me that you are to give this to Mrs. MacDowell," she instructed, referring to the registrar of the conservatory and the mother of one of America's great composers, Edward MacDowell. "You remember Frances MacDowell, don't you?"

"It's been several years, but I believe I'll be able to recognize her." He took the letter and placed it inside his suitcase.

The short, aging woman placed her hands on her son's face and looked tenderly into his eyes. "You must know how proud your father and I are of you."

"Yes, Mama, I do."

"God has a purpose for your life, Harry. Don't you ever forget that fact. No matter what happens in this audition, no matter how successful you become, always remember that, and give the glory to God."

"I love you, Mama." Harry pulled her into his arms, and they held each other for a long moment.

"I love you too, baby," she whispered in his ear. "Send me a telegram as soon as you have news," she added, wiping away tears with her handkerchief.

Harry kissed his mother on the cheek and then hugged his stepfather, the only father he had ever known. Then he turned, picked up his suitcase, and bounded onto the train. All the years of musical training; singing at weddings, funerals, parties, and in countless choirs; and the innumerable hours of vocal and piano practice were about to be put to the test.

As the cool breeze off the lake blew through the open windows of the train, Harry closed his eyes and drank it all in. His chance to actually become somebody in the musical world had finally arrived. He had paid his dues, and then some. Now the opportunity he had longed for was at hand. The rhythmic cadence of the train lulled him nearly to sleep. His mind traveled back to the time when his love for music was birthed, back to a simpler era when he would sing the plantation songs as he lit the streetlamps with his beloved grandfather, Hamilton Waters.

1875–Erie, Pennsylvania

Growing up on the hills overlooking the bayfront in Erie, young Harry had always found the sights, sounds, and smells of the piers inviting. He and his older brother, Reginald, often went down to the docks to watch cargo being loaded and unloaded from the wooden ships. The familiar smell of fresh-caught perch, walleye, northern pike, and salmon often caused their bellies to rumble in anticipation of dinner.

But what young Harry loved most about the docks were the songs the sailors and fishermen sang as they plied their trade. Some of these men were former slaves who had worked on plantations in the South. To pass the time and keep the pace of the work moving, slaves had developed an endless repertoire of songs they sang almost unconsciously. When they were freed, these former slaves carried their music with them—it was a part of who they were—and it had become a part of young Harry T. Burleigh too. For years Harry loved to wander down the hillside to the bayfront piers to hear these plantation songs as they echoed off the water.

Another favorite pastime was to visit the livery, the modestly successful business that helped his stepfather build a house and fill it with children. Harry learned a whole different set of plantation songs from the stable hands as he helped clean out the stalls or brush down the horses. But these were songs that he could never sing at home. If his stepdaddy or mama ever heard him singing those songs, his hide would be tanned with a switch and he'd be burping bubbles for a week from the soap used to wash out his mouth.

These were joyous times for the boy. Though money was often tight, the love given him and his siblings by their parents overshadowed any sense of need. If there was a lack of money, none of the children ever knew it.

In an effort to help provide for the family, Harry's grandfather, Hamilton Waters, insisted on working as a lamplighter even though he was almost completely blind. Hamilton, who grew up as a slave on Maryland's eastern shore, had been beaten severely when an overseer caught him trying to learn to read. The whipping damaged his eyes, and as he aged his sight deteriorated even further. Elizabeth sent Reginald and Harry to help their grandfather on alternate days.

Hamilton always started his rounds at the corner of First and State Streets at the top of the hill overlooking Erie's harbor, Presque Isle Bay. He lit the lamps nearest the water while the sun was still shining to avoid the bitterly cold wind that whipped off the bay after dark. He liked to face north to feel the wind and smell the fishy odor of the day's catch. To him the cold air coming across Lake Erie from Canada and the sounds and smells of the fisheries meant freedom. In the summer months, when the air became heavy with humidity and the blazing sun scorched the grass, he was reminded of an earlier time on another shore. He looked forward to the cool wind at dusk as he prepared to light the lamps. It reminded him that all was well—he was home.

Some folks complained about the snow and the long, cold winters in Erie. But to Hamilton Waters these were keepsakes of liberty.

<hr/>

"Tell me what you see," Hamilton asked young Harry as they got under way one special December evening.

Looking out over the bay, the boy described life on America's northern shore. "The men are bringing the fish off the boats and dumping them in the vats on the docks. There are boats as far as the eye can see. Their masts are poking up into the sky like a forest without any leaves. The sun is flickering on the choppy water." Harry squinted to see beyond the glare on the water. "The trees on the other side of the bay are swaying in the wind." He brought his gaze back to the docks on the near shore. "Snow is piled up along the side of the docks where the fishermen shoveled it off earlier. They're loading cut wood and coal onto the big ship." Harry turned, looked up at his grandfather and asked, "Where are they gonna take it, Grandpa?"

"Dey takes de coal and lumber from our woods to places all around de lake—to Detroit or Buffalo, maybe. Der won't be many more trips dis year. De lake's 'bout to freeze over."

Hamilton Waters, who recognized the voice of nearly everyone in Erie, lifted his cap to greet his neighbors as they passed by. "Why, good evening, Mr. Patterson. How do ya' do, Mrs. Carson. Good day, Mr. Vosburgh."

When Harry was sure they would not be interrupted, he began to ask Hamilton his usual list of questions. "Grandpa, can you tell me about the slave times?" Harry loved to hear stories of the South, and more than anything he looked forward to singing the plantation songs that his grandaddy taught him as they lit the lamps.

"You knows 'bout how I was a slave, but I done bought my freedom, and my mama's too," Hamilton answered his grandson. "De overseers was cruel, and dey'd whup ya' for talkin' or even for tryin' to take a rest. De only ting dat kept up my spirit was de plantation songs."

"Tell me about the songs. Where did they come from?"

"Well, son, you's mighty full of questions dis evening," Hamilton replied, shuffling through the snow as the boy led him on. When they arrived at the next lamp, he set down his small wooden ladder and climbed up to do his work. He pulled out a rag and wiped the soot off the glass panes. As he worked he hummed a melody that was familiar to young Harry. The old man began to sing:

> Oh freedom. Oh freedom.
> Oh freedom over me.
> And before I be a slave, I'll be buried in my grave.
> And go home to my Lawd, and be free.

Harry held on to the ladder, steadying his grandfather. The old man turned the key to start the gas and then held his thin torch up to light the lamp. Hamilton then closed the little glass door and climbed down off the ladder. They set out through the blowing snow toward the next lamp, and once again the boy asked, "Grandpa, I thought you were going to tell me about the plantation songs. What is that one about?"

Hamilton laughed, leaned his ladder against a lamppost, and sat down on a wooden bench to take a rest. Harry snuggled up next to him to keep warm. "OK, OK, I'll tell ya'. For more den two hundred years, our people sang de slave songs to comfort demselves in de troubled time. We'd sing de songs in de fields to help us keep workin'. At night, mamas and papas would sing 'em to der younguns to help 'em get to sleep.

"Der was different kinds of slave songs too. Songs like 'Deep River' or 'Balm in Gilead' told us dat God delivered Moses and Daniel and such—someday he'd deliver us too, if we kept on praisin' him." The boy listened intently as he imagined the slaves singing the spirituals to give them hope and courage to press on.

Hamilton continued, "Other songs was 'bout breakin' free." He sang a tune to the boy.

> When de sun comes back and de first quail calls,
> Follow de drinkin' gourd.
> For de old man is a-waitin' to carry you to freedom,
> If you follow de drinkin' gourd.

Harry giggled at what sounded to him like a silly song. "You tink dat's funny?" Hamilton asked as he tickled the lad. Harry squirmed like a snake, trying unsuccessfully to get away from his grandfather's grasp. When the horseplay finally subsided, Hamilton went on with the story. "Did you ever play wid a treasure map, Harry?"

The boy grew excited. "Ooh, yes, I love treasure maps!"

"Well dat song is a treasure map." Harry's face contorted in a puzzled expression. Hamilton continued. "Dat song is a map to the Underground Railroad." He stood up, lifted his ladder onto his shoulder, and walked to the next lamppost as Harry followed behind. The old man put the ladder against the pole and stepped up to light the lamp.

"What's the Underground Railroad?" Harry questioned.

His granddaddy kept talking as he went through his routine, the steam of his breath billowing around his dim eyes. "De story comes from de slave times. Der was folks like me who worked fo' de massa. More den anything, we wanted to be free. And der was brave people who'd help de slaves to run away. Der would be people hidin' in de woods who would help 'em go north. Dey'd meet up wid other slaves and work der way to freedom. Dey called dis de Underground Railroad."

"Did you walk through tunnels?" the wide-eyed lad asked.

Hamilton smiled at his freeborn grandson. "No, boy, dat's just what dey called it. Yo' daddy and mama used to work on de Railroad, and so did I."

"Really," Harry exclaimed. "What did you do?"

"Yo' daddy and I helped people get to freedom. De slave owners had mean men wid horses and dogs who'd try to catch runaway slaves when dey was headin' north. Dat's why dey sang dis song. De drinkin' gourd is de Big Dipper. Dose stars point north."

"Wow, that's pretty smart!" Harry responded with a grin.

"Dat's right," his grandfather agreed. "Dey would also sing 'Wade in de Water.'"

"That's one of my favorites," the boy said excitedly.

"Mine too," Hamilton replied. "De bloodhounds couldn't track de slaves when dey was in de water, so dey stayed in a stream if dey heard de dogs and horses comin'. Dat's what de song means—wade in de water."

The two lonely figures came to the town square. It was nearly dark and no one else was outside on this blustery evening. They crossed the frozen street, stepping over the ice-covered wagon tracks, and began lighting the lamps around the square. Harry's teeth chattered as he fought to stay warm.

"It sure is cold tonight, Grandpa. Why did you come to Erie? Why didn't you stay where it's warm?" the boy questioned.

"I came here because dis is where der was freedom," the old man answered. "Wid God's help, I worked hard and saved my money. I bought my freedom and came to Erie. Boy, I tell you," Hamilton declared as he blew his warm breath into his cupped hands, "it may be cold here, but to me, dis place is de Garden of Eden."

They approached the next lamp, and the mostly blind man went through his routine. Hamilton lit the next few lamps in silence. He wanted his grandson to think about what he had told him. By now it was completely dark, and they needed to finish the job so the shop-keepers and neighbors could see as they walked or rode their buggies down the street.

Hamilton lit the final lamp on his route and then climbed down the ladder to begin the walk home. Placing his arm around the shivering boy, he declared, "Harry, de winters in Erie are fierce, dere's no doubt about it. But I ain't gonna complain. No sir. Dis is where de good Lawd brought me, and dis is where I's gonna stay. You remember de children of Israel in de desert, before dey went into de Promised Land?" Harry nodded. "Dey went 'round dat mountain for forty years, jest 'cause dey couldn't stop bellyachin'." The boy giggled at his granddaddy, causing the old man to smile. "Now Harry, you's got a Promised Land dat you's got to find too. If you moans and complains, you might never get der. But if you praise de Lawd, no matter what be happenin' in yo' life, good or bad, you'll cross over yo' Jordan and take yo' Promised Land." The thought filled the old man with zeal, and he shouted into the frigid wind, "Hallelujah! Glory be!"

The two shivering souls stopped in front of the Russell estate, where Harry's mother, Elizabeth, was working that evening. Through the window, the boy could see the guests dressed in elegant evening wear gathered to hear the great musicians who had come from far away to perform at the patron's Erie mansion. The glow from the lamps and from the crackling fire beamed from the tall, draped windows. Every once in a while Harry saw his mother walk by the window, carrying a tray filled with hors d'oeuvres. The faint sound of the chamber quartet could be heard above the whistling wind.

The old man knew of his grandson's love for music. He put his hand on the boy's shoulder and spoke into his ear, "Son, you's got de gift of vision, jest like I did. You can see tings—tings de way dey are, and tings de way dey could be. God has given you dis gift, Harry. Use it fo' him, and don't let dis world take it away. No matter what happens, you keep on praisin' de Lawd."

Harry looked up at the old man and said sadly, "I would love to be in there listening to the music, Grandpa."

Hamilton spoke gently to his grandson, "Have patience, my boy. Yo' time's comin'."

Inspired by the music, Harry asked, "Grandpa, can we sing a song?"

"Why, certainly sir. Ain't no better ting den singin' wid my grand-son. What do you want to sing?"

"Let's sing 'Freedom,' the song you were just singing!"

A sharp wind blew through the square. "Well, I guess we's already done wid de lamps," Hamilton replied as he squinted to see the park that was now golden with the light that they had provided. "We jest have time enough to sing de song tonight on our way back." They turned and started walking toward home, laughing and singing the familiar tune:

> Oh freedom. Oh freedom.
> Oh freedom over me.
> And before I be a slave, I'll be buried in my grave.
> And go home to my Lawd, and be free.
> No more weepin'. No more weepin'.
> No more weepin' over me.
> And before I be a slave, I'll be buried in my grave.
> And go home to my Lawd and be free.

Classical music flowed from the mansion and mingled with the old plantation song as the winter wind whistled along. A dream was born in the heart of the young child that cold December night in Erie, Pennsylvania—a Christmas present that would be God's gift to the rest of humanity.

2

Nobody Knows the Trouble I've Seen

At Buffalo, the train ground to a halt, screeching into the station house, rousing Harry from that place of dreams and visions between waking and sleeping. New passengers began crowding their way into the coach, bearing various kinds of boxes and bags. Seats on the car filled quickly until Harry's was the only bench with just one occupant. Several white passengers continued to board the train, but none sat with the young black man. Harry felt disapproving stares from people standing in the aisle. Ignoring them, he turned his head and peered out the window.

"Boy." The deep voice came from above him. "What kind of uppity n—r are you to sit here while these good folk have to stand?" A white man in his late thirties dressed in a handsome blue suit hovered over him. No one intervened on Harry's behalf. It was clear that some of the passengers were scolding the young black man with their eyes, as if he were a delinquent child. Others, wishing to avoid the confrontation, merely looked away.

Harry took a moment to collect his thoughts and then responded, "I'm sorry, sir, but I'm a paying customer on this railroad. I boarded the train in Erie and have been in this seat ever since. Perhaps there are some seats in the next car."

"Yes," the man responded. "Perhaps there are seats at the back of the train. But these ladies and gentlemen should not be required to go looking for them. You have two perfectly good seats right here. Don't you think you should give them up?"

Harry looked around the train for support, but none came. He smiled and looked down at the floor, trying to find a diplomatic way to respond. Finally he looked back up and gestured to the chair next to him. "Sir, this seat is available if anyone wishes to sit here with me."

The man put his hands on the back of the benches and leaned so close to Burleigh's face he could smell his breath. Coming within an inch of Harry's nose, he half whispered, "Which of these good people do you think wants to sit with a n—r? Hmm?" Then he looked around the car, leaned back in, and whispered, "If you want to enjoy the rest of your ride, I suggest you take your ratty bag and your filthy suit and find yourself a seat at the back of the train."

Again Harry looked around the coach. Several people were grinning, clearly pleased with the man leading the attack. Others continued to look away, avoiding the uncomfortable confrontation. Harry knew the odds were stacked against him. All he could do was stand, grab his bag, and make his way through the crowded aisle to the rear of the train. He reached the final car as the train began moving again. Mercifully there were still a few aisle seats available. Most of the faces he saw around him were dark, like his. He placed his luggage in the rack above his new seat and collapsed onto the bench.

He didn't know what lay in store for him when he arrived in New York. Could this confrontation be a forerunner of things to come in the big city? Hot tears tried to force their way out of his eyes, but he fought them back. He could not allow himself to break down, not in front of these people.

As he struggled to keep his composure, he wondered if the day would ever come in America when a black man would be treated as equal to a white man. Harry remembered what his grandfather and mother had taught him of the promise of the Declaration of Independence, the lofty rhetoric that black people held on to, hoping for a day when everyone would behave like "all men are created equal." He

27

had rarely experienced equality in America. Though he had known many kind white people in his lifetime, the lines were clearly drawn between the races. In his experience, opportunities were made available first for the whites—black folks, Asians, and Native Americans got whatever remained.

Suddenly the familiar, sickening feeling of hopelessness came over him, causing his stomach to tighten. He wondered if he should be making this trip at all. Would he have any chance of earning a scholarship to such a prestigious school in the white man's world?

As the train slowly pulled from the Buffalo station, he recalled the many times when his hopes had been dashed because of the color of his skin. Throughout his young life, Harry had to fight to keep from expecting racial barriers at every turn. And now here he was again, on the way to the most progressive city in America, sitting in the back of the train with the rest of the coloreds.

Will they ever let us be free?

As the train built momentum Harry couldn't help thinking of how his beloved grandfather had tried to escape to freedom several times when he was a slave—only to be caught, whipped, and chained once again. He remembered the story his mother told him of how her father was caught trying to teach himself to read—the crime that earned him seventy lashes and damaged his eyesight for the rest of his life.

1831–SOMERSET COUNTY, MARYLAND

"N—r! You's dead, boy. You ain't fast enough to outrun these horses."

Wide-eyed, the young slave ran through the thicket, thorns and branches tearing at the flesh of his face and arms. The sound of hooting and horse hooves surrounded him. Fear filled his chest. His heart pounded in his ears. His throat constricted, feeling as if a noose were being tightened around it. He tried to catch his breath, but no air came. He gulped and sucked at the humid Chesapeake air, straining to take in the needed oxygen to keep running. Adrenaline pumped through his slim, short frame, pushing him on.

Breaking out of the brush and into an open field, he realized the situation was hopeless. Suddenly, his foot sunk into a hole and he was hurled to the ground.

The overseer and his men surrounded him with their horses. Three of the slave handlers held rifles pointed at the young man's head. Though it was the middle of summer, the young slave lay shivering in the tall grass.

The overseer of the Tilghman plantation, Jeffrey Stutzman, jumped off his horse and was joined by two of his men. He stood over the young man so that his long shadow covered him completely. "Now Ham, I'm disappointed with you," he said sarcastically with a thick southern drawl. Pulling a speller from his back pocket and waving it in the young man's face, he asked, "What's this, boy?"

Young Hamilton Waters cowered before him. He was a farm slave living on this plantation near the shores of the Chesapeake Bay in Maryland. He worked the fields, tending corn, wheat, barley, and soybeans. Hamilton lived with his mother in a small log cabin with an earthen floor. He had originally been the property of Leven Waters of Somerset County, on Maryland's eastern shore. When Leven died, his slaves were sold to James Tilghman of the same vicinity.

Unlike some of the plantations closer to Pennsylvania that were being influenced by antislavery pressure, this farm was more like those farther south, where slaves were often whipped to keep them in line. Like most plantation owners of that time, Tilghman believed that his African slaves were less than human—they were property, only slightly higher in intelligence than the animals.

For more than two hundred years, Africans had been kidnapped and brought to the Americas as slaves. All children born to a slave immediately became the property of the master. In time, millions of Africans were held in bondage in the United States. As a result of the influence of the Quakers and other religious groups, the northern states came to see the institution as evil, and slavery became taboo north of the Mason-Dixon Line by the 1830s.

But slavery's demise was also due to the growth of industry in the North. While the South in large measure tried to hold to the Jeffersonian ideal of an agrarian society, the North embraced the industrial revolution, relying increasingly on machines over manual labor.

In time the practice of slavery became the "peculiar institution" of the South, helping to maintain and prosper the southern agrarian economy and way of life. Though slavery was eventually frowned upon in the northern states, racist and elitist attitudes by whites persisted across America, both North and South.

In order to keep the massive slave population under control, federal and state governments enacted restrictive Slave Codes. Under these laws slaves were not allowed to buy or sell merchandise. They could not carry a gun or ride a horse without permission. There was to be no gambling, no liquor, no slandering a white person, and no insolence whatsoever. To keep them from becoming too "uppity," slaves were not permitted to read or write. This was especially true of the Bible. Most plantation owners agreed their slaves must not read the Bible. It was believed a slave would focus on certain provocative verses, which could then cause an uprising. The only Bible knowledge allowed, according to most slave owners, was what they learned from their master or from a white minister. Though there were exceptions, most blacks were not permitted to gather for religious services, or meetings of any kind for that matter, without white oversight.

The highest crime of all was for a black person to try to educate himself.

A new slave brought to the Tilghman plantation earlier in the summer told Hamilton how some black folks across the South had taught themselves to read using small spellers. Like any other human being, Hamilton was filled with hopes and aspirations. He dreamed of being free one day, owning his own land, and building a family. He knew that reading was essential to survival and success for an escaped slave, so he began learning his ABCs from his new friend and carried a speller under his shirt to avoid detection.

Hamilton quickly learned the alphabet and could read most small words. At night, as he lay on his cot, he recounted the lessons learned during the day, mouthing the words without making a sound. He was always ready to hide the book when he heard the handlers coming for the nightly inspection.

But this time he had been caught red-handed, and he couldn't outrun the horses and hounds.

"I thought you were smarter than that, Ham." The overseer spat into his face. "Pick him up," he barked to his cronies. They grabbed the young man and yanked him to his feet. "You're always trying to fly like a bird." He was so close to Hamilton's face the young man could smell the whiskey on his breath. Turning back to the men, Stutzman declared, "I'm afraid I'm gonna have to make an example of this ignorant wretch. He tries to run. He tries to read. We'll have to clip his wings before he tries anything else."

Most of the men in the group chuckled with evil anticipation. But not all of the farmhands were as delighted. One of the young men shook his head in disgust, earning sneers from those who saw it. While the majority of the white laborers wholeheartedly agreed with the harsh policies of the master and the overseer, a few of the hired men sympathized with the plight of the slaves. They were not happy with Stutzman's tactics and they often voiced their disapproval, much to the derision of their fellow workers. Stutzman ignored them and in contempt became even crueler.

Suddenly the overseer slapped the cowering slave across the face. "Tie 'em and drag 'em," he yelled. A rope was thrown to the two men holding Hamilton. They bound his hands tightly in front of him.

Hamilton pleaded with them, "Please, no. I ain't gonna do it again. I's sorry." Tears ran through the dirt and blood that covered his cheek.

They threw the rope to the overseer, who mounted and tied it to his saddle. "Heyah!" Stutzman kicked at the sides of his horse, and the group moved forward at a slow trot. Hamilton ran behind trying to keep up. Emotionally and physically exhausted, he finally fell to the ground after more than a mile. They dragged the young man the rest of the way to the plantation.

In front of Master Tilghman's house, the overseer stopped to receive instructions. He climbed the staircase between the large white pillars and knocked on the door. When the black doorman appeared, Stutzman ordered him to fetch the master. As the elderly house slave scurried back into the mansion, the overseer turned and ordered his men to lift Hamilton to his feet.

After a moment's wait, the plantation owner stepped out of the mansion and onto the wide porch. James Tilghman was a tall, slender man whose gaunt, pale face was framed by long, wiry sideburns. His thin, gray hair barely covered the top of his head, with several long strands combed from just above the left ear and running across the scalp to the right ear. He wore gray satin pants with pinstripes. A burgundy satin vest covered a slightly yellowed silk shirt.

Tilghman was a respected member of the Maryland aristocracy, and the plantation had been in his family since the 1660s. Slaves first came to the farm not long after his family built its first crude pine home. Master Tilghman now owned dozens of slaves, and to him they were all chattel. He looked down with a serious expression on the bruised and bloodied young man.

"What is the meaning of this, Mr. Stutzman?"

"He had this under his shirt, sir." The overseer handed him the speller. The master looked over the small book. Recognizing the insubordination, his expression slowly changed from one of curiosity to anger. His jaw shifted from side to side as he looked up from the speller to examine Hamilton. The man towered over the shivering slave from atop the wide wooden porch. Placing the speller into his pocket, he stared down and declared in a controlled voice, "Make an example of him, Mr. Stutzman. He's been nothing but trouble since he came to us from the Waters plantation. He must have a devil in him." He turned his gaze from Hamilton to the overseer. "I want it driven out. Do you understand?"

Stutzman smiled wryly. "Yes, sir, Mr. Tilghman. I'll see to it." He walked quickly down the steps and mounted his horse.

Tilghman watched as the young man was forced to run, stumbling, behind the horses toward the slave quarters. Pulling a handkerchief from the pocket of his vest, he wiped the sweat from his forehead. "Good Lord, it's hot," he said aloud. The master then turned and entered his mansion. He walked directly to the kitchen, where lunch was being prepared. The slaves working over the food smiled nervously as he entered the room.

"Afternoon, massa," they said one by one, bowing their heads as he passed by. The women moved out of his way as he approached the stove. He reached for the iron door, intending to throw the book into the fire. In his anger he grabbed the door with his bare hand, searing his flesh.

"Sweet Jesus," he cried out in pain.

"Massa!" the oldest woman in the room rushed to his side with a thick potholder. He snatched it from her hands. "Fetch de massa some ice," she ordered. A young girl scurried from the room and outside to the ice cellar.

Using the potholder, Tilghman opened the iron door and tossed the book into the flames. He stood for a moment, holding his blistering hand, peering into the stove until he was satisfied the book had been fully consumed. The women cast curious glances at each other as they stood motionless over the unfinished food. When he was confident the deed was done, he closed the oven door and placed the potholder on the counter. The young girl entered the room carrying a fist-sized chunk of ice.

"Well that was very sweet of you," the master said, smiling. She handed the ice to the older woman, who gently wrapped Tilghman's hand and the ice in a towel. "Thank you very much," he said with a slight nod. "I guess I was a bit hasty. Good afternoon." He nodded again graciously to the women, turned, and quietly walked out of the kitchen holding his wounded hand.

<hr />

Outside, the posse approached the slave quarters. "Gather every n—r on this farm," Stutzman commanded. "The master wants them to see this." The handlers fanned out through the plantation, calling every slave in from the fields, the shops, and the master's house. Stopping in front of the row of cabins where the slaves lived, the group dismounted. Stutzman directed the others to tie the young man to the well. By now Hamilton's face was swollen and bloody. The handlers pulled the dazed and crying slave to the well and tied his hands to one of the posts.

The other slaves slowly gathered, bracing themselves for the worst. Lovey Waters, Hamilton's mother, cried out when she realized they were tying up her son. She began running toward him to shield his body, knowing the cruelty Stutzman had inflicted on others. "Don't do it," she cried hysterically. "He's my baby." One of the male slaves grabbed the distraught woman and held her tightly to keep her from being tied next to the boy.

"Stop dem, please, do somethin'," she implored.

"You know dere's nothin' I can do," he replied, his teeth clenched in anger. She sobbed into his shoulder, shielding her eyes from the impending punishment.

As soon as he was satisfied all the slaves were assembled, Stutzman addressed the group.

"Master Tilghman wants you all to know the good Lord made darkey to serve. This boy somehow got it in his head he could get some book learnin'." His eyes glared at them. "Now you n—rs don't know much, but you do know you can't read or write like us white folks. Let this be an example to any of you who are thinkin' about goin' against the will of the Lord."

He pulled a leather whip from where it was tied to his saddle and walked up behind Hamilton, whose exhausted body sagged over the well.

"No, have mercy," Lovey again tried to break free from her friend's grasp.

"Shut her up," Stutzman ordered. The muscular slave pulled her head into his chest to shield her eyes. The slaves had seen this before. Many exhibited a glassy stare as they looked on, numb. Several in the group bore stripes across their own backs from just such an occasion. Some of the younger slaves turned their heads away slightly to avoid viewing the carnage. Stutzman walked over to Hamilton and tore his shirt open in the back. The young man looked up through blood- and tear-soaked eyes, moaning and begging for mercy.

"No—no, I's sorry. Please, no," he cried.

Stepping back a few paces, the overseer pulled the leather whip back and brought it forward swiftly. The leather slapped across Hamilton's dark, bare skin, causing him to scream in agony.

"Mercy, my Lawd Jesus," the cry came from Hamilton's mother, who again tried to break free.

"Shut her up or she'll get the same," Stutzman hissed.

The whip came down a second time as a welt raised up on Hamilton's back. The third crack of the whip slightly broke the skin. Blood oozed out of the wound.

To the astonishment of the overseer, Hamilton weakly began singing in halting phrases through the lashes.

> Swing low, sweet chariot
> Comin' fo' to carry me home
> Swing low, sweet chariot
> Comin' fo' to carry me home

The melody clearly enraged Stutzman. Again and again he brought the leather across the slave's back, legs, head, arms, and face. Like a man possessed, white foam gathered at the corners of his mouth as he yelled obscenities.

"Please, no mo'." Hamilton again cried out in agony. "I beg you. Please stop." Mercifully he collapsed, fainting from the pain.

Stutzman spat out, "No n—r is going to break the rules on this farm and get away with it. This will guarantee that." Tears ran down the faces of many of the slaves. With every ounce of self-discipline they possessed, they remained quiet to avoid the lash. The overseer kept striking the unconscious figure until he had counted out seventy lashes. Finally he stopped, wiped his face with a handkerchief, and ordered the men to cut the young slave down.

Hamilton's mother rushed to him as he slumped to the hard earth. Moaning and weeping, she cradled his bleeding head in her hands. "My baby. Oh my Lawd. My sweet baby."

The slaves stood frozen in horror. "Y'all get back to work," Stutzman ordered. Slowly they wandered back to the fields and the shops, many wiping away tears.

The handlers yelled at them as they dispersed, "Get back out there. Break it up. Do you want some of the same?"

But one of the white foremen did not move from his place. He stared angrily as Stutzman folded his sweat-drenched handkerchief, placed it back in his pocket, and began coiling the blood-soaked whip. As he tied it back onto his saddle, he looked up and caught the eyes of the young man. Stutzman laughed mockingly and shook his head. "Boy, ain't you got work to do?" he chided.

The man spat on the ground, then replied, "I sure the hell do." The foreman walked past Stutzman to the well and began to draw water for Hamilton. The overseer glared at him in anger, but didn't follow. The young overseer handed the bucket of water to an elderly black woman, who nodded thankfully and turned to carry it to the cabin. The man walked back over to his horse and grabbed the reins. As he mounted he looked over at Stutzman. "You're a sick man," he said, then rode off toward the fields.

A handful of Lovey's close friends gathered around her boy's bleeding body, sobbing and hugging one another. A younger woman ran to the master's house to gather some spare material from the sewing quarters to use as bandages. The large slave who had held Lovey back now got down on one knee and gathered the unconscious boy into his arms.

As he carried the limp, broken body to Lovey's small cabin, he continued the song where Hamilton had left off.

> I looked over Jordan and what did I see
> Comin' fo' to carry me home
> A band of angels comin' after me
> Comin' fo' to carry me home

The others joined in, singing quietly as they led Lovey to the cabin. She followed in shock, hanging on the arms of her friends as they sang.

> Swing low, sweet chariot
> Comin' fo' to carry me home
> Swing low, sweet chariot
> Comin' fo' to carry me home

The overseer watched as they carried the unconscious slave away. When they were out of sight, he turned to his horse and pulled a glass whiskey bottle from his saddlebag. He unscrewed the top and lustily swallowed several mouthfuls. Wiping his chin with his sleeve, he put the bottle back, then mounted the horse and trotted away from the slave quarters and down the road. He didn't look to the right or the left. He didn't allow his eyes to meet anyone else's. He merely looked ahead and galloped away from the plantation.

1891–NEW YORK CITY

Harry spent the remainder of the train ride in pensive silence. When the train finally arrived at the New York station at nine o'clock in the evening, Harry picked up his bag and exited, drained from the long ride. He walked wearily onto the platform, milling along with the crowd toward the exit.

Harry emerged onto a street filled with carriages and trolley cars, the sidewalk crowded with every kind of person he had ever imagined.

Electric and gas-lit signs hung in front of the buildings for as far as he could see. The sight jarred him from his malaise, filling his senses with the wonder of a world-class metropolis.

This was his first trip to the big city, and the night was still young. He checked the directions he had received through his correspondence with the school. They recommended an inexpensive hotel a couple of blocks from the conservatory. Harry found the train station on the city map he had purchased in the lobby. He calculated the distance from the station to the hotel. *Six blocks down and three blocks over.* He picked up his suitcase and started walking, a small man in a very big city. It was New York, and he was about to reach for the brass ring.

He smiled and began whistling the familiar tune "Freedom," tipping his hat whenever he caught the eye of passersby on the crowded city street.

3

There Is a Balm in Gilead

The lights, noises, and excitement of the moment quickly overshadowed the unpleasant train ride. Harry was finally in New York City. The sidewalk was teeming with people of every size, shape, and color. The street was busy with trolley cars, carriages, and buckboards. This was not the sleepy town he was used to. This was the greatest city in America, and Harry was ready for it. The air was filled with a mixture of the oily smell of burning gaslights and the familiar smell of manure from the countless horses on the street. He had spent many sleepless nights wishing for this moment and for the chance to sing for the world. Now it was here. Energized by the frenetic pace of the city, Harry felt as if he could walk the streets of New York all night.

After several blocks, the young man's attention was suddenly drawn to familiar music emanating from a small, dingy saloon. This was one of the songs he used to hear the stable hands singing in his daddy's livery. The melody was accompanied by the sound of a banjo, violins, a washboard, and the bones. Unable to contain his curiosity, Harry walked down the steps to the basement honky-tonk, found an open table near the back of the long narrow hall, and laid down his small bag.

On the stage a group of black minstrels with greasepaint smeared over their faces acted out a slapstick routine. One actor was dressed in knickers and a frilly shirt. He was the Ruse—the dumb, likable Negro. A woman played the part of Mammy, the plantation mother hen. Then there was Zip-coon—the cocky, scheming darkie that everyone feared, black and white alike.

Harry ordered a drink and cheerfully followed the scene as it unfolded on the stage. Zip-coon cried out that he was tired of being hungry all the time. "I's goin' over to de farmer's house, and I's a gonna steal me some fat, juicy chickens."

"Oh, you don't wants to do dat, no sah," replied old Mammy. "If'n you do dat, de debble is gonna get you fo' shuh."

"What you talkin' 'bout woman. Der ain't no such thing as a debble."

"Oh yes der is," she replied, pointing her rolling pin at him.

"Oh yes der is," echoed the man in the frilly shirt in a deep baritone voice. He stood wide-eyed with his knees knocking together in mock fear. The audience roared in laughter at his reply.

Suddenly the orchestra struck up the ominous tones of the plantation song. Old Mammy walked to the front of the stage and began singing in a strong voice:

> Dat day when you'se weary, fightin' wiv sin
> An' de debble comes 'round fo' his due
> Doan' be totin' er bag wiv three chickuns in
> Dat de Lawd only made fo' two!

The audience burst into applause as she finished the first verse. "Come on, sing it if you know it," Zip-coon shouted to the crowd. Harry sang along with enthusiasm. The minstrels finished their song to raucous applause from the inebriated patrons, and then arm in arm belted out the popular melody "Swanee."

> Way down upon de Swanee Ribber,
> Far, far away
> Der's wha' my heart am turning ebber
> Der's wha' de old folks stay

When they finished the first chorus, the young man playing Zip-coon jumped off the stage and ran into the audience. "Who is going to join us in our song? You sir?" He pointed to a large man who clenched a beer mug with his thick fingers. The man refused the invitation. "You madam? You?"—again a refusal.

He came to the table where Harry T. Burleigh sat. "What about you, sir?" He turned to the audience and pointed at the young man. "Who would like to hear this handsome young man sing?" The crowd roared its approval. Harry smiled at the sound of the applause as a tingle raced up his spine. After a short moment of contemplation he jumped to his feet and followed the actor up onto the stage.

Zip-coon placed Harry at the center of the stage as the other actors surrounded him. With the sound of the band, the glare of the lights, and that familiar sweaty smell of the stage, suddenly the confrontation on the train slipped from Harry's memory. Maybe New York would be all right after all. The banjo plunked out the familiar introduction, and the group began to sing together.

> All up and down de whole creation
> Sadly I roam
> Still longing fo' de old plantation
> And fo' de old folks at home

Harry's rich baritone overpowered the other singers. The actors gave each other curious looks as the young man closed his eyes and sang the song with great enthusiasm. They quickly took the harmony parts, allowing Harry to lead the way.

> All de world am sad and dreary
> Ebry where I roam
> Oh! Darkeys how my heart grows weary
> Far from de old folks at home
> All round de little farm I wandered
> When I was young
> Den many happy days I squander'd
> Many de songs I sung
> When I was playing wid my brudder
> Happy was I

Oh! Take me to my kind old mudder
Der let me live and die
All de world am sad and dreary
Ebry where I roam
Oh! Darkeys how my heart grows weary
Far from de old folks at home

When they finished, the audience jumped to its feet, applauding the impromptu chorus. The actors stepped back and allowed Harry to bask in the glory of the moment. He felt the thrill of the applause and drank in the audience's appreciation for his talent. His experience to this point had been in churches or at polite social receptions where there was little or no applause. But this was theater—and it was wonderful!

Harry bowed to the audience several times as their ovation continued. Then he turned, thanked the actors, and returned to his seat to watch the rest of the performance.

After the show the man who played Zip-coon jumped off the stage and made a beeline for Harry's table. "Hey, brother," he said, causing Harry to look up from his drink. "You sure can sing. Can I buy you another glass of whatever you're drinking?"

"No thanks, I think I'm fine."

"May I sit?" The actor reached out his hand and introduced himself. "I'm Anthony Galloway, and I manage this troupe."

"Sure, please join me." Harry shook his hand. "I'm Harry T. Burleigh, pleased to meet you."

"Well Harry, I've been in show business for many years, and I'm here to tell ya', you don't come along to a voice like yours very often."

"Thank you, sir. I truly enjoyed the opportunity to be onstage."

"Well, we enjoyed having you. Your voice blended nicely with the other singers." He paused for a moment. "Tell me, what do you do for a living?"

Harry smiled. "By trade I'm a stenographer, but my heart's desire has always been to sing professionally."

Anthony grinned. "Really? Well, my friend, I may be able to help make that dream come true."

Harry was shocked by the statement. "How's that?"

"I'm looking for another singer for this troupe. I have plenty of comedy players, but to give this show some style I need a straight man, someone with a voice like yours. I want someone with your kind of finesse to give us a touch of class. Audiences are yearning for class these days, Harry, and I think you could deliver it for us."

Harry shifted in his seat, looking more intently at the actor. "Well, even though I'm flattered by your offer, I'm afraid I'm not available right now."

The actor moved in closer. "Wait a minute, Harry. You can't turn me down before you hear the entire proposal. From New York we're heading south to Philadelphia; then to Washington, DC; Richmond; and Norfolk. We'll be playing all up and down the East Coast. During the winter months we'll tour the South. Harry, I'll pay you fifty dollars a week and give you room, board, and new clothes."

Harry smiled and looked down at his drink. Had he been given this kind of opportunity a month earlier, he would have jumped at it. "I appreciate your offer, Anthony, but I'm here in New York to audition for a scholarship with the National Conservatory of Music. I'm not really interested in doing theater right now."

"Wow, the conservatory." The actor was even more impressed and whistled a long, slow whistle. "Well, that's wonderful. Are you fairly confident of your chances?"

Harry grinned. "Actually, I'm fairly doubtful of my chances." Anthony laughed with him. "But I'm going to give it my best shot and leave the rest in God's hands."

"With your voice, I can see you being given a place." The actor leaned back and stroked his chin as he spoke. Harry looked up at him in surprise. It was reassuring to have his talent recognized, especially by a professional. "If by chance it doesn't work out, keep us in mind. We'll be playing this theater for the next two weeks and then it's on to Philly. My offer stands." He stood up from the table and extended his hand. "Stop by and see me if you want some solid work."

"Thank you, I'll keep it in mind," Harry responded, shaking Anthony's hand firmly.

The actor worked his way through the crowd and disappeared behind the stage curtain. Harry finished his soda water, picked up his bag, and made his way back onto the street. The horse and buggy traffic had thinned somewhat, but the street was still busy compared to Erie. Harry walked toward his hotel, considering Anthony's offer. Before he left home he had decided that no matter how the audition for the conservatory went, he would not go back to the life of a stenographer. That decision had come one cold night as he worked at Koehler's Piano Company.

1891—ERIE, PENNSYLVANIA

Nearly broke and without hope of ever becoming a full-time musician, Harry finally surrendered his dream and decided to launch into an office career. He had beautiful penmanship so he studied stenography, all the time holding on to the faint hope that one day he could find a way to become a professional singer. Remarkably, he found work as a stenographer for the Koehler Piano Company, which gave him the chance to remain in a musical environment. The Burleigh family could not afford a piano in their home, though they did own a reed organ, so Harry took advantage of his work at the Koehler Company to practice. He loved the sound of the elegant, well-tuned pianos at Koehler's and often stayed after work rehearsing late into the night.

"I'll lock up tonight, Mr. Koehler," Harry said, poking his head into the proprietor's office.

"Will you be practicing your piano this evening, or have I loaded you down with too much work, Harry?" the white-haired gentleman replied in his thick German accent.

Harry liked his job at the piano company, and even though he knew his boss was only kidding, he quickly answered, "No sir, not at all. The work is fine. If it's all right, I would like to rehearse my piano exercises."

"Of course. You can stay all night if you like. Just make sure the door is locked when you leave."

"Thank you, Mr. Koehler."

"I think I'll be leaving myself," the merchant exclaimed. Harry helped his boss pull on his coat and walked him to the door. "Good night, Harry," he said, smiling at the dapper young man. "I wish I could stay and play with you, but the missus is most displeased if I'm late for dinner."

Harry chuckled. "Good night, sir. Have a pleasant evening." Burleigh locked the door behind him and walked from the office area at the back of the store to the gallery in the front. Sitting down at a glossy black grand piano, Harry looked out the large glass windows at the gaslight flickering on the corner. His mind began to race. The lamp made him think of his grandfather, a nearly blind man escaping slavery only to toil for pennies, working in all kinds of weather to keep a roof over his family and food on the table.

He thought about his sweet mother, working as a servant to help provide for a home full of children and kin—never knowing the joy of teaching the languages she herself had come to master. He thought of her toiling as a janitress in the very school that should have given her a teaching position.

Then his thoughts turned to himself. Suddenly anger and frustration overwhelmed him. He knew he was a talented singer and musician, and yet here he was at twenty-six years of age in Erie, Pennsylvania, struggling as a stenographer. He watched the people who came by to play the pianos at Koehler's and knew he was better than any of them. He was even better than the salesmen.

He was doing everything he knew to make a living as a professional musician. He had sung in three different church choirs and at private parties, funerals, and weddings. He had traveled the country with a choir, singing the spirituals. But none of these things paid good money. Now he was nearly penniless. When would he get his break? Were the doors closed to him because he was black? He knew very well the sting of prejudice. It had kept his family down for two generations since the Emancipation Proclamation. Would he stay forever bound by the chains of hatred and ignorance? Would he ever be released to sing and write the melodies that swirled within his mind? Would bigotry hold him in the icy grip of poverty for the rest of his life?

As he stared at the streetlight, suddenly he was taken back to the endless nights lighting the lamps with his grandfather. The old plantation melodies washed over him, flooding his soul. He remembered his grandfather's admonition, spoken innumerable times over the years: "If you praise de Lawd, no matter what be happenin' in yo' life, good or bad, you'll cross over yo' Jordan and take yo' Promised Land."

He began to run his fingers up and down the piano keys like an artist moving his brush across a canvas. Closing his eyes, he released his pent-up frustration, intensely playing his scales.

"I must master this," he said out loud. "I can't be less than excellent. They won't let me be." Overwhelmed, he began missing the keys. "I must be better. I cannot fail. I cannot make these mistakes."

His emotions gained control and he was no longer playing the piano, he was pounding the keyboard, venting years of anguish. In a climax of anger he slammed the keys with his fist, hammering the insults and accusations of a lifetime into the grand instrument. The dissonant chord reflected the impatience in his soul, the longing to break free from the invisible chains of injustice. He placed his hands on the edge of the piano bench and wept as the grotesque tone slowly faded from the room.

"God, where are you?" he cried out into the darkness. "I need your help. I can't do it alone. I can't be like my grandfather. I can't master this anger." Only silence remained in the room. *If God heard me, he's not talking back*. A wave of hopelessness poured over him. After a minute of sobbing, Harry finally went silent. He sat quietly, alone in a room full of beautifully crafted instruments.

"God, I need your help," he whispered. Suddenly a great sense of warmth swept over him. He was surprised by the sudden change, the release of the anger. Though God hadn't spoken, Harry knew he was communicating. Suddenly a song he had sung dozens of times at the mission church with his grandfather began to flow through him.

Without touching the piano, he began to sing:

> Sometimes I feel discouraged,
> And think my work's in vain.
> But then the Holy Spirit,
> Revives my soul again.
> There is a balm in Gilead,
> To make the wounded whole.
> There is a balm in Gilead,
> To heal the sin-sick soul.

As the final words resonated in the empty chamber, Burleigh placed his hands on his legs. He closed his eyes and tilted his head back.

Hot tears rolled down his cheeks. He listened to the last notes fade and then sat in the dark silence, seeing nothing but the world within.

1891–NEW YORK CITY

Now Harry had one final chance. He had made up his mind. He would be a musician, either by winning the scholarship to the conservatory or by joining the minstrel troupe. Harry T. Burleigh would never go back to his old life. He would be a musician until the day he died, no matter the cost.

As Harry checked into his room, he asked the clerk if there was a telegraph office nearby so he could let his mother know he had arrived safely.

"We have a telegraph service here, but it is only open from 8 a.m. to 5 p.m.," the clerk answered wearily, handing Harry the large brass key to his room. "You can send a telegraph in the morning."

Harry thanked him, picked up his bag, and entered the elevator, pushing the scissor gate shut and pressing the button to his floor. In his room he unpacked his few belongings and remembered how his mother had always admonished him to avoid the minstrel house. He flopped down on the bed, utterly spent from the trip. As he started drifting to sleep he prayed a silent prayer. *God, if you don't want me in the minstrel show, you will need to open the door. But either way, oh Lord, I believe you have called me to music. And by your grace, I will be the best musician I can be.*

The sounds and smells of the city rose through his open window, but they were not enough to fight off his exhaustion as Harry T. Burleigh fell asleep on his first night in New York City.

4

My Lord, What a Mornin'

As the sun peeked over the Atlantic horizon to shine on New York City, Harry T. Burleigh was already up and preparing for his audition. He walked down to the lobby to ask the hotel manager where he could find a place to rent a suit. The manager directed him to a haberdashery around the corner. Burleigh thanked him and stepped outside. The hot August sun was already beating down on the stone streets. He knew that by the time of the audition in the afternoon the temperature would rise to scorching levels. Harry went straight to the suit shop and rented the best outfit he could afford. For five dollars he was able to obtain a black woolen suit with matching vest and a white silk tie. He wore his own cotton shirt that he had purchased for the occasion. He wanted to be sure he had a shirt with a collar that would not constrict his throat during the audition.

Harry returned to the hotel and dressed in the steam box of a room as perspiration poured down his face and back. He picked up his music and took one last look in the dingy mirror, adjusting his tie and collar. Taking the elevator to the lobby, he dashed out the door into the busy street. In his excitement and nervousness he forgot all about sending the telegram to his mother.

Harry arrived at the conservatory drenched in sweat, but dressed smartly with his hair greased back, music in hand. He was greeted at the door by the registrar, a kind, older woman who took his name and asked several questions for the committee. Harry thought she looked somehow familiar and took notice of her fashionable dress. When she finished gathering the information she directed Harry to take a seat inside. He thanked her and entered the room. His rented suit gave him a dose of confidence to combat the apprehension that filled his soul. *At least I look like a professional musician*, he thought as he began rehearsing his song one more time in his mind.

Every applicant was required to audition for the scholarship. Twenty-five other well-dressed candidates crowded the large, steamy rehearsal hall. The windows of the room were opened, but there was no breeze, only stifling heat. The musicians fanned themselves with their sheet music or any other item they could find to do the job. The minutes ticked by as one by one the young men and women made their way into the classroom to stand before the panel of judges.

Harry sat in a wooden chair near the corner, moving his lips without making a sound as he performed his memorized piece. A tall, thin young black man paced the floor in front of Harry while playing an invisible violin, moving his fingers in rapid motion. His head was cocked to the left and his eyes remained closed. He walked back and forth, turning around in a military manner every ten feet. When he finally tired of the mental rehearsal, the lanky musician slumped down against the wall, his long legs jutting straight out from the corner. "Are you nervous?" he asked, looking over at Harry who had been following his movements for several minutes.

"Yes, a little," Harry responded. "This is my first professional audition."

"Really," the man replied with a surprised look. "You're kidding. Where are you from?"

"I'm from Erie, Pennsylvania."

"I've heard of Lake Erie, and I've heard of Pennsylvania, but I can't say that I've heard of Erie, Pennsylvania. Where exactly is that?"

"Right on the lake, between New York and Ohio."

"Oh, the little smokestack thing on top of the state, right?"

"Yeah, I guess that's one way of describing it." Harry chuckled.

The young man reached out his long slim hand and introduced himself. "I'm Will Marion Cook."

Harry liked the cadence of the three names strung together so he replied, "Harry T. Burleigh. It's a pleasure to meet you, sir."

"What instrument do you play, Harry?"

"Actually, I'm a singer," he responded.

"Ah, then you have a reason to be nervous."

The response did not sit well with Harry, who was terribly apprehensive as it was. "Why is that?" he asked.

"Most of the people who come here are masterful instrumentalists. Yes, they do have vocalists as well, but the real focus of this institution is composition. In fact, there are rumors that the great Bohemian composer Antonin Dvorak may be installed as director of the conservatory. I met him once in Prague when I was studying under Joachim."

"You studied under Joachim?" he responded in surprise. Harry mimicked Cook's imaginary playing. "So, you play violin, right?"

"Yeah, but I'm also a composer. I've been to hundreds of these auditions, so I'll give you a little advice. This heat will make it difficult to sing. Make sure you drink plenty of water."

"Thanks for the warning." Harry had noticed that his throat was getting parched. He had wanted to find some water but didn't want to risk missing his turn. As the minutes ticked by, the dryness of his throat heightened his nervousness.

Just as he was standing to go find some water, the registrar emerged from the classroom and called for Burleigh to enter. Harry stood and adjusted the collar of his shirt, which suddenly seemed much tighter. He wished he had jumped at the chance for that glass of water. Cook wished him luck. "Thank you, and good luck to you too," Harry replied as he turned to enter the room. After he walked through the door, the registrar closed it behind him.

The committee members sat behind two long oak tables at the far end of the room. Behind them was a chalkboard with staff lines etched into it. Wooden chairs and cast-iron music stands lined the walls of the room. A grand piano stood to the side with the accompanist sitting stoically on the bench. A single music stand stood at the center of the room, about ten feet from the committee.

"Mr. Burleigh, correct?" A slender, attractive woman looked up from a stack of papers.

"Yes, ma'am."

"I'm Adelle Marguilles." She introduced the other judges one by one. Burleigh recognized several of them by name.

The final panel member seated closest to the piano was none other than the famous master Joseffy. Harry remembered how he had kept him spellbound years before at Mrs. Russell's mansion. In an instant he was overcome with anxiety. His throat tightened even more. Sweat began to emerge in large beads upon his forehead. *I dare to apply for a scholarship here? In front of these great musicians?*

"Do you have your selection with you?" Ms. Marguilles asked.

Harry hesitated for a moment. Her comment jarred him from his memories. "Uh, yes . . . yes, of course." He handed the sheet music to the accompanist and took his place behind the music stand. The young man once again adjusted his collar. The judges looked at one another with questioning eyes.

As he sang, his nervousness caused his throat to constrict. At a key moment in the piece his voice cracked on a high note. His mind was a whir of thoughts. After he sang, the committee grilled him with questions. Answers he had studied and formulas he had memorized would not come to his mind. When the trial was finally over, he courteously thanked the committee and walked quickly from the room. Cook tried to question him on the audition, but Harry walked right past him without saying a word. The registrar stopped him at the door. She could see the disappointment in his eyes. "It's Harry, right?" she asked him.

"Yes, ma'am," he replied, trying to remain polite.

She wrote his name in the appointment book. "Harry Burleigh. All right, you are scheduled to receive the grade for the audition at 10 o'clock tomorrow morning. My name is Mrs. MacDowell, and I'm the registrar. You can come to my office."

"Thank you, ma'am," he said, nodding his head. Harry looked into her eyes. *So, this is Mrs. MacDowell. I knew she looked familiar. She doesn't look that much different from when I saw her at Mrs. Russell's home.*

Still upset over his performance, he turned and rushed out of the building. Harry was able to contain his emotions long enough to walk half a block. Finally, he couldn't hold the feelings inside any longer, and he ducked into a small alleyway. Safely out of view, he burst into tears. *How did I get so flustered? Why didn't I get a drink of water before I went in?* He had known the correct answers to every question they asked but he just hadn't been able to put them into words. He lifted his foot and kicked back against the stone building behind him.

"Now what do I do?" he said out loud. He leaned his head back and looked up into the sky. "God, what do I do now?" His mind flashed back to countless nights practicing piano at Koehler's. "I cannot . . . I will not go back," he shouted into the alley. Burleigh wiped the tears from his eyes and looked out into the crowded street. A blur of people passed the alley, unaware of Harry's anguish. He was alone. Harry didn't know a single soul in the city of New York. He didn't want to go back to the hot hotel room. Instead he decided to take a walk to sort out his thoughts.

He stopped at the hotel to change into some more comfortable clothes. It was now late in the afternoon, but the air was still stifling. He returned the suit to the haberdashery and set out to walk the streets of the city. Over and over again he asked himself, *What am I going to do now?* He had made up his mind before leaving Erie that no matter what happened in the audition he would not return to his hometown. The only future he had there would be as a stenographer. One way or another, he planned to make his living in the world of music.

Harry entered one of New York's gilded parks and slumped down on a wooden bench. Engrossed in his thoughts, he didn't even notice the children who joined a flock of small birds splashing in the fountain. As he contemplated his future, he thought of the band of minstrels from the night before.

Throughout his life his mother had exhorted him, "Harry, the minstrel house is the playground of the devil. God only knows what sort of debauchery, drunkenness, and crass behavior take place in that house of sin. They take the jubilee songs—the spiritual songs of our ancestors—and desecrate them in those brothels. These were songs given to our people by God to strengthen them to endure all kinds of suffering. But for the love of money, those folks turn them into a plaything for Satan."

But Harry hadn't seen any of that at the theater the night before. The songs they sang were the plantation melodies he had heard at his father's stables and on the lake steamers. They made him happy. They made him feel good, like he used to feel when he worked the boats with his brother Reginald. Harry T. Burleigh wanted to sing. He wanted it more than anything else in the world. He was sick to death of breaking his back just earning a wage to get himself from day to day. What would be wrong with earning a living making people happy?

But in his gut, questions still gnawed at him. These were his black brothers and sisters, and they were making fun at the expense of other Negroes. It didn't sit right in his heart that they painted their faces with clown makeup to overemphasize their features. He didn't want to be a part of ridiculing poor black folks. But according to Anthony, that wasn't what he would be doing. The actor promised he would be the straight man. He would bring class to the act. That would be a good thing. He could show audiences that the black man could be sophisticated too.

A sophisticated musician, Harry thought. *That's all I've ever wanted to be.*

Lying on the park bench, he recalled the exact moment when he decided to become a distinguished musician. It was a frigid night in Erie, Pennsylvania, as he stood in the snow and watched the great Joseffy through a plate glass window performing for the wealthy patrons inside the Russell mansion.

1876—Erie, Pennsylvania

In order to make ends meet, Harry's mother worked as a servant in the homes of several of Erie's leading families. From her mother she had learned the manners and etiquette needed to impress the aristocrats. Elizabeth spoke with sophistication and carried the refined qualities that her mother had learned when she worked in the governor's mansion in Albany, New York. This training served her well, opening many opportunities for employment, though the pay for a black woman remained relatively low. But it was work, and she was grateful for it.

On one particularly blustery winter night in 1876, Elizabeth was called upon to work at the Russell home. The icy Canadian wind had been blowing across Lake Erie for days, carrying with it snow that quickly descended in large, heavy flakes. A winter storm from the north could blanket the land with several inches of snow in a matter of minutes. Erie was usually so cold in the wintertime that ice cutters worked well into March on Presque Isle Bay, carving large slabs to be stored for use throughout the warm months. Teams of horses harnessed to wooden buckboards, with iron sled runners installed to replace the wheels, pulled the ice squares to shore where they were transported to storage cellars across northwestern Pennsylvania and beyond.

It was common to see children rolling snowballs until they became large and heavy, with the wet white snow mixed with multicolored fallen leaves. Placing one ball on top of another, the children created a torso and then a head for a plump, frozen snowman. Youngsters often would sneak extra scarves and hats from a closet to dress their creations. Two lumps of coal were borrowed for eyes, a carrot for a nose, and fallen branches for arms. Winter scenes such as these lasted from mid-November, when the first snow stuck to the frozen ground, until mid-March, when it finally melted.

It was just such a winter's day that changed the course of young Harry Burleigh's life forever.

"Children, I'm leaving now." Elizabeth called up the stairs to the youngsters ruckusing about in the spacious, wooden home she and her husband had recently built.

"Mama, who's playing tonight?" Young Harry came barreling down the stairs with his brothers and sisters. He stopped just in front of his mother. She was dressed smartly to serve as a maid for another concert at the stately mansion of Erie's leading socialite.

"Mrs. Russell is hosting a famous Hungarian pianist, Rafael Joseffy," she said with a smile. "Do you remember when we learned about him?" Elizabeth thoroughly instructed her children in music education as they grew, teaching them the basic classical music theory that she had learned from her mother and her classes at Avery College. She also taught them music history, as well as acquainting the children with the great musicians of the day—several of whom came to Erie to perform at the Russell home.

"Oh yes, Mama, I remember him. Please can I go with you, pleeease?" Harry asked in a preadolescent whine.

"Now you know you can't go with me to Mrs. Russell's house, sugar."

"But Mama, I'm nine years old. I can behave myself. Please, Mama."

"Honey, I know you can, but you just can't come to this recital," she said as she pulled on her coat, gloves, and hat. "Mrs. Russell is a very particular woman, and she just won't abide having children around for such an occasion. I'm sorry, baby, but you'll just have to stay here with your daddy." The dejected boy turned and began slowly walking up the staircase. "Now, aren't you gonna give your Mama a kiss before she leaves?"

Harry turned and walked back down the stairs. "Yes, Mama." He wrapped his arms around his mother's neck, kissing her on the cheek. "Mama, I just love to listen to the music. I hear the piano play and I have to go and watch. I don't know why, Mama, but I don't want to miss a single note."

"You've got too much of your grandfather in you, Harry." She smiled as she held his shoulders. "You definitely have his voice." She hugged him tightly. "Don't worry, baby. There will be other concerts. Someday, maybe little boys will run to hear you sing."

His face lit up. "Really? Would they come to hear me sing if I practice really hard?"

"Honey, I'm sure of it." She kissed him on the forehead. "You be good for your daddy, all right?" Harry nodded and watched his mother kiss his brothers and sisters good-bye. She then wrapped her scarf around her face and stepped out into the harsh winter wind.

Harry turned and walked slowly back up the stairs to his room. He plopped down on his bed with a thud and stared up at the ceiling. From down below he could hear his father in the kitchen, cleaning up the dinner dishes and singing a happy, familiar melody. Harry turned and put his head off the side of the bed to listen through the floorboards.

> Roll Jordan roll, roll Jordan roll,
> I want to go to heaven when I die,
> To hear Jordan roll.

He couldn't resist the urge to take the music in—to make it a part of himself. Suddenly an idea popped into his head. He stopped singing along and mulled the thought over for a moment. Jumping out of bed, he began furiously lacing up his boots. Just then his older brother, Reginald, walked into the bedroom. "Where are you going?" he asked, as Harry finished with his boots.

"I'm going outside to play."

"I'll come too," Reginald replied.

"No," said Harry. "I need to go alone."

Instantly suspicious, Reginald asked, "Why, where are you going?"

"It's a secret. I just need to be by myself."

"OK, but what do I tell Papa, if he wants to know where you are?"

"Tell him I went out to play, and I'll be home soon."

Harry ran past his brother and down the stairs. He grabbed his coat and quickly ducked out into the dark, cold January evening. Running quickly down the block, he turned the corner onto French Street and headed south toward the Russell mansion. It was already after seven o'clock and the winter sun had set nearly two hours before. The gas lamps that Reginald and Hamilton had lit earlier that afternoon now burned brightly, lighting up the snow-covered sidewalk in front of him.

In his haste to get out of the house undetected, Harry had left behind his woolen cap and mittens. The wind swirled around him, throwing hardened snow crystals up into his face like wood chips coming off a sawmill blade. He squinted and turned his head to avoid the sting. Coming to the large square in the center of town, he crossed the street and walked along North Park Row. In the distance, through the falling snow, he could see the lights of the Russell mansion. He leaned into the wind, which was whipping in from the west, and made his way toward his goal. Passing the Vosburgh Barber Shop and the Dispatch Building, he could see the dim lights of Park Presbyterian Church on the far side of Perry Square. Crossing the street to the park, Harry stood behind a tree, spying out the Russell estate. His hands, ears, nose, and toes were already beginning to sting from the cold.

As a child, Mrs. Margaret Russell, the matron of the home, had been trained in European music. From her youth she loved listening to classical musicians. Her father, one of Erie's first bankers, sent her to the best schools where she received formal instruction in music theory and history. Having married R. W. Russell, a wealthy industrialist,

Margaret soon achieved her goal of becoming a leading socialite in the city. Soon the Russell home became a familiar stop for the great musicians of the day traveling by rail from New York to Chicago.

The mansion was a large redbrick structure with tall mahogany doors hung under a granite entranceway. A low granite wall surrounded the property. At the entrance, four white Roman pillars supported a portico, and a bright gas lamp hung from the ceiling. Two brass angels stood like sentries on either side of the staircase. In their hands were gas torches under glass domes that lit up the walkway in front of the mansion.

"It's freezing out here," Harry scolded himself as he stared at the grand home. "Why did I leave my gloves behind?" He remembered what his brother Reginald had told him about little kids freezing to death in a blizzard. "The wind and the snow sting your skin like a switch," his brother had said. "Then you start to shiver so bad that you can't stop your teeth from chattering. All of a sudden you lose the feeling in your feet and hands, and even your nose. And just before you die, you start to feel really good, like you're warm all over."

Harry spoke into the cold night air. "Well, as long as my hands sting I'll be all right."

He could see the doorman's silhouette inside the vestibule and decided to sneak around to the side of the house. The boy knew there was an ornate window box on the south side of the mansion. Maybe he could watch the concert from there. As he made his way across the street, his feet slid on the ice and he nearly fell as he tripped in the wide ruts left by the wheels of numerous carriages and wagons. He climbed over the low granite wall and trudged through the knee-deep snow to the window box. The boy was shivering from the cold, and his teeth began to chatter.

Harry slowly raised his head up above the windowsill and peered inside. He quickly forgot his pain when he heard the faint music from the other side of the window. As he peered through the window, the grand scene unfolded before him. What he saw took his breath away. Men in black suits sat sipping brandy and smoking thick cigars. Some of the gentlemen were clean shaven with waxed mustaches curled up on the ends, while others had long, wiry beards that flowed down to their cummerbunds. The women wore elegant evening gowns covered in lace, their hair standing high on their heads. Every neck was adorned with sparkling diamonds, rubies, or emeralds. Harry could see the grand piano and hear its wonderful tones.

Suddenly he saw his mother walk into the room carrying a tray filled with delicious-looking little foods. He ducked down to be sure he couldn't be seen.

As he pressed his ear against the glass his heartbeat began to quicken. A rush of excitement filled his chest as he heard the muffled but powerful notes of the piano being played masterfully.

I've never heard anything so grand. He is amazing.

The steam from his breath fogged the window and he repeatedly wiped it with his coat sleeve. After some time, the chill in the air created frost on the glass from his wet breath, obstructing his view. The cold, wet snow trickled over the edge of his boots and slid down to his feet. A battle ensued between the frigid winter night and the warmth of the music inside the mansion. For the moment the music was winning.

The notes emanating from the piano at the hands of the master pulled the lad through the window and into the great hall. He saw himself inside the mansion, dressed in a black suit and white tie, standing next to the grand piano. Harry imagined bowing to the ladies and gentlemen and then turning to Joseffy. The master begins to play an elegant melody and the child prodigy, the spectacular Harry Burleigh, sings along as golden tones resonate from deep within him.

The boy savored every keystroke. As the virtuoso pounded out the notes Harry saw them spring to life like ballroom dancers, clinging to one another on top of the piano. Every time Joseffy hit a high chord, another emerged onto the dance floor. The notes were dressed as beautifully as the dinner guests and spun round and round in a frenzy. The faster the pianist played, the more the notes spun, moving around the ballroom like phantom spirits, propelled by the master musician. The sight was marvelous to behold.

Jesus, I want to be as good a singer as he is on the piano. The prayer rose to heaven with the steam of his breath, accompanied by the glorious music.

To Harry it seemed like mere moments, but in reality the boy had been standing at the window for more than an hour. From within the home Joseffy played the final, thundering chord and the guests roared their approval. As the clapping ceased and people began to mill about inside, a strong gust of wind reached its icy hand and wrenched the boy back into the snow. The warm music remained in the house, but Harry was left alone to grapple with the ice and the frigid arctic air.

He shivered violently and could not keep his teeth from chattering. He knew he needed to get out of the cold, and quickly. Panic began to grip his mind as the words of his brother screamed in his ears. *All of a sudden you lose the feeling in your feet and hands and even your nose. And just before you die, you start to feel really good, like you're warm all over.*

"I can't feel my feet!" Harry screamed into the howling wind. He jumped up and down in the snow, but no feeling came. He hit his hands together and could hear the clapping, but did not feel a thing. "Oh no. Oh no." For a moment he considered going to the door of the mansion, but he knew that his mother would be outraged.

Harry decided to make a run for home. He worked his way back through the snow, pulling his feet up and down through the deep, heavy drifts on the mansion lawn. When he finally reached the wall he noticed that his nose and ears had stopped stinging. The wet snow, driven by the wind, slapped again and again at his face, making it difficult to breathe. The blizzard was growing in intensity as he ran back across the icy street and down North Park Row. He began to cry as the wind howled and panic gripped his heart. He imagined himself in a snowbank on the side of the park, frozen in a large chunk of ice. He pictured his father wailing in the night air as he chipped away the ice to free his little blue body.

"If I m-make it home, will they have t-t-to cut off my hands and f-feet?" he chattered into the darkness. Dread pushed him to run faster. With the wind at his back, he turned the corner and slid on a smooth sheet of ice, falling to the ground. When he made it to his feet, he once again broke into a run, trying to avoid the ice patches. Fear pushed him on and he flew down French Street to Third Street and around the corner. Partially frozen tears covered his cheeks as he burst through the door of his home.

John Elmendorf sprang from his chair. "Where in heaven's name have you been, boy? I have looked everywhere for you." Harry was still panicking. He jumped up and down to try to get the feeling back in his feet.

"I d-d-don't want to die, D-Daddy!" he screamed as he ran in place. "I can't f-feel my f-f-feet."

The man tried to calm him down. "It will be all right, you're not going to die." He reached out and touched Harry's cheek. Ice crystals had solidified in the boy's hair, and his skin was terribly cold. "Oh my Lord," John exclaimed. "Boy, let's get you out of those wet clothes."

The boy was still whimpering as his stepfather led him up the stairs to his bedroom. He pulled off the lad's wet boots and clothes as quickly as he could. As warmth slowly started coming back into Harry's feet and hands, the stinging resumed.

"It hurts, D-Daddy. It h-hurts so b-bad." The boy was wheezing now and began to cough. John dressed him in warm clothes and wrapped him in a big blanket. He placed him on the bed and lay down next to him to help the boy get warm. Within minutes Harry began coughing from deep in his chest.

"I'm sorry, Papa. I shouldn't have stayed out so long." He was finally gaining control over the shivering.

"Where were you? I looked all around the neighborhood."

"I was just out playing and didn't realize how late it got," Harry lied. He began coughing again.

"We'll talk about this tomorrow with your Mama. For now, you get to sleep." John kissed him on the forehead and stayed until the boy fell asleep.

It seemed like only moments later that Harry woke up alone in his bed with a violent cough. His toes and fingers still ached and his chest was tight. It was becoming difficult for him to breathe. "God, I'm sorry for lying. Please forgive me. Don't let me die," Harry prayed.

As he lay in bed agonizing over his deception, the sweet notes he heard through the windowpane began to roll over and over again in his mind, bringing comfort and a slight smile to his face. Suddenly his chest tightened and he coughed a deep, hoarse cough. Again fear clutched his heart. "Please forgive me, God." Slowly the music returned and he drifted back to sleep.

It was a fitful night for Harry. His chest had filled with fluid and he coughed so hard he woke himself up several times. The next morning he was flush with a fever. Elizabeth had come home late the night before and heard about the incident from her husband. As daylight crept into the boy's bedroom, she quietly checked her son's temperature. His fever was 104 degrees, and he was coughing from deep in his chest. He opened his eyes and saw the worried look on his mother's face.

"Harry, what in the world were you thinking, child?"

"Mama, I just had to hear him," he wheezed.

"Hear who?" she asked. "What are you talking about?"

"I know it was wicked of me, Mama, but when you told me that Joseffy was playing last night . . ." He coughed violently, then continued, "I just had to come to see him."

"Child, don't you know you could have caught pneumonia?" She remembered watching her own mother's painful death, and in her heart she feared that Harry faced the same peril. "Don't you ever disobey your mama like that. If you weren't so sick I'd put you over my knee right now." She reached up and felt his forehead. "Dear Jesus," she prayed out loud, "heal my foolish boy."

Harry lay in bed throughout the day, drifting in and out of sleep. His temperature remained high, despite Elizabeth's attempts to bring it down. That night he coughed right through, keeping his mother and father awake. The high fever brought on strange hallucinations. He dreamed of a handsomely dressed Joseffy sitting at the grand piano playing Mozart. Suddenly the room began spinning and the pianist was transformed into an evil-faced circus clown. The frightening apparition began pounding on the piano, which turned into a large coffin. Shrill noises and screams began emanating from the instrument. Spirits like demons or gargoyles began seeping out of the wooden box. They stood on top of the casket and danced together, twirling and spinning to the ghoulish music. As they danced, they screamed and cackled, swooping close to the boy's face with hellish delight.

Harry cried out in the night, bringing his mother rushing to his side.

"Make them stop, make them stop," he screamed.

Elizabeth grabbed her son and held him close. He was burning up. "It's stopped, Harry. I'm here. Don't fret, child. Jesus won't let anything happen to you."

"God, help me. Please, Lord, make them go away."

"John, fetch the doctor, now," Elizabeth begged her husband.

John Elmendorf grabbed his coat and ran out the door. He drove his horses as fast as they would run through the snow to the doctor's house. The hallucinations had returned by the time the doctor arrived. Harry drifted in and out of consciousness, screaming and crying out at what he saw.

"Draw a cold bath, immediately," the doctor commanded. "We have got to get this child's fever down or he'll die." John ran to the bathroom and began filling the tub. Elizabeth and the doctor pulled the boy's sweat-drenched clothes off of him. She carried him into the bathroom and placed him in the water.

Harry started to splash and scream. "It's too cold, Mama."

"Stay in there, Harry. We've got to cool you down." Elizabeth held her son's hands while John and the doctor held his feet. After a moment he stopped struggling and lay still in the water, his teeth chattering, tears streaming down his little face. When the doctor felt enough time had passed, they lifted Harry from the tub, dried him off and laid his shivering body back in bed. With the fever down, Harry slowly drifted back to sleep.

The doctor gave Elizabeth some medicine to break up the congestion. "This should ease the coughing. Don't let his fever spike again, whatever you do. Come and get me if there's an emergency."

Harry's fever finally broke after the third day, but the cough lingered on. Elizabeth made him stay in his room another two days. As punishment for disobeying his mother, he was required to write a composition on truth and deception. And he had to keep up with the schoolwork that Reginald brought from his teacher.

As Elizabeth thought about the situation, she realized that with Harry's insatiable love for music, such an event could happen again. She decided to see Mrs. Russell to ask what could be done.

"Pneumonia! What happened to the poor child?" the mistress inquired. Elizabeth removed her scarf and coat and told of Harry's ordeal. When Mrs. Russell heard the whole story, she nearly cried. "That sweet thing. He loves music so much that he would listen out in the snow? Well, we're just going to have to do something to make music more readily available to the lad." She pondered the situation for a moment as Elizabeth sat in silence. Suddenly an idea came to her. "Is the boy responsible?" Elizabeth nodded. "Perhaps there may be some way young Harry could help in the house when artists performed?"

"That would be wonderful," his mother responded with a smile. "He is a good boy and would take orders well."

After another moment of thought, Mrs. Russell came up with a plan. She insisted that Harry be given the job of doorman at the recitals so that he could hear the concerts. She had an outfit tailored for the boy that consisted of a white shirt, black vest, and black knickers with a satin stripe running down each side.

Harry was thrilled at the proposal and couldn't wait to try on his new uniform. Three weeks later, a handsome, young Harry T. Burleigh stood in the lobby of the palatial home and opened the door for the distinguished guests who arrived to hear talented Venezuelan pianist Teresa Carreno. Later in the evening he helped the maids wait on the guests and made himself useful by emptying the ashtrays, offering cigars, and wiping up spilled wine. Elizabeth smiled at her dapper son and winked at him from time to time as she walked past.

One person who captured the boy's attention was a magnificent-looking woman, the traveling companion of Ms. Carreno. She was a kindly, older soul who was dressed as elegantly as anyone he had ever seen. On the way through the door she stopped and greeted the boy warmly. "My, what a handsome-looking fellow. Good evening to you, young squire," she said.

Harry smiled, looked into her face, and said, "Good evening, ma'am," just as his mother had instructed him to. Later he learned that this kind, older woman was Mrs. Frances MacDowell, a friend to Mrs. Russell and a frequent visitor to her home. She also just happened to be the mother of the great American composer Edward MacDowell.

But on this, his first night in the service of Mrs. Russell, his heart was filled with joy to be so close to the music that he loved. As Ms. Carreno began her recital the mansion was once again filled with distinguished men and women, the cream of society. But this time, in the warm vestibule was nine-year-old Harry T. Burleigh, who stood at attention and watched the beautifully dressed notes as they waltzed on top of the piano.

1891–NEW YORK CITY

The rumble of a passing fire wagon brought Harry back to the park. He sat up and rubbed the slumber from his eyes as he pondered an intriguing thought. *Maybe in time I could launch my own theater group that would only perform artistic pieces?*

He was still discouraged by his failure at the audition, but the thought of launching an artistic touring company gave him a small sense of comfort. Maybe a black man from Erie, Pennsylvania, wasn't meant to attend the greatest conservatory in America.

Harry stood up from the bench and slowly walked back to the hotel. As he entered the lobby, he realized that he had forgotten to send the telegram to his mother. He pulled his pocket watch from his vest. *4:45 p.m.—just enough time to send a note to Mother.* He stopped at the front desk and wrote out the message for the telegraph office.

> Audition did not go well. Will receive grade tomorrow. Offer given to travel with minstrel group. Thinking of accepting.
>
> H.T.B.

Harry handed the hotel clerk the telegram and boarded the elevator. The hot, stale air rushed out at him as he opened the door to his room. The familiar, hopeless feeling once again overtook him in the stifling heat. He opened the window wider to let in some fresh air, but it made no difference. Harry leaned his head out the window and looked down the cavernous avenue. The sun was setting in the west above the bustling city street. *Tomorrow I'll take the position with the minstrel show.* The smell of the horses and garbage on the street below wafted up to his window, causing him to feel nauseous.

He pulled his head back into the room, stripped to his underwear, and lay down on the bed, hoping that his stomach would settle. As the light slowly faded from the room, questions reverberated in his brain. *Who will give me a break? When will my chance come?* He lay in bed, staring at the ceiling and listening to the din from the crowded street below. When a slightly cooler breeze blew through the window, the nausea lifted and he finally fell asleep.

5

Didn't My Lord Deliver Daniel?

Early the following morning Harry rose with a pounding headache and began getting dressed in his best suit. Even though he fully anticipated rejection, he wanted to maintain a sophisticated appearance. Looking in the faded mirror above the dresser, he adjusted his bowtie and collar, then turned and walked out the door toward the small metal elevator.

As he was about to exit the hotel, the clerk called out, "Mr. Burleigh, there's a telegram for you." The wire was from his mother.

Don't despair. God is with you. Give the letter to Mrs. MacDowell. Stay away from the minstrels. Love,

Mama

As he read the telegram Harry didn't know whether to laugh or cry. He had completely forgotten about the letter from his former employer. He went back to his room and rifled through his suitcase, looking for Mrs. Russell's letter. Harry pulled out the slightly wrinkled envelope and looked at the familiar handwriting. He folded it over and placed it in his jacket pocket. It was a small piece of home and for a moment the note, along with his mother's telegram, lifted his spirits.

He walked the few blocks from his hotel to the conservatory in the hot sun. The time had come to receive the verdict. Harry went straight to the registrar's office. "Good morning, Mrs. MacDowell. I wanted to reintroduce myself to you." He extended his hand across the desk.

The lady shook his hand and responded, "Yes, Harry Burleigh, I remember you from yesterday."

"Actually, we met before. It was many years ago," Harry replied.

"Really? Forgive me, but I don't recall."

"It was in my hometown of Erie, Pennsylvania. You were visiting the home of Mrs. Russell, and I was working as the doorman."

"My, that was some time ago." She gave him a quizzical look. "Mrs. Russell? Why I haven't seen her in years. You aren't the cute little boy I met at the door, are you?"

Harry smiled. "As a matter of fact I am."

"Well, now you are making me feel positively ancient." She chuckled and paused. Looking him up and down she finally blurted out, "Yes, I remember you. How good it is to see you again. How is Mrs. Russell? I haven't been to Erie for quite some time."

"She's doing fine. My mother still works for her."

"Is that so? Well, isn't that delightful? I am so happy to meet you again." Suddenly she remembered the business at hand. "Well, Mr. Burleigh, let us see how you did. I seem to recall that you were somewhat nervous."

Harry blushed. "Yes, ma'am. I must admit, it was a bit intimidating."

"It's meant to be, dear. That is how we separate the wheat from the chaff." She smiled and looked down at the ledger. "Let me find your record." Harry held his breath as she read his score. She looked up at him with a sympathetic smile and announced, "Harry, you were given an ABA for reading and a B for voice." She paused, clasped her hands in front of her, and pulled them up to her chin as if in prayer. "Unfortunately, the required mark for a scholarship is an AA. I'm sorry, but your scores are too low to be considered for a position at this time."

Though he had braced himself for the worst, the news hit him like a blow to the stomach. He stared at her for a moment and then looked around the room as if searching for a hiding place.

"I am truly sorry, dear," the elderly woman said softly.

"I—I don't know what to say." He laughed at the hopelessness of the situation and looked up at the ceiling, blinking continually to keep from crying. After a long pause he looked back down at the registrar. "For as long as I can remember it's been my unquenchable ambition to become noted as someone of importance in the realm of music. Ever since I saw Master Joseffy at the Russell home when I was a boy, I have longed to be a professional musician." Mrs. MacDowell could not find any more words of comfort, and for a moment they both stared at the floor in awkward silence.

Suddenly Harry remembered the letter from Mrs. Russell. He reached into his pocket and pulled out the folded envelope. "Here you are, Mrs. MacDowell, I almost forgot to give this to you. It's a letter from Mrs. Russell."

"Oh, thank you, dear. I'm glad you remembered," she said with a slight smile as she tore open the envelope.

Harry stood motionless as she read, trying to decide what to do next. He only had enough money for a few more nights in a hotel. As the woman read the note he decided to leave, but when he turned to go it was as if something was holding him there. He could only stand still and watch as the kind woman read the letter.

When she finished, Frances MacDowell slowly looked up at the young man. "Well, Harry, this is very interesting." She looked back down and reread the words she held in her hand. "It seems that Mrs. Russell thinks very highly of you. I'm sure Master Joseffy will be interested in reading this letter." She pondered the thought for a moment. "Why don't you return tomorrow morning? I will see if we might reconsider your situation."

Harry couldn't believe his ears. He hesitated for a moment and stammered as he processed his thoughts. "Rea—really? Tomorrow morning?"

"Yes, be here at ten o'clock. And bring another selection with you."

The young man couldn't help but let his emotions show. "Thank you Mrs. MacDowell." He grabbed her wrinkled hand and shook it vigorously. "Thank you very much."

"I recommend that you go and review your theoretical concepts, young man. I'm quite sure the committee will have a question or two for you in the morning."

Harry tried to be serious but couldn't help grinning. "Yes, ma'am. I'll run right to my hotel and look over my papers." He turned to leave, then quickly turned back. "And I'll stop at the library too." He briskly shook her hand again as she laughed. He bowed, then turned and nearly ran out of the building.

Burleigh flew from the conservatory with renewed joy and strength. This was the chance he was looking for. He would not make the same mistakes again. Harry spent the night in study, rehearsal, and prayer.

The next morning, he dressed in his own faded but comfortable suit and walked casually back to the conservatory. He greeted Mrs. MacDowell when he arrived in her office. "They are ready for you," she said with a wink, then ushered him into the same room as before. "You will do fine," she whispered into his ear just before closing the door.

The room and the faces were no longer foreign, and he felt much more comfortable in his own clothes. He gave the accompanist the sheet music and took his place in the center of the room. Harry's voice was rich and smooth as honey, and this time he hit every note effortlessly. The committee members were drawn to his performance from the first note. Some of them had a hard time believing this was the same young man from the earlier audition.

"You should have used that selection the first time, young man," Joseffy remarked with a slight grin when Harry finished. The panel grilled him with questions and he answered every one flawlessly. Harry had done everything he could to secure the scholarship; now it was in God's hands. Leaving the rehearsal hall, Harry walked over to Mrs. MacDowell's office. She brought him a glass of water and gently rubbed his shoulder. "I gave it all I have," he said, smiling.

"That is all you can do," she answered with a smile. "Why don't you have a seat? The committee will make their decision quickly."

The young man sat pensively in the registrar's office, waiting for word. After what seemed like an eternity, Mrs. MacDowell opened the door and walked right past him, setting a stack of papers on her desk. She sat down and began working without looking at him. Harry stood in confused silence, watching her for nearly a minute. Finally, she looked up and said in a terse manner, "Now that you are a student here, you will likely need some form of employment."

Harry jumped in the air. "You mean . . ."

"I need custodial help," she continued without missing a beat. "Are you interested in a part-time job?" she asked, her eyes twinkling with delight.

Harry laughed out loud. "Yes, ma'am, I surely am."

"Fine, consider yourself gainfully employed. Report to work at eight a.m. on Monday morning. Classes begin two weeks after that."

"Monday morning, yes, ma'am. I'll be here." Harry ran out the door, then turned and poked his head back into the registrar's office. "God bless you, Mrs. MacDowell." She smiled and regally nodded her head as if to say "You're welcome." Harry turned and ran down the hallway. Breaking through the doors to the outside, he hollered into the street, "Hallelujah! Glory be!"

6

Wade in de Water

"It was like a romance," Burleigh said when telling about his time at the conservatory. He worked for Mrs. MacDowell both as a handyman and a personal secretary. People quickly discovered his stenography skills, and he was also given manuscript work from time to time. His scholarship covered only tuition, not room and board, so the extra work helped keep his stomach full and his expensive New York City rent paid.

While Harry was thankful for the janitor's job, he preferred to work as often as he could in his chosen field of music. During his time at the conservatory he also found employment as a private tutor, a vocalist, and a teacher, training choirs throughout the city. Whenever he started to get discouraged he reminded himself that he was a student at the greatest musical school in the country.

Harry knew in his soul that the sacrifice he was making would be worth the pain, just as the sacrifices his grandfather and his mother had made before him had been made to prepare him for this moment. Harry determined to never forget the price that his mother, stepfather, and grandparents paid to give him a step up in life. He often remembered the stories his mother told of her struggle to make it as a teacher in the years following the Civil War.

1851–Erie, Pennsylvania

Three daughters were born to Hamilton and Lucinda Waters: Elizabeth, Louise, and Jane, who died as a young girl. Young Elizabeth Waters grew with the city of Erie, from a baby born in the wilderness to a sophisticated teenager in a growing American city. Her mother passed on to her daughters the manners she learned early in life. She taught the girls how to speak courteously to others, especially to elders and persons in authority. They learned how to walk with an air of grace and dignity. The children were instructed in all things domestic, but they were also encouraged to follow their dreams, wherever they might take them. Elizabeth inherited a graciousness from her mother that would serve her well in the years to come.

She also inherited her father Hamilton's gift for singing. On countless nights in their modest wooden home the family sat around the fireplace telling stories and singing cheerful melodies. As she matured, Elizabeth was often asked to sing in church or at community events. Over time she gained a reputation as a natural singer and became a favorite in the gospel choir.

Elizabeth and Louise attended the little mission school in Erie established by abolitionist William Himrod, who also operated the mission house and church. Himrod sold parcels of land in Erie to black families, many of them former slaves, at an affordable price to help them get a start in life. He named this neighborhood on the western fringes of town "New Jerusalem." He sold the lots to both whites and blacks with the provision that they would eventually build a house and reside on the property.

From her earliest years, Elizabeth yearned to become a teacher. She was diligent in her studies and was especially gifted at learning foreign languages. One day in her final year of preparatory school she burst into their small wooden house, startling Hamilton, who was sitting in his rocking chair. Elizabeth ran over and knelt on the floor beside him.

"Papa," she said excitedly, "I would like to go to college to learn to teach the French language."

The man was pleased but not surprised by the request. "Well, Liz'beth, dat's very interesting," he declared as he placed his pipe in the ashtray and stroked his stubbly beard. "How'd you decide on dis profession?" he asked.

"I've been learning French at school and speaking it with friends. Sometimes we go to the docks and talk to the French traders from Canada. They tell me that I can speak the language rather well," she replied. "I know I can do it, Papa. You know how hard I work in school."

Hamilton laughed and put his arm around his precious teenage daughter. "If'n anybody works hard at school it's you," he declared as he gave her a big hug. Hamilton and Lucinda had been thinking about Elizabeth's future for quite some time. The teachers at the mission school told them they had an extremely gifted child. Through Hamilton's abolitionist friends, they had heard of a progressive school near Pittsburgh called Avery College. In 1849 one of Pittsburgh's wealthiest men, a staunch abolitionist named Charles Avery, founded a school for the education of black Americans, both freeborn and former slaves. Like Himrod, Avery was a white abolitionist who believed that one of the key means for the black race to rise from slavery was through education.

Hamilton was also a strong proponent of this view. "Your mama and I done heard of a school near Pittsburgh, run by godly folk—it's called Avery College. I's been told dat it's a good school. We'll pray and ask de Lawd to let you go der."

Elizabeth shrieked with joy, causing Hamilton to start. The young girl bounded to her feet and jumped up in the air, clapping her hands for joy. She hugged her father, squeezing him with all of her strength. "I'll work really hard to be accepted by the school. I know my grades will be good enough."

"Honey, if God has called you to do dis, den God will make a way," he said, as once again she hugged him. "I'll find out what needs to be done to get you into de school," the proud father told her.

"I'm going to go tell my friends," she cried and raced out the door. Before she was able to get outside, she turned and rushed back to her father. "I love you, Papa," she said as she gave him one more hug and kissed him on the cheek.

"I loves you too," Hamilton said with a laugh. After she left the room he sat in his chair and smiled as he puffed vigorously on his pipe. His daughter, the child of a slave, was interested in becoming a teacher—it was a thrilling and utterly rewarding thought. His mind suddenly raced back to the whipping he himself had received for trying to learn to read. He remembered his mother, Lovey, who had passed away when the girls were still very young. She hadn't had a day of formal education in her entire life. Now her granddaughter wanted to go to college to learn to teach an entirely different language. *Hallelujah! Glory be!* he thought to himself.

He rocked quickly back and forth as the joy welled up like a fountain. Finally he could hold it in no longer. He stood up and began dancing a jig. He twirled and kicked, holding his pipe in his mouth. Suddenly he leapt into the air, and with all of his might he shouted, "Hallelujah! Glory be!"

Hamilton had diligently set money aside for his daughters' education. Here was a chance for the family to rise another step out of poverty and into a better life. Through self-denial and sacrifice, Hamilton saved enough money to send Elizabeth to Avery. The college specialized in the various branches of science and literature, along with ancient and modern languages.

After four years, Elizabeth graduated from Avery on July 11, 1855. She received a bachelor's degree in language, having become proficient in French, Latin, and Greek. She was one of three women graduates and gave a commencement address in French.

During the graduation festivities, she also delivered an essay titled "American Institutions." In it, she spoke of sorrow for her race, with so many still in bondage. Like her father, Elizabeth believed that slavery was a stain upon America's soul. The *Pittsburgh Gazette* covered the event, describing Elizabeth as "a very intelligent young lady in appearance, whose pronunciation of the French language was impeccable and indicated an excellent knowledge of the tongue."

The *Erie Weekly Gazette* also reported Elizabeth's graduation from Avery nearly a week later:

> The first-named of these graduates is the elder daughter of Mr. H. E. Waters, of this city—a colored man of unusual intelligence. Superadded to her well-known natural talents, she has now an education qualifying her for the position of a teacher in the first seminary in the land. We

are happy to have it in our power to record the fact. It is a glorious commentary on the progressive tendencies of the age.

Unfortunately, the directors of Public School Number 1 in Erie did not subscribe to the same "progressive tendencies of the age." When Elizabeth inquired about a teaching job, she was courteously refused. Though she applied for teaching jobs across the country, she was rejected again and again. After months of searching, she finally took a job teaching at the Himrod Mission School where she had attended as a child. While it was a joy to actually be a teacher, the pay was far below what she could have made at a public school.

Soon after Elizabeth's graduation, the heat of rhetoric surrounding slavery reached a fever pitch in the nation. With the election of Abraham Lincoln, the Civil War erupted and men both young and old throughout the northern states began marching out to defend the Union. Reports returned periodically concerning major battles and the overall state of the troops. The daily newspaper carried lists of Erie boys killed or wounded in action.

President Lincoln insisted that the war was an effort to preserve the Union, but most folks instinctively understood the root cause of the conflict was slavery. Sentiments concerning African Americans were strong, both positive and negative, as the war dragged on. Some whites couldn't understand why their boys had to go off to fight a war and die merely to free the southern slaves. It was only a few years earlier that people in Erie had also owned slaves. The climate made it impossible for many black people to find work. As the war raged on, there were few positions for educated Negroes—especially women.

Elizabeth made do the best she could, teaching the youngsters at the mission. She also worked as a language tutor and as a servant in the homes of Erie's most wealthy people—a skill she had learned from her mother that came in handy when times were tough.

During her time at Avery, Elizabeth's eyes were opened even wider to the indignities of slavery. When she came back to Erie, she quickly volunteered for various abolitionist activities with her father. It was through these acquaintances that Elizabeth met a handsome young Civil War veteran named Henry Thacker Burleigh.

Originally from Massachusetts, he was dispatched to Erie by the Navy to help coordinate the defense of the Great Lakes. Henry was a gifted organizer and quickly became involved in abolitionist causes in the Erie area after leaving the Navy. Working with a network of abolitionists that stretched from the Gulf of Mexico to the Great Lakes, Henry transported hundreds of fugitives along the Underground Railroad. His military training served him well in this endeavor, and he was often sent to serve in some of the most dangerous missions.

Henry would escort runaway slaves to the old Methodist church in Wesleyville, just east of Erie. For many years the church served as a place of rendezvous and concealment. Other than the regular Sunday services, Thursday night prayer meetings, and an occasional funeral, the church was unused. It was as safe a place as could be found on the edge of the growing city. Runaways hid in the bell tower until visitors to the church had finished their business and moved on.

Through his abolitionist connections, Henry Burleigh was able to secure a job as a janitor in the church. The position was merely a cover for the dangerous work that took place there. As a strong young man, Burleigh quickly became a key conductor on the Railroad, receiving fugitives from Ohio at the church and then helping them to move east to Buffalo. Of course, assisting a runaway slave was illegal under the strict Fugitive Slave Act, but Henry used all of his energies to help his brothers in chains. There were some nights Henry wouldn't come home until nearly four a.m., only to rise at seven a.m. and head for work. This kind of activity continued throughout the war.

Elizabeth and Henry soon fell in love and were married in 1864. The couple moved in with Hamilton and Lucinda and quickly started filling the house with children of their own. Their firstborn, Reginald, was born on November 14 that same year.

After the war, Henry found work as a bank messenger for Mr. W. C. Curry, founder of the Second National Bank of Erie. He also labored as a servant for Curry's daughter, Mrs. Margaret Russell. Henry was well liked throughout the city, and he soon became a leader in the black community.

Two years after the birth of Reginald, a second son was born on December 2, 1866. He was christened Henry after his father, but he soon came to be known as Harry T. Burleigh.

Like all African Americans, the Burleighs and the Waterses rejoiced with the Emancipation Proclamation, the passing of the Thirteenth Amendment, and the end of the Civil War. But with the cessation of hostilities came the burden of reconstructing the tattered nation. More than 750,000 Americans had died in the bloody struggle. The national debt was now nearly five times as great as it was before the war. Cities throughout the South were devastated and needed to be rebuilt. A soldier from Atlanta returned to his once-fair hometown and remarked, "Hell has laid her egg, and right here it hatched."

Throughout the South, economic life had ground to a standstill. Without slavery, the agricultural system that sustained the southern way of life foundered. Once-vibrant plantations yielded only weeds. Seed was scarce and much of the livestock had been killed or driven off by starved former slaves and Confederates or by plundering Yankees. In some regions, the transportation system had been nearly destroyed by Union troops. Much of the black labor supply fled to the northern cities to enjoy their new freedom.

One of the most pressing concerns of the postwar government was what to do with approximately four million blacks who were suddenly thrust from slavery into liberty. As the Union army occupied town after town, plantation owners gathered their human chattel and announced their freedom. It was finally the Day of Jubilee, and the news was met with wild rejoicing by the black multitudes. Thousands of former slaves gathered their things and set out to find long-separated loved ones, a promised job up north, or a new life in the Wild West.

As they pursued these dreams, however, some were lured back into slavery in parts of the country where Union troops did not police. Inexperienced ex-slaves were swindled out of the little money they had with the false promise of "forty acres and a mule" from the government in Washington. Still others were caught by roving gangs of former slaveholders and were beaten and even hanged from tree limbs and gallows throughout the South.

All across the country, African Americans experienced the backlash of reconstruction. It soon became apparent that life for black folks in the years after the war would not be much better, in many cases, than it had been before. In some ways it was worse. Though Henry was working, his pay was minimal. Elizabeth still could not find a good paying job, so she continued to teach at the mission school. Both were able to make extra money serving at special occasions for wealthy Erieites and through private tutoring.

After the war, Henry Burleigh became active in helping former slaves who had come north to find work. He found places for them to stay and helped them search for decent employment. He and Elizabeth worked with the Himrod Mission to provide education for their children. Many who were abolitionists before the Civil War became active in conventions of freedmen—societies designed to fight for their newly gained rights. Ministers and freeborn blacks like Henry Burleigh often led these groups. They lobbied Washington, seeking aid to help fellow ex-slaves during reconstruction. Henry was called upon to make several trips outside of Erie as a leader in this movement.

This was very satisfying work, but the pay was modest at best. Even with the labor of all four adults in the household, the family struggled to make it financially. But the house was filled with love and laughter, which compensated for any shortage of material things. They were free people in a free land, and they had much to be thankful for. This was the world into which Harry T. Burleigh was born.

1891–NEW YORK CITY

While Harry found himself physically hungry many times in those early years in New York, there was no famine in his academic life. The professors at the conservatory were some of the finest musical minds in all of America. During his years at the conservatory, Harry studied voice, harmony, and counterpoint. He also studied music history, stage deportment, and fencing. He was the orchestra librarian and played double bass and timpani in the orchestra.

Though he did well in his classes, he did not yet possess the training to enjoy the privilege of studying advanced theory. There were strong rumors floating around the conservatory that the following semester this high-level class would be taught by none other than the great Bohemian composer Antonin Dvorak. Harry noticed that students were pronouncing the man's eastern European name in all sorts of ways, so he decided to ask Mrs. MacDowell what the proper pronunciation should be.

"His name is pronounced Dah-Vor-Zhok, dear," she said, slowly and clearly. "And we are so fortunate that he will be our new director!"

Mrs. Jeanette Thurber, founder of the National Conservatory and a fanatic patron of the arts, had first contacted Antonin Dvorak in early spring of 1891. Mrs. Thurber was both bold and savvy. She vigorously pursued Dvorak with the hope that through him her lifelong dream of building the conservatory into a vibrant artistic institution rivaling the great European schools would be fulfilled. Dvorak declined Mrs. Thurber's early attempts to persuade him to become director. He was content in his position as professor of composition at the Prague Conservatory, where he was recognized as a prolific and honored composer. Headstrong Jeanette Thurber, however, refused to take no for an answer.

Her husband, Francis Thurber, was the owner of a wholesale grocery business with retail outlets throughout the state of New York and beyond. He was one of the first businessmen in America to sell shares of a corporation to employees, giving them part ownership of the enterprise. Employing wise business practices, he had risen from humble beginnings to become one of the wealthiest men in the United States. Through his wife and the conservatory, he also became an ardent supporter of the arts. As a result of the Thurbers' persuasion, Carnegie, Belmont, and others had given hundreds of thousands of dollars to support the conservatory.

Through what she called "the personal touch," Jeanette was also able to convince her husband to contribute funds to bring the Bohemian master to America. She finally approached Dvorak with the handsome offer of fifteen thousand dollars a year to teach, perform, and compose in America. At long last he gave in, agreeing to become director of her National Conservatory.

But it was not only the money that persuaded him. He had heard the Fisk Jubilee Singers as they traveled in Europe and was intrigued by the rich melodies of the spirituals. Many Europeans viewed Americans as uncultured and unsophisticated, but Dvorak's impression was that this was not entirely true. He wanted to observe firsthand the musical, social, and political culture of the United States. And he was very interested in helping to cultivate the seedlings of a truly American style of music.

Antonin Dvorak strongly believed the source of an American musical style would be found in folk music, including African American and Native American themes. It was time for a musical revolution, he believed, to wean the child from the musical mother. He was convinced that America would have her own music, and it would one day affect the rest of the world.

By the time Harry T. Burleigh arrived in New York, he had received a deep appreciation of his own folk music heritage and also training in European American art music through his mother and grandfather. The combination served the young singer well at the conservatory.

Jeanette Thurber also recognized the genius of America's black musicians and had established the scholarship that Burleigh won in order to attract the greatest musical minds in the African American community. Burleigh had already been in school for a semester when Dvorak arrived in the United States, setting the stage for an unlikely encounter that would change the course of American musical history.

7

Little David Play on Your Harp

Jeanette Thurber was a persistent woman. When she set her mind on an idea, it was difficult for anyone to persuade her otherwise. When she read an article on how Antonin Dvorak was encouraging musicians around the world to use folk music as the inspiration and basis for their classical compositions, she decided he would be the next director of the National Conservatory of Music in New York City.

"I am so glad that Dr. Dvorak has finally come to his senses," Jeanette told her husband. "There is nowhere else in the world where he can put his theories about folk music to such good use."

As a child growing up in Bohemia, Antonin Dvorak had been the son of a butcher and an innkeeper. Though his father loved the music that was played and sung in the inn, he had little musical talent himself. Young Antonin taught himself to play the violin and was somewhat of a musical prodigy. He often entertained the guests at the inn by playing the violin. Dvorak's papa had misgivings about the boy's love for music at first, and enlisted him at eleven years old as an apprentice butcher. The son, however, was interested only in music and spent all his spare time learning to play the organ, viola, and piano.

In 1857, Dvorak's father finally gave in and allowed the lad to enroll in the Prague Organ School. After classes Antonin attended as many concerts as possible, following the wand of the conductor and studying the orchestra.

Upon graduation, Dvorak began earning a living as principal violinist in Prague's Provisional Theatre Orchestra. He also taught to supplement his income. In 1871 he finally stepped down from the orchestra in order to do the thing he loved more than anything else in the world—compose.

The great musician, Johannes Brahms, was the first person to recognize Dvorak's gift for composition. Brahms was on the board of the Austrian State Commission, which considered applications for a prize to assist "young, poor, and talented artists." Dvorak was the recipient of this grant and came to the attention of the respected Brahms.

In time, Brahms wrote a supportive letter to his publisher, Fritz Simrock, encouraging him to consider Dvorak's work:

Dear S.

In connection with the State grant, I have for several years past had great pleasure in the works of Antonin Dvorak in Prague. This year he sent in, among other things, a volume of duets for two sopranos with piano accompaniment, which seems to be very practical for publication. There is no doubt that he is very talented. And then he is also poor. I beg you to think the matter over. The duets won't give you much thought and will sell well.

> *With best greetings,*
> *Yours,*
> *J. Br.*

Dvorak received a copy of this letter from Simrock, and it became one of his most prized possessions. Whenever he read the kind words of his mentor he was taken back to those happy, hungry years of study under this musical colossus.

Simrock issued Dvorak's *Moravian Songs* for two voices and piano in 1877. Their reception was overwhelming and the publisher quickly called for dances for a piano duet similar to Brahms's *Hungarian Dances*. The product, *Slavonic Dances*, was so popular that Dvorak was soon able to devote the majority of his time to composition and teaching.

The instant and overwhelming success of these pieces led the Bohemian to worldwide fame. Not long after the success of the *Dances*, Dvorak wrote a note of thanks to Brahms:

> *Your last most valued letter I read with the most joyful excitement; your warm encouragement, and the pleasure you seem to find in my work, have moved me deeply, and made me unspeakably happy. I can hardly tell you, esteemed Master, all that is in my heart. I can only say that I shall all my life owe you the deepest gratitude for your good and noble intentions towards me, which are worthy of a truly great artist and man.*
>
> *Yours ever grateful,*
> *Antonin Dvorak*

As Jeanette Thurber had predicted, Dvorak's purpose in coming to America was, in part, to study the beautiful melodies of African Americans and Native Americans. He believed that artistic music should find grounding in folk expression, a belief that was spawned while listening to countless drinking songs in his father's inn. In Bohemia he had written operas about peasant life. He composed patriotic and folk songs, as well as instrumental pieces patterned after popular folk songs and dances. He also used folk legend and popular myth as basis for several concert works. The pursuit of an American school of music was one of Dvorak's main reasons for traveling to the United States.

After accepting Jeanette Thurber's invitation, Dvorak sailed across the Atlantic on the S.S. *Saale*, arriving in New York with his wife and two of his children on September 27, 1892. He quickly fell in love with America.

Earlier in life, Dvorak had developed a fascination with trains during his years in Prague. The port of New York, with its numerous docks, provided him with a new fascination—ocean liners. After some time he likened America to a steamship or a train, saying, "This country has the means to transmit its culture throughout the world." Dvorak predicted that in the future, American values and culture would be spread across the globe. He believed this would not only be a good thing for America, but also for the rest of the world.

The Bohemian musician was intrigued by the way many Americans worked to narrow the gap between social and economic classes. Once, while visiting Boston, he was impressed by a theater that presented operas and symphonies at inexpensive prices, giving the common man the opportunity to attend. Part of the reason he decided to direct the conservatory was to interact with the many black students, to learn their music, and to study their culture. And when he heard Burleigh's golden baritone, he was eager to get to know this bright young man.

1892–NEW YORK CITY

As snow fell on the streets of New York City in giant white flakes, students rushing in from the cold tracked the slush and mud onto the floors of the old building that housed the National Conservatory of Music. Joining the throng hurrying through the halls after the last afternoon classes were dismissed, Harry stopped at Mrs. MacDowell's office to receive instructions for the evening.

"Harry, we will need to have these floors mopped this evening. The slush from the street is making a terrible mess," she instructed, looking up from the open file she held in her hand. "Dear, have you finished with those papers I gave you earlier?"

"Yes, Mrs. MacDowell, I put them right there on your desk."

"Oh, my goodness, my desk is a dangerous place." She sifted through the mountain of papers in front of her. "I have so many things on my desk that I don't know whether the legs can support it. Ah, here they are! Thank you, Harry."

"You're welcome, Mrs. MacDowell." Burleigh smiled at the sweet elderly woman. "If it's all right, I'll be getting to those floors."

"Yes, of course, dear." He turned to walk out of the office. "Harry," she called. He turned back to her. "Please also be sure the walks are shoveled. I nearly broke my neck slipping on the ice in front of the school this morning."

"I'll throw some salt on them. That should take care of the ice."

"Thank you, my dear. Good night."

"Good night, Mrs. MacDowell."

Harry went right to work on the sidewalk in front of the school. He shoveled the steps and sidewalk and scattered salt to melt the ice. Coming back in from the cold, he hung his coat in the janitor's closet, turned on the faucet, and began filling a metal mop bucket with hot soapy water. As he waited he whistled one of his grandfather's favorite songs, "Wade in the Water." Harry pulled the bucket out of the tub, grabbed a mop, and wheeled it down the long, dark hallway that was now empty of all students. He loved the echo caused by the hardwood floors and the plaster ceiling. When he was alone in the building, he liked to whistle and sing as he mopped the floors.

> Wade in the water, wade in the water, children.
> Wade in the water, God's gonna trouble the water.

He continued singing as he worked his way down the hall. He often sang up-tempo songs while keeping rhythm with the mop.

> Wade in the water, wade in the water, children.
> Wade in the water, God's gonna trouble the water.

"What is this sound?" The voice boomed from a nearby doorway and echoed in the hallway. Startled, Burleigh jumped and spun around as Dr. Dvorak, the master himself, exploded from his office. He slipped on the freshly mopped floor as he rounded the corner, nearly falling. Regaining his balance, he looked up at the startled student. "Who was just singing? What is this sound?" he asked again in his thick Bohemian accent.

Burleigh swallowed hard. "It was me, sir. I'm sorry if I disturbed you. I didn't realize anyone was still in the building. I will stop immediately."

"Stop? No, no, no," the director exclaimed, carefully approaching him on the soapy floor. "You must sing for me these melodies."

For a moment, try as he might, no sound would come from the young student's mouth. "Right here—now?" he asked, finally.

"Yes, yes, finish the song," Dvorak insisted, placing his hands in the pockets of his satin vest. The two men stood in silence for a moment,

Harry searching for how to respond, and Dvorak staring at Burleigh with a quizzical look as if to say, "Well, get on with it."

Harry placed the mop against the wall, turned back to the master, took a deep breath, and continued to sing:

> I looked over Jordan, and what did I see?
> A band of angels coming after me.
> They're gonna take me to the heavenly place,
> Where the streets are paved with gold and they got pearly
> gates.
>
> Wade in the water; wade in the water, children.
> Wade in the water, God's gonna trouble the water.

Dvorak stood stroking his wiry gray beard, listening intently to the notes that flowed flawlessly from Burleigh's throat.

The composer embodied the spirit of the rapidly approaching new century—Dvorak lived in the present while vigorously pursuing the grand and wondrous future. He wore the traditional clothing of the era: black suit and tie, white silk shirt, slightly yellowed by constant cigar smoke, and his trademark raffish emerald-green vest. He loved spending time with his children in the countryside, but he was energized by the city—in awe of modern skyscrapers, locomotives, and especially ocean liners.

In music—and in all of life—he surrounded himself with a balance of the grand and the beautiful. He was the picture of confidence, taking control of any room or situation with his powerful persona. He was a true artist, drinking in the beauty of any expression, from music to architecture to painting. He came to America to experience and to promote the folk music he believed would be the foundation of an American style of music. Now, within days of his arrival, he had found the personification of this music right outside his office door.

When Harry finished the song the older man clapped his hands together and beamed with joy. "This is wonderful. What is your name, my young friend?"

"Harry T. Burleigh," he replied.

"Are you a student at the conservatory?"

"Yes, sir."

Dvorak struggled with the name. "Well Mr. 'Barley,' you will come home with me tonight. I want you to sing these melodies to my family."

This was a most unusual situation, and Harry wasn't quite sure what to say. "I would be glad to come to your home, Dr. Dvorak, but I must finish mopping these halls."

"Cannot the halls be mopped later in the evening?" the director asked.

Burleigh rubbed the back of his neck, smiled, and said, "I suppose they can, sir."

"Then you will put your mop away and come with me to my home across the park."

Burleigh had no further argument. He stored the mop and bucket in the closet, grabbed his coat, and followed Dvorak out the door. They walked down 17th Street and past Stuyvesant Square through the wet, freshly fallen snow, finally climbing the stairs leading to the Dvorak townhouse.

As soon as they walked through the door, the men were surrounded by the high-pitched voices of more than thirty birds. Kicking the snow off of his shoes, Dvorak laughed at the noise. "It is like a tropical paradise with this sound, yes?" Burleigh nodded in agreement as he removed his coat. Scattered throughout the townhouse were intricately decorated birdcages of every sort. In the corner of the living room was one large cage that housed more than twenty small singing birds. The legs of the cage looked like vines with gold-covered leaves. These thrushes filled the house with melodious song.

"You are finally home," Anna Dvorak, the composer's wife, rushed out from the dining room and grabbed their coats. "We have kept the food warm for you." She looked at Harry, then turned and spoke to her husband in their native tongue. "*We have no need for further servants, Antonin. Who is this Negro?*"

The master answered her in English. "He is a student at the conservatory, and he's here to sing for us. Come young man, welcome to our home." He put his arm around Burleigh and led him through the living room into the dining room where the table was set for dinner. The tableware was meticulously arranged on a silk cloth, with fine china and silverware placed neatly at each seat.

Anna called up the stairs to the children. "Otylia, Antonin, please join us for dinner." Otylia was a beautiful fourteen-year-old with dark hair and deep steel-blue eyes. She wore a white cotton dress with a blue bow. At nearly ten years old, her younger brother Antonin was a whirlwind of energy. The Dvoraks had lost their three oldest children while they were very young, and they couldn't face the idea of the entire family perishing together if the ship were to sink during their transatlantic voyage. They had decided, therefore, to take the eldest girl, Otylia, and the eldest boy, Antonin Jr., and leave the other children with relatives in Prague.

As Anna was being seated, the two children rushed into the room. "Papa!" they cried simultaneously, throwing themselves at Dvorak.

"My children!" He gathered one in each arm like a bear drawing in its prey. The faces of the children disappeared within his great outcrop of whiskers as their father kissed them. He pulled them away from himself, twisting them around. "Otylia, Tony, I want you to meet one of our students. This is, ah, ah," he fumbled for the name.

"Harry T. Burleigh," the young man responded, reaching out his hand to the girl. She extended her hand slowly, intrigued, but also unsure of how to respond to this dark-skinned young man. She had not seen very many black people before coming to America. The family had a couple of black women who cooked and cleaned in the townhouse, but this was a handsome young man. She smiled and bowed her head as he grasped her hand. Young Tony merely waved and ran to his seat.

Two servants entered the dining room carrying silver dishes brimming with liver dumplings, sauerkraut, pork chops, and roast goose. Wine was poured out for Mrs. Dvorak, pilsner ale for the master and Burleigh. After a blessing from the father of the house, the family dove into dinner.

"Ah," sighed Dvorak, finishing his dinner and wiping the remnants of roast goose from his thick whiskers. Suddenly he issued a tremendous belch, bringing roars of laughter from the children and a disapproving scowl from Mrs. Dvorak. Burleigh muffled a laugh with his cotton napkin.

"And now for music." The master pushed himself away from the table and announced, "Tonight our guest shall sing for us the interesting melodies he was singing to his mop earlier this evening."

Burleigh blushed as he and the family rose from the table and went into the living room. Dvorak lit a thick cigar, blowing a plume of blue smoke into the air. He unbuttoned the bottom three buttons of his vest and sat majestically in the corner chair. Mrs. Dvorak and little Antonin sat on the green velvet couch that matched the master's vest. Otylia took the chair next to the large birdcage, while Burleigh assumed a concert position in the center of the room next to the grand piano. In the dining room the servants quietly removed items from the table.

This was a familiar ritual for this musical family. Dvorak brought students and professors home to play and sing almost every evening. At times one of the master's children would play a piano piece that they had perfected.

"What will you sing for us tonight?"

Burleigh thought for a moment and then replied, "How about a song called 'Weepin' Mary'?"

"Yes, yes, I am familiar with it," Dvorak said in his broken English. "Sing us this, please."

The young man smiled, nodded to the master, and then grew somber. He looked down for a moment and then raised his head, looking out as though he were viewing a scene unfolding before him. On his face was a sorrowful expression, reflecting a witness of endless cruelty with little hope of freedom. Gently parting his lips, he began singing to the family as if imploring their help.

> If there's anybody here like weepin' Mary,
> Call upon your Jesus, and he'll draw nigh.

His baritone voice was rich and clear. It flowed like golden honey. The master sat with his eyes closed, a look of pleasure on his face. Little Antonin slid over closer to his mother and rested his head on her shoulder. Otylia's eyes sparkled as she watched the handsome young singer perform. Mrs. Dvorak's demeanor relaxed, though she continued to sit properly erect. As she listened to the vibrant voice and watched the sincere manner with which he presented the song, she became more comfortable with the young stranger.

As Burleigh finished the second verse, the sound of his voice grew in intensity with the beginning of the chorus. He finished the song with a crescendo.

If there's anybody here like weepin' Mary,
Call upon your Jesus, and he'll draw nigh.

With the dramatic conclusion, the family broke into applause. Both the master and Otylia rose to their feet. "Ah, that is wonderful," Dvorak exclaimed. "Wasn't that wonderful, Annie?" His wife nodded rapidly, closing her eyes, a slight smile on her face.

"This music—this is the music of American soil." Turning back to Burleigh, he declared, "It is why I have come to this country, for this glorious sound!"

"Where did you learn this melody?" asked Otylia.

"Originally I learned it from my grandfather. He was a slave in Maryland before he moved to our hometown in Pennsylvania."

Dvorak bent over to tap the ash off of his cigar. "And this song, did he learn it on the . . . the . . ." He struggled again for the word, twirling the stogie in the air. "How do you say it? The plantation, yes, that is it."

"He most likely learned it from his mother."

Just as curious as her father, Otylia asked, "Did she write this song?"

Burleigh chuckled. "No one knows who originally wrote the plantation songs. They grew out of secret religious gatherings and work times and were passed on orally from generation to generation."

Cigar smoke circled the master as he exhaled. His eyes glistened with intrigue. "It is 'Barley,' yes?"

"Uh, Burleigh, sir."

"Yes, yes." He paused and spoke more slowly. "Bur-leigh. Will you sing another for us?"

Harry happily sang several more plantation melodies for the family, each one ending with appreciative applause. The kitchen help stayed to listen through the door long after the dishes were cleaned. As the hour grew late, young Antonin drifted off to sleep, his head resting in his mother's lap. Mrs. Dvorak finally led him and a reluctant Otylia up to bed as Harry and the composer remained in the living room.

"My wife didn't want us to come to America," Dvorak confided to Harry once he knew his wife had closed the door upstairs. "We were quite comfortable in Bohemia. But there was something that drew me to this land. In Prague I was fortunate enough to hear your Singers of the Jubilee."

"The Fisk Jubilee Singers?" Burleigh asked.

"Yes, yes, of course. They sang many of the melodies you have sung for my family tonight." The great musician placed his large, tobacco-stained hand on the young man's shoulder, looking intently into his eyes. "These songs of the slave, these melodies have haunted me from that time until today."

Burleigh was overwhelmed at Dvorak's transparency. He felt both awe and joy at what the master was confiding in him.

"These songs brought me here, Barley." The young musician didn't correct him. "You say that you know many of these songs?"

"Yes, my grandfather taught me dozens of them."

"Then you must teach them to me."

Burleigh was stunned. He stood speechless.

"Yes, and tell me of your grandfather too. How did he find his way to freedom? Tell me of the plantations. I want to know everything."

Harry sat and pondered the questions for a moment. He had heard the story a myriad of times from both his grandfather and his mother. Now he didn't know where to begin. After collecting his thoughts for a moment, he finally unfolded the story for Dvorak. "My grandfather, Hamilton Waters, was a slave on the Tilghman plantation on the Chesapeake Bay in Maryland. He had tried to escape several times, but he was always captured, beaten, and returned to his chains.

"Then one day a slave from another plantation was purchased by Master Tilghman. He told my grandfather how other slaves had taught themselves to read using small spellers. Granddaddy knew that he needed to learn to read if he was going to survive as an escaped slave. His friend began giving him lessons and my grandfather learned to read.

"But one day the speller accidentally slipped out from under his shirt and was discovered by one of the overseers. My grandfather knew the punishment for this act of insubordination, so he took off running, even though he knew that he would never escape."

A look of anger and disgust came over Dvorak's face as he listened to the tragic tale.

"It wasn't long before they caught my granddaddy and gave him seventy lashes. The whip hit him in the eyes several times, causing him to lose most of his eyesight. After that he wasn't of much use to the plantation, so the master allowed him to purchase freedom for himself and for his mother."

Harry smiled at the thought, tilting his head back. "I'll never forget how my granddaddy told us the story of the day he purchased his freedom. The first thing he did was run to tell his mother, Lovey Waters."

8

Steal Away

1832–MARYLAND'S EASTERN SHORE

Hamilton ran from the master's house as fast as a nearly blind man could run. His heart was dancing as he worked his way to the dirt-floor cabin that had always been home. Though he could only make out hazy figures, he knew the box-shaped shadows in the distance were the slave quarters.

"Mama, Mama," he cried out as he approached the hut. His mother, Lovey Waters, came running to the door. "He done it, Mama. He went and done it." He clutched a piece of paper in his hand and waved it over his head triumphantly. When he reached the doorway, Hamilton thrust it into her hands. Panting and nearly out of breath, he relayed the news. "The massa let me pay fo' my freedom."

Though she didn't know how to read, Lovey recognized the elegant signature of James Tilghman at the bottom of the paper. She had seen it dozens of times on papers lying about the mansion. One of the other slaves, who had secretly learned to read, told her that the curling line was the signature of the master. She memorized the pattern and recognized it whenever she saw it. Lovey began to tremble and tears rolled down her cheeks. "Praise you, Jesus," she whispered. She looked up at her son who stood before her, smiling so wide it would be impossible to stretch a face any farther.

"And Mama," he said slowly as he held her shoulders in his hands, "I paid for yo' freedom too."

"Oh my Lord. Oh my Jesus!" She looked up to heaven and bellowed as the tears kept rolling down. The two held each other tightly, weeping and swaying back and forth. It had been a long, torturous journey. Slavery was all they had ever known—and now they would be free.

Hamilton had tried to escape several times, but the slaveholding network throughout the South was just too tightly knit. He was always captured and beaten severely. After the whipping he received for trying to learn to read, his eyes were permanently damaged. It took more than a month for him to fully recover from the wounds, and since that time he had not been able to do much manual labor. There were days when exhaustion from a long, difficult day's work caused his eyes to swell, leaving him completely blind. The overseer put him to work in the mansion, pressing the family's clothing, but he was not nearly as fast as the women who worked alongside him.

Master Tilghman grew impatient with the blind man's handicap. Though they continued to be fed and clothed, neither Hamilton nor his mother was making a significant contribution. Allowing Hamilton to buy his freedom would save him the expense of two relatively useless slaves. One day the master approached him. "Hamilton," he began, "a lot of slaves these days are purchasing their freedom across the South. Did you know that?"

The slave was well aware of the practice, but he didn't want to let on. Master Tilghman was such a stern man he didn't want him to know the extent of his knowledge of the world beyond the plantation. "No sir, I didn't know dat," he answered.

"Well, a strong young man like yourself might want to think about raising the money to buy your freedom." He looked for a reaction from Hamilton, but the young man played it cool, continuing to iron the clothes. "What do you think of that, boy?"

Hamilton looked up at his master. "I think dat would be jest fine, sir."

"Good," Tilghman replied. "It would be all right with me if you go into town after you're done with your duties here and hire yourself out."

Hamilton could hardly believe what he was hearing. He tried to control himself, but he couldn't help but smile. "Thank you, sir. I will do jest dat."

"Very well," Tilghman replied. "Good day." The master walked out of the room, leaving the smiling young man working feverishly to finish his chores so he could rush into town to look for work.

For more than a year Hamilton offered his services wherever he could. Sometimes he hauled lumber for the mill. Other days he swept the floor in the tavern. Folks in town got to know the young man, and a few of the merchants hired him as often as they could. They paid cash when the work was done. He hid the growing wad between the logs in the wall of his cabin to keep it safe. Other than an occasional gift for his Mama, a needed tool, or an article of clothing, Hamilton saved his money like a miser. It was precious. It was his freedom.

Lovey brought her son up to love freedom and to love God. By loving God, they believed, freedom would follow—either on earth or, as the slaves liked to say, "over Jordan." On cold nights, as the wind howled through the openings between the logs of their small cabin, the two slaves huddled together around the fire to keep warm. Lovey would sing the plantation songs to Hamilton in a rich, soothing voice.

> Steal away, steal away, steal away to Jesus
> Steal away, steal away home
> I ain't got long to stay here.

Their favorite songs were the spirituals—biblical songs of hope and songs of sorrow. They often sang them to each other throughout the night as they prepared for bed. Both Lovey and Hamilton had beautiful voices and the tunes brought warmth to their cold, gray lives. These songs comforted them in their times of grief and gave them hope to press on even when it seemed there was little to be hopeful for.

Like his mother, Hamilton was an amiable person, but the toil of slavery often drove the joy of life from even the brightest of souls. Along with his brothers and sisters in chains throughout the South, he sang the plantation songs as he worked to sustain his spirits. The rich African legacy of music and rhythm passed naturally and seamlessly from one generation to another. To endure and maintain their dignity and sanity in the face of the dehumanization that was forced upon them, the slaves created their own culture, separate from the world around them. These folk songs were the slaves' positive answer to their wretched existence. They helped to create some sense of order and purpose from the insanity of slavery.

Some of these tunes were merely entertaining ditties, crafted to bring joy to a nursing mother who knew her child would live a life of toil and labor. They brought comfort to a father whose children were wrenched from his arms and sold to a plantation in some distant state.

The spiritual songs gave them the courage they needed to press on in spite of the hardship and sorrow. They adopted syncopated melodies, handed down from their African ancestors, to help them endure hours of unrewarded labor. As a team of slaves worked a field or cut down timber, they sang together in rhythm. A leader with a bellowing voice would sing a phrase:

> I know moon-rise.

The others would repeat:

> I know moon-rise.

They sang like this from sunup to sundown:

> I walk in de moonlight,
> I walk in de starlight,
> To lay dis body down.
> I walk in de graveyard,
> I walk thru de graveyard,
> To lay dis body down.
> I lie in de grave an' stretch out my arms,
> To lay dis body down.
> I go to de jedgment in de evenin' of de day,
> When I lay dis body down.
> An' my soul an' your soul will meet in de day,
> When I lay dis body down.

The syncopation of the tune was the anchor of the song, helping them to continue to work despite endless, mind-numbing fatigue.

The plantation overseers were always suspicious of a silent darkey, so they wanted to hear them singing. If they were not singing, perhaps they were plotting a rebellion or an escape. If the tired workers grew silent or there was whispering among the group, the overseer would holler from atop his horse, "Sing up, n—rs. Make some noise, now."

Over time, southern slaves developed plantation songs that also carried coded messages that were sung right in front of their overseers. Only the slaves knew their meaning. It was through these songs that important information was passed along a system of communication throughout the South. Coded songs conveyed messages about rebellions or escapes through the Underground Railroad.

They were also a way for the slave to "sass the massa" without fear of retribution. The plantation owners and overseers never suspected their smiling chattel who sang such simple songs.

Or at least they assumed they were simple.

There was one final group of haunting melodies, rich with emotion and deeply moving. They were songs of hope and anticipation. Some folks called them the sorrow songs. Eventually they would come to be known as the spirituals.

They were the soul cry of the black slave longing for freedom. They were born in the fields, among the hoed rows of cotton and tobacco. They sprang to life among the salty wharves of the Atlantic harbor and the Mississippi bayou. These songs rose to heaven above the whine of the sawmill and the roar of the waterfalls that drove them. From the painful cries of the Negro wench, enduring yet another violation by the master, these ballads arose. They issued forth from the sweat and heartache of a lifetime of dehumanizing toil and humiliation.

Often these spiritual songs had their beginnings in the fervent heat of a backwoods religious meeting. Slaves gathered secretly to encourage one another and to cry out to God for freedom. This activity was against the law, and they knew that a severe beating or even death could face them if they were caught. But the joy and peace that they received from heaven in these meetings made it worth the risk they faced here on earth. The atmosphere in the midst of the woods was always charged with emotion. As they mourned their wretched existence, songs would develop spontaneously—psalms, hymns, and spiritual songs. In time, these melodies were memorized and passed along from plantation to plantation.

Like a captive eagle, a man's spirit cries out under the tethers of oppression. In the same way that a caged bird yearns for freedom, the Negro slaves cried in anguish under their captivity—and the spirituals were born from those cries.

As the lashes came down on their backs, the pleas to God for justice and a homeland of freedom across the Jordan rose from their bellies. The spirituals became a lifeline, bringing a vital flow of hope and faith to the emotional and spiritual heart of the slave. Through these melodies they held on to the hope of survival. By them, a unique and vibrant community formed. They served as a second language that only the slaves understood. Through these songs they expressed in subtle words and melody their pain, loneliness, weariness, and sorrow—but also their hope and determination to live on.

Though the slaves were not allowed to read the Scriptures, they learned Bible stories at the village church or on the plantation in religious meetings with the white folks. The Sunday morning routine included Sunday school, singing hymns, Bible reading, and the sermon, where the preacher told them to obey the missus and the master.

But the slaves also learned God's Word from abolitionist preachers from the North—both black and white—who bravely traveled through the southern states. After the "Great Awakening," some southern whites who had come into the "new light" became Baptists. Much to the annoyance of many southerners, these new evangelicals began teaching the slaves about the way to salvation. Black and white evangelists alike poured out their lives, preaching the gospel to the captives in secret late-night meetings.

A favorite analogy from the Scriptures used by these circuit preachers was the plight of the Hebrews of Exodus and God's handpicked deliverer, Moses. The African slaves identified with this ancient oppressed people. They grew to understand that it was through their faith in the God of the Bible that freedom was given to these slaves of old.

The Old Testament fired their imagination. Had not the people of Israel been enslaved in Egypt? And did not God rescue them, leading them out of bondage and into the Promised Land? Quickly they formed a close kinship with Israel. Would not God do the same for them in their enslavement? Moses became their man too, and figuratively they implored him in song:

> Go down, Moses—way down in Egypt's land
> Tell old Pharaoh, let my people go!

The capacity to funnel the troubles of their daily lives into song was the unique genius of the American slave. They were helped in this creation by their own black preachers who identified with what the congregation had been through since their last meeting. They saw husbands sold away from wives and children from parents. Their women lived under the chains of their master's lusts and their men at the end of an overseer's whip. Their environment, with the lash in frequent use, told them they were in no way significant as persons— that they were important only as property. But as the slaves learned of the God of the Bible, they began to see themselves as his children.

"No, no, no!" their black preachers dramatically exhorted them. "You are not slaves. You are the apple of God's eye, made in his very own image." They learned that it was through a good and benevolent God, who heard the cry of the Hebrew slaves, that freedom came. They realized that they were not inferior to the white man, just as the Hebrews were not inferior to the Egyptians.

The spirituals attested to this and proclaimed the goodness of this God and his ultimate triumph over evil. They would taste freedom, they believed, across the Jordan River of death—and some sweet day in the here and now. Looking forward to that day of freedom, the slaves sang of the "deep river," with its mighty waters flowing into distant horizons. As the embers glowed in the campfire, deep in the heart of the forest, they would sing:

> Deep river—my home is over Jordan,
> Deep river, Lawd, I want to cross over into campground.

For a time, the slaves simply bypassed the New Testament, especially since their white taskmasters used it to justify slavery as an acceptable way of life. But there was something about Jesus hanging there upon the hard, wooden cross that captivated their spirits. Here was a man who was beaten like they were. He was spit upon. He was falsely accused. He was imprisoned for a crime he did not commit. Finally, he was hung on a tree, a method of execution familiar to the slaves. Through all of these indignities, Jesus prayed, "Father, forgive them, for they know not what they do."

"How was he able to forgive?" they questioned. "What was it that enabled him to love those who were unlovable?" Was he in pain? They were in pain. Did he have to drink the cup of suffering? They had to drink theirs too. Yes, their cross was one with his cross. They came to believe that Jesus died for the sins of all men, of every color. He had to be who he said he was. How else could he have done what he did?

In time, they embraced Jesus as their Savior, and they experienced his peace, his grace, his forgiveness—and remarkably, they found hope for the future. From this relationship they were able to sing:

> Sometimes it causes me to tremble, tremble, tremble.
> Were you der when dey crucified my Lawd?

From the cross they felt a mighty emergence of the divine will, breaking down the barriers that separated man from man and man from God. And so, instead of taking the destructive road to violence, many began to hum, then to sing, and sometimes to shout the spirituals— a cry to God for freedom and a declaration of faith in his ability to provide it.

Lovey and Hamilton shared that faith and carried the spirituals in their hearts. Whatever they did, they set to it with all their energies, singing the spirituals and the plantation songs throughout the day as a source of strength.

―――――◇――――――

Hamilton's goal was freedom, one way or the other, so he worked diligently for the shopkeepers in town. One of his jobs was delivering food for a local grocer, Mr. Carl Johnston. He was a kindhearted man who employed several black folks, along with Native Americans and other less fortunate people.

One of the laborers in his household was an attractive Scotch-Indian woman named Lucinda Duncanson. Mr. Johnston first met her while visiting the home of his friend, Governor Enos Thompson Throop of New York. Lucinda had worked as a servant in the governor's household for several years. Johnston complimented her on her refined manners. The governor's term in office was nearly complete, and he planned to reduce his staff before he moved back to Ithaca. The governor informed Lucinda that Mr. Johnston had a position open for a maid in his home in Maryland.

Lucinda's parents had moved to Michigan, and she was alone in the world. Though she was close to the Throop family, she didn't think that they would have any need for her services after they left the governor's mansion. On the day before Mr. Johnston was set to end his visit, she informed him that she would take the position. Lucinda traveled back to Maryland with the Johnston family, the trunk with all her earthly belongings strapped to the back of the carriage along with the others.

Hamilton often delivered supplies from the mercantile, and in time he became friendly with many of the servants on the Johnstons' household staff. Lucinda was a slender, attractive young woman with a sharp wit. The two often sparred with each other in the large kitchen, exchanging wisecracks and backhanded compliments. It wasn't long before the barbs softened and they were speaking more delicately to each other. Soon the young man was looking for excuses to make deliveries to the Johnston home. On occasion, when Hamilton worked late into the evening, the two found themselves alone in the kitchen. She would offer him a slice of sweet potato pie, and they would sit across from each other, sharing their dreams.

She told him how her father had come from Edinburgh, Scotland, as a servant to the Throop family and had married her mother, an American Indian. He had remained in the employment of Mr. and Mrs. Throop for years and had arranged for Lucinda to work for them as soon as she was old enough. When Lucinda's father decided to move the family to Michigan, Lucinda stayed in Ithaca, working as a servant for the Throops. After Mr. Throop was elected governor, she moved to Albany with the family and worked in the executive mansion.

Hamilton told her of his life growing up on the Waters plantation. His old master, Leven Waters, had been much kinder than his current owner. When Master Waters died, he and his mother were sold, along with most of the Waterses' property, to Master Tilghman, where life was much more difficult. He told her about the beatings and how he had lost most of his eyesight. He explained that he was working hard to raise the money to purchase his freedom.

When she heard that, she became excited. "When you finally purchase your freedom, would you take me with you?" she asked one night. "We could go and stay with my family in Michigan until you find work." Lucinda missed her mother, and she did not like the humid summer air of the South. She longed for the day when she could move north again.

Hamilton could hardly believe what he was hearing. "I would like dat very much," he answered. "But I's plannin' to bring my mama along."

"That would be all right," Lucinda answered, smiling. "Does your mama like needlepoint?"

"She loves it. She worked for a long time mendin' clothes in the master's house."

"Well, then she and my mama will get along just fine."

Hamilton reached across the kitchen table and grabbed the young woman's hand. He squeezed it gently as he looked into her eyes. Her hand was soft and slender. She held his hand for a moment and then gently ran her other hand over his callused palm. They both smiled. After a moment, Hamilton stood, put on his cap, and bid her good night. As he walked out the door and headed for the plantation, he felt as if his chest would burst with excitement.

In the next few months he made the final preparations for the journey. Master Tilghman had set his price, so Hamilton knew what it would take to buy his freedom. He saved extra money for their travels and to buy a used covered wagon and a mule. One of the town merchants allowed him to store the wagon in his barn. He also packed some extra food and blankets, along with other supplies he thought they would need on the trip to Michigan.

Finally, on a warm spring afternoon, Hamilton gathered the required amount—fifty dollars for his own freedom and five dollars more for his mother—and took it to the master's house. He stood and watched as the tall, thin plantation owner counted every dime.

Earlier that spring, after his initial meeting to set a price for the slave's freedom, Master Tilghman had prepared the proper legal items needed to obtain Hamilton's official papers. He composed a letter and sent the package to the state of Maryland's Department of General Services. The letter described Hamilton as "five feet, eight inches in height and of a bright mulatto complexion, partially blind, orderly and intelligent, about thirty-two years of age, and a native of Somerset County." The final manumission was entered into the Somerset County deed book on March 5, 1832. The deed, titled "Bill of Sale," was for the purchase of Hamilton Waters and his mother, Lovey.

"We gots to go quick before dey changes der mind," Hamilton told his mother after showing her the papers. "Do you have yo' tings?"

"I's already packed 'em—der ain't much to take."

"We's got to keep de papers in a safe place. We can't never leave dem where dey can gets lost." Losing your freedom papers could result in being returned to slavery, an unthinkable fate that they could not allow to happen through carelessness. Hamilton and Lovey smiled and wiped their tear-stained cheeks. They decided to wait until after sundown to leave. Though they had their papers in hand, they did not want to chance running into the overseer as they left the plantation for the last time.

Hamilton went into town to fetch Lucinda. Together they hitched up the mule to the wagon and loaded their supplies and the carpetbags filled with all of their earthly possessions. He returned to the plantation after dark for his mama. After loading her few belongings, Hamilton helped Lovey into the wagon and she took her place in the back. He walked around to the front, climbed aboard, and snapped the leather reins on the back of the mule. Slowly they worked their way from the slave quarters and past the great house.

When they reached the end of the drive, Hamilton turned to say one last good-bye. He could only make out the blurry dots of light from the slave quarters, where fires burned into the evening. Hamilton's eyes filled with tears as he looked at the windows of the master's house, illuminated by the candles inside. This man had inflicted so many wounds, but in the end he gave them their freedom. Hamilton's emotions were a mixture of anger, sorrow, and joy.

"Good-bye, forever," he whispered into the darkness. Lucinda took his hand and squeezed it tightly. He looked into her eyes. Her face brought renewed peace. Hamilton returned a slight smile, squeezed her hand, and repeated softly, "Good-bye, forever."

He looked forward into the blackness with Lucinda's hand in his and drove out onto the hard dirt road.

They turned to the right, because every slave on that plantation knew that at the end of that drive, to the right, the road to freedom led north.

9

Were You There?

1893–NEW YORK CITY

After that first night in the Dvoraks' home, Burleigh made himself available in any way he could to the maestro. Harry wasn't advanced enough to be in any of Dvorak's classes. His main ambition was to become a concert singer, and he was just glad to have been admitted to the conservatory at all.

Harry played double bass and timpani and served as librarian for the conservatory orchestra. One day during rehearsal Dvorak's young son, Antonin, wandered into the hall and slinked over toward the timpani. Since Burleigh spent so much time at the Dvorak house, he had become friends with the boy. The young lad made a beeline for Harry's kettle drums. Dvorak was a perfectionist and was demanding with his students in order to bring them to the level of expertise he expected. He almost took Burleigh's head off when he heard the extra drumbeats.

"Stop, stop, stop. What in the sweet name of God are you playing, Barley?" The young musician blushed, sitting speechless. Suddenly a panicked young Tony popped up from behind the large drums. "Oh, it is you." He reprimanded the youngster in Czech and then, switching to

English, growled from the podium, "Push him out!" Burleigh obeyed immediately, showing young Antonin to the door.

Dvorak was fascinated by the spirituals and asked Burleigh to sing them to him again and again, particularly after supper when he was tired. The melodies and rhythms were radically different from anything he had heard in Europe. He made it his mission to become intimately familiar with them.

Burleigh's training as a stenographer also aided him in his relationship with Dvorak. When the master realized Burleigh's skill, he entrusted to him the task of copying his manuscripts.

But Dvorak was interested mostly in Burleigh's knowledge of the spirituals. And he loved to hear the stories of Harry's grandfather, Hamilton Waters.

"Barley, come we must go now," Dvorak shouted one beautiful spring afternoon. The young singer stood in the next room chatting with Mrs. MacDowell. The director continued, "I have two hours before my next class. Bring your notebook."

Any time with the maestro was precious, so with an apology to Frances MacDowell, Burleigh grabbed his music notebook and pencils and was off to catch up with Dvorak. The Bohemian walked at a brisk pace, causing the shorter student to almost jog to keep up. It was a glorious late April day in New York as the flowers and trees were coming into bloom. The elegant Stuyvesant Square was nestled halfway between the conservatory and Dvorak's townhouse on 17th Street. An ornate wrought iron fence surrounded the neatly manicured park, which was located directly across from the tall brownstone spires of St. George's Episcopal Church. Dvorak loved to sit on the iron park benches and watch the birds bathe in the fountain. Burleigh sat down next to him, laying his notebook on the seat.

"It is so lovely here, so peaceful! It reminds me of my home in Bohemia."

Burleigh smiled, thinking of the Russell estate and Park Presbyterian Church on Perry Square in Erie. "It's like my home too," he replied. "In fact, I come here from time to time to remember."

Water from the fountain sparkled in the sunlight as New Yorkers walked quietly through the park. Some sat on benches, reading their newspapers or talking. A small family played with a ball on the grass.

"The songs of the slaves, these are melodies of the earth." Dvorak paused to take a long puff on his cigar. "This is why you must sing these songs to me, Barley. I want to swim in their melodies." The master stretched his long legs, leaning back on the bench, his face turned toward the sky. "It's a splendid day. Sing a happy song for me."

Burleigh was not intimidated by the public setting. He was in the presence of one of the greatest musical minds of the age. Dvorak had been a student of none other than Brahms. If he wanted him to sing standing on his head, Harry would do it. He stood, and began:

> Joshua fit the battle of Jericho, Jericho, Jericho.
> Joshua fit the battle of Jericho and the walls came tumblin'
> down.

A small crowd gathered. Anything out of the ordinary drew a crowd in New York, and here was a black man singing a slave song to a world-famous composer. The onlookers were intrigued.

> You may talk about your men of Gideon,
> You may talk about your men of Saul,
> There's none like good ol' Joshua at the battle of Jericho.

The master was oblivious to the spectators. Dressed in his usual attire—gray woolen pants, white silk shirt, black felt homburg, flamboyant necktie, and the familiar emerald-green vest—he closed his eyes tightly, guarding his mind from distraction.

The family stopped playing ball and walked to the edge of the grass. The gathering crowd spooked the small flock of birds. They flew to the far side of the fountain to continue their bath. Dvorak took another puff of his cigar.

> Joshua fit the battle of Jericho and the walls came tumblin'
> down.

The bystanders began clapping, assuming the young man was a street minstrel. Burleigh smiled and nodded his thanks.

Dvorak ignored the applause. "Very good, Barley. Good tone, good control. Now, sit." The children went back to their games and the crowd trickled away. During times like these Dvorak asked Burleigh hundreds of questions about slavery, the plantations, the American Civil War, and Hamilton Waters.

"You say your grandfather taught these songs to you?"

"Yes, when I was a boy. He learned them while he was a slave."

The Bohemian shook his head in disgust. "It's disgraceful, Harry, a man owning another man. If there is one truth that is absolute, it's that God has created man to be free." He pondered the thought for a while, staring at the birds that had returned to the near side of the fountain. "Your grandfather was fortunate to taste freedom, Harry. Next to love, it's the greatest thing in the world."

"Yes," Harry said slowly. "But he paid a terrible price to obtain his freedom."

"This is true," Dvorak said, shifting on the park bench. "After your grandfather left the plantation, where did he go?"

"Well, you may remember that my grandmother was half Scottish and half Indian."

Dvorak laughed out loud. "Harry Burleigh, you never cease to astonish me. I have been nearly as fascinated with the American Indian music as I am with the plantation songs. Now you're telling me that you have ancestors from both the slaves and the Indians? You are an amazing man."

Harry laughed along with Dvorak. "Thank you sir, but I had very little to do with it."

Dvorak chuckled and then took a long puff on his cigar. "I've been studying American Indian music along with the plantation melodies. There's a Bohemian colony in Spillville, Iowa, near an Indian village. I'm taking my family there for the summer to learn more."

Again, Harry was amazed at the breadth and depth of Antonin Dvorak. He smiled and slowly shook his head. "That, um." He scratched his cheek with his thumb as he looked for the right words. "That will be a tremendous opportunity for your children. I've never been farther west than Ohio."

Dvorak smiled and his eyes brightened at the thought of expanding the understanding of his children. He turned to Burleigh. "Yes, we will take the train all the way to Iowa. You know how much I love locomotives. It will be a great adventure." The great musician looked around the park, took a couple of long puffs from his cigar, and then turned back to Harry. "Now, continue the story."

"My grandmother left with Granddaddy and his mother, and they all traveled to Michigan to meet her parents and look for work."

1838—THE WILDERNESS OF PENNSYLVANIA

Hamilton was able to save just enough money to travel north into the free territory of Pennsylvania. As they made their way west toward Michigan, they stopped in towns along the way, working as laborers for months at a time until they could raise enough money to move on. Whenever they entered a town, Lovey stayed with the wagon to watch their things while Lucinda and Hamilton worked odd jobs.

From their first meeting, Hamilton had considered Lucinda a friend. Now they were spending every day together, depending on one another for their survival. Soon he realized his feelings for her were stronger than mere friendship—he was falling in love.

While he was still a slave, Hamilton and Lucinda could not allow themselves to explore any notions of romance. They were unsure of the future, and no free woman married a slave. Now as they walked back and forth from their campsite to town, their love blossomed. As soon as they realized their feelings, they sought a preacher to make them man and wife. They had been friends for more than a year; why should they wait to marry? Hamilton and Lucinda exchanged vows in a small Methodist-Episcopal church in southeastern Pennsylvania, with Lovey and a small group of black freedmen looking on.

Over the next few years they worked from town to town, making enough money to get them to the next place. Hamilton knew of a former slave named Thomas Wilson from Somerset County who had settled in the small port town of Erie, in northwestern Pennsylvania. Since it wasn't too far out of their way on their trek to Michigan, he decided to try to find Thomas to line up some work. They slowly worked their way through the dense western Pennsylvania woods to the shores of Lake Erie. At times the road narrowed to nothing more than an overgrown footpath through the forest, causing Hamilton to get out and cut back encroaching branches with an ax. The terrain was mountainous, and they made little daily progress. They lived off of what they could gather, the animals they trapped, and the fish they caught along the way. After several months of difficult travel, they finally arrived in the remote town of Erie.

Hamilton looked for his friend while Lovey and Lucinda set up camp. After a few inquiries, Ham found him loading lumber onto a large ship. After a warm greeting, Thomas informed Hamilton that Erie was a growing port and fishing village with plenty of jobs for former slaves. Hamilton reminded him that his eyesight was poor and asked if there was any work for someone as a presser of clothes. The man knew of a job available mending and pressing clothes for one of Erie's wealthy families. He thought Hamilton might be able to find work with them.

"Hamilton, that sounds like a good position for the time being," Lucinda said when he told her about the possible job. She smiled brightly as she grabbed hold of his arm and pulled up close to him. "But I think it can only be a temporary job."

"What do you mean?"

"Well, dear, I think we should stay here just long enough to raise the money to go on to my parents' home in Lansing. A woman should be with her mother when she delivers her first baby."

Hamilton's features froze into a shocked gaze.

"Dear, did you hear me?" she asked, looking up into his eyes.

Slowly, Hamilton looked down at his young bride as his expression of surprise melted into a smile. "A baby? We's gonna have a baby?" He lifted Lucinda nearly a foot off the ground. "Hallelujah! Glory be!"

Hamilton took the job pressing clothes. Though he enjoyed the people of Erie, he planned to make his way to Michigan as soon as possible. After three months of work, Hamilton had raised enough money to begin the final leg of the journey. Though she was close to her time to deliver, Lucinda wanted to be with her mother when the baby came. Lovey made up a bed in the back of the covered wagon for the difficult journey. Once again they loaded the wagon and headed west toward Michigan.

"Hamilton, we've got to stop now. This baby's not going to wait," came the painful plea from within the covered wagon.

"But Lansing is just a day's journey. Can't you wait until—"

Lucinda screamed as the pain of childbirth overtook her. There would be no more discussion of the subject. The bumpy ride had taken its toll and the child was determined to come into the world. Hamilton could do nothing to stop it.

Lovey comforted the young mother, singing soothing melodies and holding her hand. She had birthed many babies on the plantation; now she would help to bring her own grandchild into the world. She kissed the forehead of her daughter-in-law. "Der, der, chile. It will be all right. Soon you's gonna be holdin' dat sweet baby, and you'll forget 'bout de pain." Lucinda grimaced and looked into Lovey's eyes to gather strength as she braced for the next contraction. They were coming quickly, with growing intensity. Again she screamed in agony. "Ham, we needs to pull dis wagon to de side of de road now," his mother insisted.

In the late afternoon, after considerable travail, Lucinda gave birth to a beautiful baby girl—an entire month ahead of schedule. Lovey wiped the blood off of the child, then cut the umbilical cord with a sharp knife and tied it in a knot. She wrapped the baby in muslin cloth and handed the crying child to Lucinda as Hamilton peered in over her shoulder.

"My little precious one, welcome to the world," Lucinda spoke softly as she gently bounced the baby to quiet her crying. Hamilton laid his hand on the baby's soft, moist head. "Do you want to hold her, honey?" Lucinda asked.

"Can I?" he asked.

Lucinda lifted the tiny infant into his hands. Tears filled his eyes as he wrapped the blanket tightly around her. "Hallelujah, glory be!" he declared, smiling at his mother. He held her for several minutes, placing his finger into her tiny grip and kissing her forehead. "What is we gonna call her?" he asked as he tenderly placed the baby back into his wife's arms.

Lucinda smiled as she looked down at the child. "Since my mama couldn't be here to see her born, I think we should name the baby after her—let's call her Elizabeth Waters."

Hamilton looked over at Lovey. She smiled and said, "Dat's a wonderful name—little baby Lizbeth." Hamilton kissed his wife and then the baby. "Lizbeth Waters it is."

Arriving in Lansing the following day, Lucinda weakly introduced Hamilton and Lovey to her parents, Gordon and Elizabeth Duncanson. Lucinda's father quickly rode off to fetch the doctor to examine the tiny infant and his daughter. The doctor gave both mother and daughter a clean bill of health and encouraged Lucinda to get some sleep.

———◇———

After dinner, as Lovey and Elizabeth prepared a place for the new mother and her baby, Hamilton and Gordon went out onto the front porch to talk. The two men sat on rocking chairs and lit celebratory cigars, purchased earlier that day by Gordon on his way back from town. "There's just not that much available for former slaves in Michigan since the Blackburn riot in Detroit," Lucinda's father explained.

"I heard people talkin' 'bout de Blackburn riot as we was comin' through Detroit," Hamilton responded. "What happened to dem folks?"

"The Blackburns were fugitive slaves from Kentucky who had settled in Detroit," Gordon began. "Everything was going fine for them for the first two years. Then someone from Kentucky spotted them, and their owners sent slave catchers to bring them home. These bounty hunters met with the sheriff in Detroit and convinced him to arrest them until they could stand before the judge.

"When the black community heard what was happening they rallied together with their white abolitionist friends to call for the immediate release of the former slaves. The sheriff refused. When it became clear the sheriff intended to send the couple back into slavery, the black community decided to act.

"A couple of Mrs. Blackburn's friends had a tearful visit with her in the prison. After an hour the two ladies left their weeping friend behind in prison. But what the sheriff didn't know until the next morning was that it wasn't Mrs. Blackburn who sat in the jail cell, but her friend who'd exchanged clothing with her during the visit. The real Mrs. Blackburn was safe in Canada after being shuttled across the Detroit River under the cover of darkness."

Hamilton clapped his hands and burst into laughter. "Dat was smart," he howled. "Dat was very smart."

Gordon chuckled as he took a few puffs on his cigar. "This infuriated the sheriff something awful," he continued. "Now he was more determined than ever to send Mr. Blackburn back into slavery."

Hamilton could hardly believe what he was hearing. "And dis is in de North?" he said, the cruel recognition sinking into his consciousness.

The old Scot shook his head and spit off the side of the porch. "As you can imagine, when word of this got out people all around Detroit converged on the jail to protest—both black and white. On the day they planned to move Mr. Blackburn, the crowd surrounded the jail, demanding his release. Despite the growing tension, the sheriff and the bounty hunters decided to make their move. But as soon as they walked out the door, men in the crowd started waving clubs and shotguns.

"All of a sudden somebody tossed a pistol to Mr. Blackburn, who quickly pointed it at the sheriff's head. When the sheriff tried to reach for his gun, Blackburn fired two shots into the air. The slave catchers turned and ran back into the jail, closing the door behind them and leaving the sheriff to face the angry crowd all alone."

Hamilton whistled low and long. "My, my, my," he declared. "De hunter is de hunted."

"That's right. Someone came up behind the sheriff and hit him over the head with a club. They knocked him out cold and took the keys to undo the prisoner's shackles. Loading Mr. Blackburn into a wagon, they raced to a waiting ferry boat that had been secured to shuttle him across the river to the Canadian shore.

"As you can imagine, the escape of the Blackburns infuriated the white politicians, who clamped down hard on any black folks coming in from the South."

"But I's got my freedom papers," Hamilton quickly responded. "I has every right to be here."

Gordon shook his head and gathered his thoughts as he rocked back and forth on the porch. From inside the small clapboard house they could hear the muffled cry of little Elizabeth. After several moments Lucinda's father turned and looked at Hamilton. "Son, ever since the riots, the white folks in this area don't seem to care if a colored man has his papers or not. They don't trust anyone from the outside, especially former slaves."

Hamilton immediately shot back, "Then we'll just cross over into Canada."

"Son, I don't mean to discourage you. I truly don't. But I need to tell you the rest of the story. The Blackburns weren't in Canada for more than a day when officials from Detroit met with the Canadian magistrate, accusing the couple of causing a riot and wounding the sheriff in a jail break."

"But that's not what happened," Hamilton said, frustrated.

"You and I know that," Gordon answered. "But the Canadian officials didn't want to take any chances of harboring dangerous fugitives, so they immediately arrested them again. They're sitting in jail just across the river from Detroit even as we speak."

Hamilton stood up like a shot. "You knows what will happen if dey sends 'em back to Detroit."

"I know exactly what will happen," Gordon replied. "They will be shipped back to slavery faster than you can say George Washington."

Hamilton began to pace back and forth on the porch, puffing on his cigar as Gordon gently rocked in his chair, staring out at the starlit sky. Finally Hamilton turned and announced, "Well maybe de good folks of Lansing will be more hospitable. I will go tomorrow and see if der is any work to be found 'round dese parts."

Gordon didn't say a word. He just puffed again on his cigar.

"Sir, thank you for everything you has said. I appreciates it. I'll be goin' to bed now. Good night."

"Good night, Hamilton. And good luck."

The next morning Hamilton was up early to get into town. The stress of the journey and the early arrival of the baby had caused his eyes to swell, and he had tremendous difficulty as he walked through the unfamiliar town the next morning. He began to wonder if his dream of freedom would be even more difficult than he had anticipated. He had to grapple with his handicap while supporting an elderly mother, a wife, and now a small daughter. As he made his way through the town, he met with resistance to his inquiries.

"A blind Negro. What kind of work can you do?" The sarcastic response came from a local hotel owner. "There's nothing here for you. Why don't you move along, boy?" He received similar reactions from nearly every shop owner. After a long and arduous day, he worked his way back through town, shuffling his feet along the dusty main street. He had to hurry back to the log cabin before the sun set and he could no longer see the road in front of him.

When he finally made it back, Hamilton could hear the cries of the newborn child and the muffled sounds of Lucinda and her parents talking inside. He stood outside the window and listened quietly. Soon the crying stopped and the night was calm. He sat down against a tall poplar tree, put his head in his hands, and cried out to God. "Lawd, you's been good to us. You's done blessed us with dis beautiful chile, and I's grateful." Tears welled up in the man's eyes. He went on, looking to heaven for comfort and assurance. "God, now I needs to find work so I can provide what dis chile needs. You knows what I heard today. You knows dat dese people don't want to hire a half-blind former slave."

He looked out into the darkness. He could tell by the singing of the crickets that the sun had now completely set. Peering up toward an ocean of stars that he couldn't see, he declared, "Lawd, you delivered Daniel from de lion's den, and Jonah from de belly of de whale, and de Hebrew children from de fiery furnace. Now I asks you to deliver dis family, and dis tiny little baby. We can't do nuttin' widout yo' help."

He paused and listened as the crickets grew louder. Soon a sweet serenity flooded his soul, and he sensed a familiar presence. In his heart he heard the words, *Peace, be still*. He smiled and sat quietly, listening to the symphony of night sounds.

Finally, he took a long, deep breath. "Thank you, Lawd," he whispered as he stood and walked over to the log cabin. Hamilton opened the door and stepped inside. It was late, and everyone was asleep. He felt his way to where Lucinda was lying on a straw-filled mattress on the floor, next to a tiny crib for the baby. He quietly removed his tattered shoes and lay down next to her. He could hear the deep, slow breathing of his sleeping wife and the faster-paced breathing of the little baby. He felt to make sure both were covered with blankets. Again he whispered into the darkness, "Thank you, heavenly Father." He closed his eyes and drifted off to sleep.

The next morning Hamilton awoke to the realization that his dream of paradise in Michigan was gone, replaced by a sober recognition of reality. Only days earlier he thought he had entered into a land flowing with milk and honey. Now he just wanted to find a place where they could be safe. In the time since they left Maryland, the most hospitable place for them had been the small port city of Erie, Pennsylvania. Now that little Elizabeth had come, Hamilton knew that he had to settle somewhere and make a life for his family. He and Lucinda talked it over and decided to go back to the little fishing town. Perhaps his laundry job would still be available.

Later that day he loaded Lucinda and the baby into the wagon, along with his mother and the gifts given to them by Lucinda's parents. He checked again to make sure he had his Bill of Sale and Certificate of Freedom in a safe place. A freed slave needed all the legal proof he could obtain to protect his status from roving bands of slave catchers. Waving good-bye to Gordon and Elizabeth Duncanson, Hamilton slapped the leather reins on the back of his mule with a "Heyah."

Turning to the east, the small, discouraged family started back down the dusty trail, making their way to their new home—in Erie.

10

Go Down, Moses

By the middle of May the flowers in Stuyvesant Square had fully bloomed, painting the park in green, yellow, purple, and red. Harry walked past the blossoms and down 17th Street from the conservatory to the Dvorak townhouse.

"Come in, Barley, welcome." Dvorak was in his shirtsleeves, while Otylia and Antonin ran around the townhouse in a circle from kitchen to dining room to living room. "Children, go upstairs now. Harry T. is going to sing for me."

The children had grown fond of the young singer and wanted to stay. "Can we listen? Please, Papa. We will sit quietly."

The master was firm. "No, I must have no distractions. To your rooms."

"But Papa—"

He interrupted in a growl. "I will have no distractions."

The two looked to Burleigh, but he did not dare intervene. They trudged slowly up the stairs.

"It's been a long day. Huneker gave me fits today." The master referred to fellow faculty member James Huneker, who didn't share

115

Dvorak's vision of a national school of music that would be thoroughly American. The maestro slumped in his corner chair and reached for a cigar. "Sing of your grandfather. What songs did he like?"

Burleigh sat down at the piano to accompany himself. As Burleigh sang, the composer brooded in his chair, taking short, continuous puffs on his cigar.

> Go down, Moses,
> Way down in Egypt's land,
> Tell ole Pharaoh, let my people go!

With the bellowing finale, Dvorak bounded from his chair. "Did they really sing it that way?"

"To the best of my knowledge, sir," Harry responded.

Dvorak paced the floor, the cigar in one hand, his other hand furiously rubbing his brow. The student watched him walk back and forth. Suddenly Dvorak turned and exclaimed, "Barley, that is as great as a Beethoven theme. I am more convinced than ever that these plantation songs and your Indian melodies are the seedbed for an American school of music. I don't care what that bag of wind Huneker, and MacDowell, and the whole lot of them think."

Harry smirked and looked down at the keys.

"They don't realize what they have right here," Dvorak concluded and collapsed back into his chair, puffing furiously on his stub of a cigar. "Our students at the conservatory—and all American composers, really—must learn to value the music of their own land."

"Like you did with the *Slavonic Dances*?" Burleigh asked.

"That is it, exactly." The master stood up and began to pace again, the ash of his cigar now an inch long. "My people are like yours, Barley. My ancestors were the slaves of the Romans. We both sing songs coming from the groans of people under an evil burden, like the children of Israel."

Abruptly he sat and closed his eyes. Harry noticed the master's hand began slowly moving in time, as though he were leading an orchestra. After a moment, Dvorak lifted his other hand and waved them together. Several minutes later, the director suddenly opened his eyes and stood back up. "Take dictation, Barley."

The young man grabbed his notebook, opened to a blank page, and began writing furiously as the great composer dictated the notes to him. The two worked for nearly an hour before the music was fully written out. Burleigh had been receiving dictation from Dvorak for several weeks now and was curious as to what this beautiful music would be.

When he completed the final line, Burleigh shook the cramp out of his hand and declared, "Sir, this is wonderful. What are your plans for this music?"

"A symphony, Barley. I am writing a symphony from the New World."

Harry's heart suddenly felt like it would burst with excitement. "Sir, that is wonderful. When will it be completed?"

"Soon, my friend." Dvorak took another long, slow drag on his cigar. "Very soon."

The spiritual that Harry sang had lifted Dvorak's spirit. He wanted to know everything he could about these haunting melodies and the institution of slavery that produced them. "Tell me more of the slave times. Didn't you say that your father and your grandfather helped slaves find freedom on the Underground Railroad?"

"Yes, that's true," Harry said proudly.

"Tell me, tell me," Dvorak begged in an almost childlike manner.

"But what of the symphony? Aren't we going to continue working on it?"

"As the inspiration comes, my friend. Your song inspired me for one more piece. Now I would like your grandfather's story to inspire me further."

Harry smiled and sat down on the couch to convey the story. "When my grandfather first crossed the border into Pennsylvania, he jumped down from his wagon, kissed the ground, and thanked the good Lord for his liberty. He vowed then and there that if he ever had the opportunity to help another slave to freedom he would do whatever he could to make that possible."

1830s—Erie, Pennsylvania

The remote western town of Erie, Pennsylvania, was experiencing the same growing pains as many frontier villages in the 1830s. Rich with natural resources and a beautiful protected harbor with fishing and logging interests, Erie had grown since the War of 1812 when Commodore Perry built the ships there that defeated the British in the Battle of Lake Erie.

In 1780, during the War of Independence, Pennsylvania passed the first legislation in the United States designed to abolish slavery. It was a gradual abolition, a compromise that would allow current owners to keep their slaves but banned the practice in the future. The law stated that no black child born or imported from abroad after that date could be a "servant for life."

By an act of the legislature, "All servitude for life or slavery of Negroes, mulattos, and others is utterly taken away, extinguished, and abolished forever."

From that point on, however, the children of slaves and other servants in Pennsylvania were still bound to serve until they were twenty-eight years of age, and those who were slaves in Pennsylvania in 1780 would be so for the rest of their lives.

In the eastern part of the state, where abolition fervor was strongest, fueled by Quaker sentiments, many people freed their slaves with the passage of the law. But such progressive thought took much longer to catch on in the rugged wilderness of the western counties. Several of Erie's prominent families owned slaves. The 1800 census of Erie County listed more than 1,400 free whites, seventeen persons of color, and two slaves. Of the seventeen free persons of color, however, only two were living in an independent household. The others were the children of slaves serving out their twenty-eight years. As late as 1821, notices appeared in the Erie newspaper advertising the sale of the time of Negro servants.

In 1825, landowner P. S. V. Hamot offered a six-cent reward for the return of a runaway slave. The notice in the newspaper said:

> Runaway from the subscriber on the evening of the 12th, a Negro BOY Servant, aged 19 years, indented to serve until the age of 28 years. Do not know of any physical marks, except of his being fat, short, and thickset. Of his moral marks, he has many; much of the spirit of Cain. He is, in fact, a very bad character. Although at first appearance and

acquaintance would seem clever, but ought not to be trusted. He is a very bad subject and is capable of every bad deed.

P. S. V. HAMOT
Erie, June 15, 1825

By the late 1830s, life in the town of Erie was still somewhat primitive, though the population had nearly tripled in the previous decade from 1,300 to almost 3,500 souls. Of that number, there were ninety-two black and mixed-race persons living in Erie. They worked as laborers, blacksmiths, cooks, sailors, barbers, servants, grocers, and porters.

It was not an easy life for persons of any race. One farmer wrote of the town, "To live in this country is a continual warfare and contention between the crops, the adjoining forest, and the wild animals. It takes vigilance to eke out a living with scanty crops by carefully saving the remnants that the mischievous animals failed to destroy."

In time, railways and steamship routes passed through Erie, making it an important trading post of the still-wild western frontier and bringing with it people of all races with the goal of seeking fortune or building a new life. It was here that Hamilton Waters came to make a home for himself and his family. Upon arriving in Erie, Hamilton added clients to his business of cleaning, dyeing, and ironing clothing, tasks he could perform with his limited eyesight. He purchased an ironing board and an iron and became a presser of garments for some of the wealthier families in Erie. He diligently completed his work and frugally saved all the money he could.

As time passed, Waters grew to admire the hearty people of Erie. He and his wife built a small cabin from the abundant woods and set up housekeeping. The Waters family was welcome among both the poor and the wealthy residents of the rough pioneer town. Upper-class residents commended Lucinda's good breeding and sophistication, attributes that impressed Erie's white society. The training Lucinda had received in the governor's mansion provided employment for her, and later for her children and grandchildren.

Through his hard work, creativity, and versatility, Hamilton also soon came into favor with some of the leading citizens of Erie. They quickly recognized his intelligence and reliability. But like other free blacks before the Civil War, Waters had to constantly demonstrate that he was not inferior to whites.

In 1844, after several years of diligent labor and saving, Hamilton purchased three-quarters of a city lot for five hundred dollars. On the property, at 71 East Third Street, he built a modest, two-story clapboard home in this middle-class neighborhood.

By 1850, Erie's population had grown to nearly six thousand people, large enough to be designated as an official city in the state of Pennsylvania. It was already one of the most successful freshwater fishing ports in the world. As the city grew, so did the fortunes of its citizens. Hamilton had proven that he was a person who could be trusted, and local politicians offered him the job of lighting the newly installed gas streetlamps. Every evening, just before dusk, Hamilton could be found singing the plantation songs as he carried his torch and ladder through the streets of Erie.

That same year a reign of terror erupted in the United States when Congress passed the Fugitive Slave Act. This infamous law expanded the original law of 1793, allowing bounty hunters to track down and capture runaway slaves anywhere in the United States. It also became illegal to assist fugitive slaves who were trying to reach freedom in Canada. Since Erie was located on the northern boundary of the United States, it increasingly became a hotbed for abolitionist activity. The busy Underground Railroad had routes coming to Erie from safe houses to the south in Pittsburgh and from the west in Ohio. Once a passenger arrived in Erie, they were either shuttled across the lake to Canada by boat or transported along the lakeshore east to Buffalo, New York, where they could cross the border on foot.

Crossing the lake by boat was terribly risky for several reasons. The busy harbors of the growing industrial North were closely watched by federal agents. It was nearly impossible to travel through the ports with a runaway slave. Also, the weather on Lake Erie was highly volatile. Storms rose on the lake frequently and without much notice. Travel in smaller watercraft was dangerous and at times deadly.

Several stops on the Railroad existed in and around the city. As abolitionist activity increased in the area, it became routine to see posses riding through Erie on the trail of a fugitive. Professional slave catchers, with vicious hounds trotting along beside their horses, were not an uncommon sight. Southern slave owners were uncompromising in their pursuit of what they considered to be their runaway property.

Newspapers throughout the United States carried offers of reward for the return of fugitive slaves. Incentives to turn in runaways and collect the bounty were very tempting. Even free Negroes were not immune to capture and deportation.

It was inevitable that Hamilton Waters would come into contact with both black and white abolitionists in Erie. Free blacks throughout the North were part of a cohesive and complex community of individuals from different backgrounds and walks of life. Many blacks in Erie were either freed slaves or the children of former slaves. They shared a legacy of servitude, and thus a bond of understanding and compassion.

One of the best-known stations in the Erie area was the Himrod Mission—a refuge for freed slaves and downtrodden white folks. It was situated just east of the busy port at the foot of French Street. Overlooking the harbor, up on the high bluff, the mission was sometimes used as the last point in the long journey toward freedom. It was not, however, an easy boarding point for ships leaving Presque Isle Bay. After passage of the Fugitive Slave Act, ships traveling out of Erie were closely watched by sheriff's deputies. Often conductors transferred their passengers to Harborcreek, ten miles to the east, to board small ferry boats. Sympathetic captains on the Cleveland to Buffalo steamers would pause their vessels and load passengers from these ferries for the trip across the often-treacherous Great Lake.

Several abolitionists made Erie their home, including a black freedman named Albert Vosburgh, a longtime resident of the city and a member of the Pennsylvania Abolition Society. As a business leader and property owner, he had the means to provide assistance in the form of food, clothing, and cash to fugitives.

Over the years, Hamilton and Vosburgh developed a friendship, and the businessman introduced him to other abolitionists. Soon Hamilton was busy with all sorts of political and social activity, including the harboring of fugitives.

Like most slaves in the South who had heard of the Declaration of Independence, Hamilton was raised with the belief that all men were created in the image of God, and thus were entitled to freedom. In the decade before the outbreak of the Civil War, the efforts of the abolitionists along Pennsylvania's northern shore rose to fever pitch. As in the South, where plantation songs became a code for sending messages along the lines of slave workers, northern abolitionists devised ways of sending clandestine information through a variety of means.

Being partially blind, Hamilton was not able to do the labor of other men his age. His family survived through the various small jobs that he patched together, and also through Lucinda's service to wealthy families. There was always food on the table, but they were never well-to-do. A new opportunity arose for Waters when some of Erie's leading abolitionists devised a new scheme for sending messages to their members. Because of his reliability, Hamilton was recruited to take the position of town crier. His responsibilities included walking up and down Erie's streets and boulevards declaring the news of the day at the top of his lungs—while also passing messages along to key abolitionists.

Erie's newspapers were printed only once a day, so when important events took place, the town criers were sent out to announce them. As Hamilton walked slowly through the center of the city at all hours of the day or night, he called out the news: controversy at the previous day's city council meeting, a freighter sinking off of Long Point, an increase in barge traffic from Pittsburgh along the Beaver and Erie Canal, and so on. If a local citizen died, the town crier went through the streets ringing his bell, telling the hour of the funeral. He carried any news of importance to the community.

Hamilton looked at the job as his way of helping the cause of freedom. In front of key abolitionist businesses, he stopped and added cryptic messages to his cries. "Railroad traffic increases, local freight is delivered."

In the summer of 1851, Jehiel Towner, a white abolitionist, sent just such an encoded message to the home of Frank Henry, a conductor living in Harborcreek:

Dear Frank:
  The mirage lifts Long Point into view. Come up and see the beautiful sight. I can't promise a view tomorrow. Truly,

Jehiel Towner

Frank Henry contacted Albert Vosburgh for help, and he, in turn, called on Waters.

"Hamilton, I need to speak with you a moment." The robust Vosburgh was an intimidating figure who carried himself with style and sophistication. He stood more than six feet tall and sported wiry sideburns and a rotund belly, which he kept in place with a lavish silk vest. Pulling Hamilton by the arm, he turned off French Street and into the entranceway of one of his buildings.

"Yes sir," Hamilton replied. "How can I help you?"

Vosburgh shut the door behind him and spoke quietly into Hamilton's ear.

"We have passengers who need to be transported and the railroad is running late. We need a conductor to see the cargo through to Harborcreek."

In those days one never spoke of runaways or fugitive slaves. The Underground Railroad transported "passengers" and "cargo."

"Do you think you can handle this for us?" Vosburgh asked.

The opportunity to actually transport fugitives was both exciting and frightening. The penalty for being caught with a runaway slave could be a fine, imprisonment—or for a black man, even deportation back into slavery. Yet Hamilton was firm in his conviction that helping another to freedom was more important than his personal safety. He had been helped when he tried to escape and after he had purchased his freedom. He'd sworn that when given the opportunity to help someone else find freedom he would not turn down the chance.

"Mr. Vosburgh, I's your man," Hamilton replied, his eyes wide with excitement.

"Good. Meet me tonight at eight o'clock just beyond Jerusalem at the Gleason Fishery on Cascade Creek. We'll load the passengers there and you can deliver them to the home of Frank Henry, one of our conductors in Harborcreek."

As the evening approached, Hamilton mulled over the situation in his mind. His eyesight was passable in full daylight, but once the sun went down he could barely see his hand in front of his face. He would need to find a guide to travel with him. He crossed busy State Street, full of buckboards loaded with all sorts of items being transported from the docks to locations throughout the city and beyond. He made his way to the house of another freedman, Eldred Davis, who lived on the western bluff overlooking the bay in the black section of town that had come to be known as Jerusalem.

"Eldred, I wants to talk to you privately," Hamilton said after being greeted at the door by the handsome man in his midthirties. The two walked around behind the wooden home and into the small grove of trees at the end of the property.

"What's up, Hamilton?" Davis questioned.

"I's been asked to move some cargo on de railroad tonight," Waters said quietly. Davis knew exactly what Hamilton meant. "You knows I has trouble wid my eyes from de slave time. I sees all right in de day, but at night I's blind as a bat. I needs a set of eyes to go wid me to lead the way. I can takes care of de cargo and drive de hawses, but someone has to be out in front with de lantern."

"I'll go with you, Ham," Davis responded quickly. "Just let me tell the wife."

"Dat's kind of you, Eldred." Hamilton responded, rubbing the back of his neck with his hand. "But if we gets caught, it'd be terribly hard on yo' family if you's thrown in jail, or worse." Hamilton paused, searching for the right words. "Eldred, I was thinking it'd be better if yo' boy, Charles, was to help me." Charles was twelve years old, but he was strong and mature for his years.

Eldred folded his arms tightly in front of him, then rubbed his forehead hard with his right hand. The dangers of transporting runaway slaves were enormous. Slave hunters were known to shoot those who helped fugitives at the slightest provocation. Yet Eldred himself had come out of slavery when his father purchased his freedom as a child. He felt obligated to help in any way he could. But if he were caught his family would lose their provider, and he saw the wisdom in Hamilton's suggestion.

"I'll need to talk to my wife," he finally said. Hamilton nodded his understanding as the two men stared for a moment into each other's eyes. Eldred turned and walked slowly through the grove toward his house. Outside, in the small yard, Hamilton waited and prayed for what seemed to be an eternity.

Suddenly Eldred and Charles appeared at the door. Both had a stern look on their faces, and Hamilton could see Eldred's wife inside the house, holding a handkerchief over her mouth as she fought her tears. The risk they were taking for the sake of freedom was great. This could be the last time they would ever see their son. Eldred took the boy into his arms and held him tightly as he kissed the top of his head. "You know how proud your mama and I are of you, don't you, Charles?" The boy nodded vigorously. "This is a mighty brave thing you are volunteering for. Are you sure you want to do this?"

"Do you think it's the right thing to do, Daddy?"

Eldred looked off in the distance and blinked as tears forced their way to the surface. Wiping them away with his sleeve, he smiled, looked back at his son, and said, "Yes, son, I do."

The boy blinked his eyes several times and shifted his jaw back and forth. Finally he answered, "Then I am sure that I want to do it." The two embraced as Charles's mother burst out in sobs, turned, and walked away from the door.

After a long embrace, Eldred turned to Hamilton and said through his tears, "You take care of my boy, now. I'm trusting you, Ham."

Hamilton nodded somberly and put his arm around the lad. "We'll both trust Jesus to get us back safely." The two men shook hands and Hamilton led young Charles out of the yard and down the street. They made their way back across State Street and toward the Waterses' home as the late afternoon shadows grew on the pavement.

After they lit all of the streetlamps, the pair hitched up Hamilton's wagon and headed west. As they made their way through Jerusalem, the sun began to set over the lake, turning the sky a mixture of red, orange, purple, and gray.

Hamilton held the reins as they made their way down the hill to the fishery at the mouth of Cascade Creek. "When it gets dark, I's gonna need you to walk in front of de wagon wid de lantern," he told the boy. "We'll be all right in de city wid de gas lamps. But once we's past town you's goin' to have to get down and hold de light wid one hand and de reins wid de other."

The lad nodded his understanding.

They arrived at the large wooden building that housed the fishery just as the last rays of light disappeared behind the trees on the peninsula at the far side of Presque Isle Bay. The strong odor of fresh-caught perch, salmon, and northern pike filled Hamilton's nostrils. Vosburgh greeted them and guided the pair to the back of the Gleason Fishery. There they entered a long, dark room lined with the large wooden vats used to store the fresh catch. Reaching the far end of the room, Vosburgh opened one of the containers. Crouched inside were the runaways—a large, middle-aged man and a younger couple with a baby.

"It's time," Vosburgh said, extending his hand to the woman. She handed him the baby and then climbed out of the large container. "I've packed some food and fresh clothes for your journey. They've been loaded onto the wagon. You can change when you get to Harborcreek."

The woman was dark-skinned, slender, and quite attractive. Her name was Sara and she appeared to be in her early twenties. Her baby boy was wrapped in a thick muslin carrier. Her husband, Martin, was an intelligent-looking man in his midtwenties. Sara had been sold away from him and the child to a plantation in the Deep South. The young couple could not bear to be separated, and they had escaped the night before she was to leave.

The older man was named Sam, and his face was never without a large, toothy grin. He carried with him an antique hunting rifle that he called "old smooth-bo." He was barrel-chested, with a large, round head that matched his large, round belly. His arms seemed overly long and his feet were just about as big as any Hamilton had ever seen. He wore an old shoe on one foot and a heavy boot on the other. The clothes packed by Mr. Vosburgh would come in handy for Sam. It was obvious that he hadn't had a new set in quite awhile.

"These men will guide you to the next stop on the line," Vosburgh declared. The three nodded, their eyes still adjusting to the light of the lantern. Vosburgh handed the woman her infant. "Keep that baby quiet through the city," he said somberly. She nodded vigorously. The group made their way to the wagon, where the fugitives lay down under a canvas cover. On top of them, Hamilton, Charles, and Vosburgh heaped loose straw to camouflage the precious cargo.

"The Henry farm is near the mouth of Four Mile Creek," Vosburgh instructed as Hamilton climbed up onto the wagon. "There will be two lanterns hanging on the front porch. Knock on the door and tell them you're there to deliver the packages. Do you understand?"

"Two lanterns on de porch, right," Hamilton responded and turned to the boy. "Well, son, we best be goin'."

"Yes, sir," Charles responded and climbed aboard next to him.

"Godspeed to you, my friends," said Vosburgh as the horses pulled the wagon forward.

The small band made their way up the hill from the fishery to First Street, overlooking the bay front. The gas lamps that made night travel less treacherous for most were now making it easier for people to see this wagon filled with contraband. Hamilton slapped the reins to make the horses move faster. He could make out shadows in front of him, but needed the boy's eyes to be sure he was on course. From time to time he leaned over to the lad and said quietly, "How we doin', son?"

Charles looked straight ahead and calmly replied, "We're fine, sir."

As the pair made their way across town, Hamilton sang quietly to himself a plantation song from his youth.

> He delivered Daniel from de lion's den
> Jonah from de belly of de whale
> An' de Hebrew chillen from de fiery furnace
> Den why not every man?

Between verses, he prayed, "Lawd, send yo' angels. Get us der safely."

Suddenly the quiet of the warm night air was pierced by the high-pitched cry of the baby buried next to his mama in the straw. "Quiet dat baby," Hamilton said in a stern tone.

Under the straw, the mother struggled to hush the infant. Her husband clenched his teeth, wincing in fear. He whispered in her ear, "Pull him tight." Perspiring under the weight of the warm straw, Sara put the infant to her breast, hoping the familiar feeling would quiet the child. She had heard stories of desperate mothers on the

Underground Railroad who had literally suffocated a crying baby while attempting to keep it quiet, and she was terrified that she might do the same. Even against the familiar warmth of her bosom, however, the child continued to wail.

"Dat baby's got to hush," Hamilton spoke to the night air. "We's almost to town, and if it be cryin' den, we's in trouble fo' sure." The woman began to silently weep. If she pulled the baby closer, she feared it would not have sufficient air to breathe. She had worked hard to keep a channel of air for the child, but now she had no choice. She pulled the baby tightly to her chest, wrapping her arms around his little head. Just as the bright lights of State Street began to appear in front of Hamilton, the baby went silent.

Charles looked to the left and to the right as they approached the main drive. Even at this late hour, folks were out walking along the wooden promenade. Dockworkers stumbled out of a saloon, laughing loudly as they staggered down the sidewalk. Carriages with lanterns lit carried wealthy Erie residents to formal occasions at the large mansions that surrounded the public square a half mile to the south. Charles held the lantern in his right hand and with his left he guided Hamilton's hands on the reins as they crossed the busy intersection.

"How are you this evening, Hamilton?" the voice came from his right just as they paused at the intersection. Hamilton recognized it as Judge John Grubb. "Working late tonight?"

Hamilton tried to control his anxiety. "Yes, sah. Can't seem to get de day put to bed," he replied, laughing. *God, don't let dat baby cry*.

In earlier years the Judge himself had been a slave owner in Erie. He walked up next to them and put his foot up on the side of the wagon. "I see you have some help with you. Aren't you out a bit late, son?"

The boy replied respectfully, "We're on our way home now, sir."

"That's good. You shouldn't keep this pickaninny out so late, Ham."

Under the straw the three fugitives lay motionless. Sara held the baby so tightly she was sure he would suffocate. Tears flowed down her cheeks, but she didn't make a sound. Her husband closed his eyes tightly, holding his breath. Sam moved his hand down his gun, placing his finger on the trigger. The slightest noise and they would be discovered and quickly transported back to their plantations. None of them could bear the thought of going back to slavery.

"You surely is right, Judge. The time got away from me. I'll see him home right dis minute."

"Very well. Good night, Ham."

"Good night, Judge Grubb." *Thank you, Lord Jesus.* Hamilton tipped his hat to the man, who stepped away from the wagon, turned and continued his walk down State Street. "Heyah." Hamilton slapped the reins against the backs of the horses.

The young boy had kept his wits about him, and there was no sound from below. Hamilton breathed a long, if premature, sigh of relief. They rode on for another mile without a sound from the baby. Hamilton could not afford to stop and check on his passengers; it was just too dangerous. *Lord, keep that baby in your hands*, he prayed silently.

When they reached the eastern edge of the city, young Charles turned to the older man and said, "It's awful dark, Mr. Waters. I'm gonna get out in front now."

"Good boy," Hamilton replied, patting him on the shoulder. The boy jumped down from the wagon with the lantern. He grabbed hold of the reins, and they made their way down the dirt road that hugged the shoreline high up on the cliff overlooking the lake. Soon they were beyond Presque Isle Bay. As they came upon a clearing on the bluff, young Charles could see the moon reflecting off the water of Lake Erie. The warm August breeze came off of the lake, whipping at the straw in the cart. It was a moment of peace in the midst of a night of potential terror.

After hours of slow going, they finally approached the farm owned by Mr. Frank Henry. "Mr. Waters, there it is. There are two lanterns hanging on the porch, and I can hear the creek off in the distance."

"Sho' nuff, boy, I hears it too." They made their way to the home and stepped up onto the porch. By now it was approaching midnight, but Mr. Henry was up waiting for them. Hamilton knocked firmly at the door. A tall dark-haired white man, still dressed in work clothes, opened the door to them.

"Can I help you?" he asked suspiciously.

"Mr. Henry?" Hamilton asked the shadow standing in front of him.

"Yes, what can I do for you tonight?" he replied.

"Sah, we's got some packages for you," he responded, handing him the duffel bag filled with the clothes and food that Mr. Vosburgh had provided.

"Thank you, sir. I've been expecting these. You can unload your wagon out back."

Mr. Henry led them around behind his home. They pulled the wagon into the barn and closed the large wooden doors. Once they were safely inside, Hamilton jumped up on the side of the wagon and quickly pulled the straw off of the precious cargo. Charles and Mr. Henry instinctively joined him.

"How is de baby?" he called as he threw the straw to the side. "How is de baby?" he repeated. With the weight of the straw removed, the men pushed the canvas out of the way and pulled the woman up from the wagon bed. As they did, the baby lurched forward—and woke from sleep. The child cried out at the interruption, bringing hoots of joy from the men and great sobs of relief from his mother.

The sound of that baby crying was like an angelic choir to Hamilton. "Hallelujah, glory be!" he exclaimed in the darkness.

"Thank you, Jesus," the woman said quietly through her sobs as she gently rocked the baby and looked into her young husband's eyes. "Thank you, dear Jesus."

"Welcome to Harborcreek, friends." Frank Henry smiled as he extended his hand to help them out of the wagon. "I can't wait to hear your story."

Up in the hayloft, the three passengers changed into their new clothes and quickly gulped down the warm meal prepared by Mrs. Henry. "We have a room for you inside, if you want to stay the night," Frank told Hamilton as they closed the barn doors.

"Dat would be mighty generous of you, Mr. Henry. Charles here is about to drop." Hamilton rustled the boy's hair as he led him to the farmhouse. The lad quickly fell asleep in the large iron bed in the guest room. Hamilton stayed in the kitchen with Mr. Henry and chatted for a while. "Where will our friends go from here?" he asked the conductor.

"In the winter, when the lake is frozen, we shuttle passengers up the coastline to Buffalo. But during the summer, we have a few steamboat captains who take them across the lake to the Long Point lighthouse on the Canadian shore. If we can't arrange that, we know of some sailboats that are big enough to safely make the journey."

"Glory be," Hamilton said out loud. He couldn't help but praise God for allowing him to be a part of such an adventure.

Early the next morning, Hamilton and Charles climbed up into the loft of the barn to say good-bye to their new friends. "I wants to see dat baby now dat it's light," he declared as he stepped into the loft. Sara brought the infant to Hamilton and gently placed the little boy into his arms.

"We can't thank you enough for your kindness," she said, running her hand across the baby's face.

"Yes sir, we're in your debt," her husband added.

Hamilton looked down into the deep brown eyes of the baby. "You raise dis little one to love Jesus," he said. Looking back up at them, he continued, "And when you get de chance, you help someone else." Martin put his arm around his wife and nodded his head.

"We'll do that, we promise."

Hamilton kissed the baby's forehead and handed him back to Sara. He turned to the gentle giant standing next to them. "Watch over these two, will you, Sam?"

For the first time since they met, the man's face turned from a smile to a stern expression. "I will do dat, sir," he said with determination. Then, looking down at the gun in his hands, he added with a smile, "Me and old smooth-bo." Hamilton chuckled and gave the giant man a hug.

The young mother turned to Charles, who was standing quietly next to Hamilton. "And thank you, too," she said. "What you did was very brave."

Charles smiled awkwardly. "Thank you, ma'am," he replied. "Good luck on your way to Canada."

"Thank you, young man," Martin added and patted him on the back.

"Well, we must be goin'," Hamilton declared. "Godspeed to you."

He followed Charles down the ladder and jumped up onto the seat of his wagon. Charles opened the large wooden doors, and they drove the wagon out of the barn, waving good-bye to the Henry family, who were seated on the front porch.

"Thank you for the delivery, sir," Mr. Henry shouted. "You're welcome at our home anytime."

"De pleasure is mine," Hamilton replied. "Come see us when you's in town."

"I'll do that, sir. God bless you both."

Hamilton tipped his hat to the family, slapped the back of his horses with the reins, and headed back toward the city. The trip that took several hours the night before lasted just over an hour in the morning light. As they approached the boy's house, Mrs. Davis came flying off the porch when they came into view. Charles jumped down from the buckboard and ran into the arms of his crying mama. Eldred Davis burst through the front door and bounded down the steps, a large smile spreading across his face. After embracing his son, he turned to the weary driver and asked, "Did the packages arrive safely?"

Hamilton jumped down from the wagon and with a bright smile replied, "Didn't my Lawd deliver Daniel?" Eldred shouted for joy and the two men embraced, slapping each other on the back and bursting with raucous laughter. Young Charles looked up at his mother and beamed. The woman hugged him tightly and said, "Praise Jesus." Still embracing, the men began jumping up and down, laughing uproariously. Once again Mrs. Davis cried out loudly, "Praise you, my sweet Jesus."

11

Swing Low, Sweet Chariot

1893–New York City

Over the months that ensued, Burleigh and Dvorak spent hundreds of hours together. Harry would sing the spirituals, and then the composer would scribble out a stanza of music and give it to Burleigh to rewrite in his pristine handwriting. Burleigh's fellow student Will Marion Cook called Harry "Dvorak's pet," displaying jealousy over the inordinate time given to the vocalist by the great composer.

Years later, Ambassador James Weldon Johnson would write of Burleigh's relationship with Dvorak:

> Harry not only studied with Dvorak, but spent a good deal of time with him at his home. Dvorak often listened hours at a time while Burleigh played the spirituals he had learned during his youth. Although he never really was a pupil of the master, he knew him better and perhaps saw more of him than any of his regularly enrolled students.

One warm day in May, Dvorak summoned Burleigh to his home for a special surprise. Harry was ushered into the living room, where he found the master seated at the piano. Dvorak stood and greeted his student, shaking his hand. "Come, Barley, sit at the piano. Please will you sing something for me?" Harry walked over and sat at the piano bench. The maestro stood next to the piano, tapping the ash from his cigar into his favorite tray. "Sing for me my favorite, Barley. Sing 'Were You There?'"

Harry turned to the keyboard and slowly began to play.

> Sometimes it causes me to tremble, tremble, tremble.
> Were you there when they crucified my Lord?

Dvorak was a godly man. Though he was a Roman Catholic, he felt a bond with all Christians. He even wrote a symphony to honor John Huss, a Czech hero and a forerunner of Luther, one of the first Christian leaders to break free from the Roman Church, paying for it by being burned alive. Whenever he heard "Were You There?" he sat, placed his hands over his heart, and closed his eyes as if in prayer. Burleigh finished the song and both men sat in silence for a moment, the chirping of the thrushes and the muffled sounds of the children playing upstairs the only sounds in the room.

The master stretched out his legs and puffed on his cigar. "Ah, it is such a wonderful day. Sing some more. What is the one that reminds you most of your grandfather?"

Burleigh paused for a moment, thinking back to the family gatherings when they would sing their favorite songs and tell stories of the South. What an honor it was to share these experiences with such a great man. "My grandfather's favorite spiritual was 'Swing Low, Sweet Chariot,'" he answered.

"Ahhh," Dvorak sighed as though he had just sipped a fine wine. "Yes, it is one of my favorites as well. Sing this for me, would you please, Barley."

Harry felt warm tears come to his eyes and he had to breathe deeply to collect himself. He closed his eyes and began the sweet refrain.

> Swing low, sweet chariot, comin' for to carry me home.

As he sang, Burleigh pictured his granddaddy, Hamilton Waters, telling his grandchildren the story of how angels came on a golden chariot to pick up God's people and bring them to the Father's arms when they died.

1873—ERIE, PENNSYLVANIA

In February of 1873, Harry's father, Henry Burleigh, traveled to Chicago to attend a freedman's rally. He had distinguished himself as a friend to former slaves, not only in Erie but throughout the Midwest. As he had before the war, Henry worked late hours for several years, pouring himself into the cause in which he believed so strongly. Walking with some colleagues down a snow-covered Chicago street after a late-night meeting on February 26, 1873, Henry suddenly slumped forward and fell to the ground. His friends gathered around and tried to resuscitate him, but to no avail. He died of a massive heart attack before he hit the snow. He left Elizabeth with four children all under eight years of age.

Harry Burleigh was less than six years old when Henry died. The sudden loss of their father and his income forced the children to take odd jobs as soon as they were old enough to work. To help the family survive, Reginald and Harry sold newspapers, worked as errand boys, and began accompanying their grandfather on his daily rounds of lighting the gas lamps of Erie.

As a widow, Elizabeth was forced to take any job she could find to supplement her teaching at the Himrod Mission. After an extensive search she finally found work as a janitress at Erie Public School Number 1—the same school where she had once aspired to teach.

Before her husband died, she and Henry had helped make ends meet by working at private parties held by Mrs. Russell. The Erie socialite made it a point to call on Elizabeth when Henry passed away. After extending her sympathies, Mrs. Russell asked if Elizabeth would be interested in serving at her home on an ongoing basis. Elizabeth agreed to work at these functions whenever Mrs. Russell would arrange a party for her friends. But even between cleaning the school and serving at the Russell estate, it was all Elizabeth and her father could do to keep the wolf from the door.

Things were difficult for the family, but they banded together and somehow managed. Elizabeth was a beautiful young woman with a great deal of charm. It was only a short time before eligible bachelors began calling on her. Two years after Harry's father died, Elizabeth was courted by another Civil War veteran, John Elmendorf. He had also served in the Navy and was involved in abolitionist activities. He was a friend of Henry's, and Elizabeth had met him before her husband passed away. Over time, their friendship blossomed into romance. At the time of their marriage in 1875 he was a coachman for Congressman William Scott, a decent job with a salary that relieved the pressure.

———————— ◇ ————————

In the next few years the couple had two more children. Now the humble house that Hamilton Waters built when he first came to Erie was home to him, all his grandchildren, Elizabeth, John, and Elizabeth's sister Louise, who had come to live with the family after the death of their mother. It was simply bursting at the seams.

Eventually John Elmendorf worked his way into his own business, operating a boarding stable. The company prospered and within a few years the family was able to build a second house on the family property. John and Elizabeth moved into the larger house at the front of the lot with the children, while Hamilton and Louise stayed in the older dwelling in the back.

Elizabeth often took her husband and her two eldest sons with her when she cleaned the public school. But she did most of the cleaning while John played with the youngsters.

"All right, you silly boys, I have to finish my work," Elizabeth scolded Reginald, Harry, and her husband as they crawled around on the hard wooden floors. "Get off the floor right this instant. I just sewed patches on the knees of your trousers, and I am not going to do it again anytime soon."

"Yes, ma'am." John Elmendorf stood at attention, saluting his drill sergeant wife. The boys quickly mimicked the Civil War veteran. He had trained the boys on the proper stance at attention and they loved to stand stiff as a board with their hands up to their forehead in salute. The children adored their new stepfather, and he had quickly taken the role of protector and provider for the growing brood. Along with Reginald and Harry, the family included the two other Burleigh children, sisters Adah and Eva, along with another brother and sister, Elzie and Bessie Elmendorf.

"Permission to speak, ma'am," Reginald barked.

"At ease, soldiers," Elizabeth said in a deep voice. "Now what is it that the young private wishes?"

Reginald broke from the military game. "Let's sing one of Grandpa's songs."

"Can we sing 'The Gospel Train'?" young Harry added. This was one of his favorite songs.

"'The Gospel Train' it is," his mother said, ruffling his hair. "But we have to work while we sing, or we'll be here all day. Daddy, you start us off."

John Elmendorf tugged on the invisible whistle to start the train moving. "All aboard," he called, cupping his hands around his mouth. "This train is pullin' out of the station." He began moving his arms and legs in the motion of a locomotive and the boys quickly jumped behind him, playing the part of the coal car and caboose.

> The gospel train is a-comin'; I hear it just at hand
> I hear them car-wheels rumbling, and rolling through the land

Elizabeth went back to her dusting, giving up on the playful trio. They all sang together,

> Then get on board, chillen, get on board, chillen.
> Get on board, chillen, there's room for many a-more.

Elizabeth provided all her children with a thorough understanding of music. The family sang wherever they went, and they all had wonderful voices. Hamilton and John Elmendorf taught the children the spirituals, so they were sung almost continuously throughout the course of a day's work.

For entertainment, the family often gathered in the sitting room to read Bible stories or fairy tales and to sing the plantation songs. One evening after they finished a chorus of "Swing Low, Sweet Chariot," little Eva asked her grandfather, "Grandpa, why do we sing about a chariot comin' to take us home. Aren't we home already?"

The old man laughed at the sweet question. "Honey, dat song talks 'bout our heavenly home. Dis here's only our earthly home."

"Whose chariot is it?" Harry asked.

"De chariot is what de heavenly Father sends down to gather up his childrens. Den he takes 'em home to heaven."

"Did he send one for Grandma when she went to heaven?" Eva asked him.

Hamilton looked over to Elizabeth, who smiled at the thought. The question brought tears to Hamilton's eyes, and he sat for a moment puffing on his pipe. Finally, when he regained his composure, he answered the youngster. "Yes, our heavenly Father sent a golden chariot and took Grandma right to his throne, baby."

Elizabeth decided to add her thoughts to the story. "You see honey, the good Lord sends his angels with the chariot when it's time for one of his children to come home to him. When he wants to bring someone up out of this world, he just swings it down low, and the angels help the person into the chariot. Then the Lord pulls the chariot up to himself."

"What color is the chariot?" a skeptical Reginald asked.

"It's the color of the leaves in autumn, honey," his mother answered. "It's covered in gold, red, and brown."

"Do we know when the chariot is coming for us?" Harry asked, his eyes wide with wonder.

The wise old man answered the lad, "Sometimes we know dat our time is coming close, sometimes we don't. He sends down de golden chariot for de righteous persons. De wicked—dey don't have nothin' better den a wheelbarrow to dump dem off at Hades's gate." The family broke out in laughter at the thought.

"All right, everyone. It's time for sleep," Elizabeth said as the giggles died down. "Give us all kisses and go up to bed."

"Everyone say their prayers," John added as he followed the little ones up the stairs.

Hamilton and Elizabeth were left alone together next to the fire in the cozy sitting room. They sat quietly for several moments, listening to the children running about upstairs. Elizabeth worked on her needlepoint as Hamilton stared into the fire. He loved to watch the glowing embers, one of the few things that he could still see clearly. As the flames licked at the neatly stacked logs, his mind went back in time to the wonderful and awful journey from Maryland. Fire was a daily necessity, and the trio—Hamilton, Lovey, and Lucinda—carried hot embers in an iron pot so that they would always have the warmth and utility of fire, rain or shine. On many nights, after Lovey had drifted off to sleep, Hamilton and Lucinda had stayed up talking across the fire pit late into the evening.

"Yo' mother first told me she loved me next to a burning fire in de mountains of central Pennsylvania," Hamilton told his eldest daughter as he continued staring at the flames.

"I know," Elizabeth replied quietly. "Both of you shared that with me many times."

They continued in silence for several more minutes. Finally, Hamilton turned to his daughter and said, "I'm glad that she still lives." Elizabeth smiled and cocked her head as if to ask what he meant by the statement. But before she could utter the words, her father leaned forward and smiled. "She still lives in you, and in yo' precious childrens."

Elizabeth smiled and sighed. Laying the needlepoint to the side, she rose and walked over to her father and kissed him on the cheek. "I love you, Papa," she whispered in his ear.

"I loves you, too, sweetheart," he replied, hugging her around the neck.

1877–Erie, Pennsylvania

Harry's mother, Elizabeth, was a devout woman. She labored to impart to her children the cherished values passed on to her by her father. Though she worked at the Himrod Mission, Elizabeth faithfully attended St. Paul's Episcopal Church, where she found friendship and freedom from bigotry. She wasn't allowed to teach in the public school, but for years she taught the largest integrated adult Sunday school class in the city from a Greek New Testament. Harry and the other children were confirmed in the Episcopal Church. It was there that Harry first learned the hymns and liturgical songs by German, French, English, and American composers.

On Sunday mornings Harry attended this church with his mother and stepfather. Later in the afternoon he took his grandfather, who was now completely blind, to services at the Himrod Mission, where Hamilton felt more at home. He loved the way the mission choir sang the spirituals, and the service was much more free-flowing.

Hamilton and Harry loved to harmonize as they sat on the hard wooden benches. Harry never complained about having to attend two services on Sunday. He enjoyed the music in both churches and loved spending time with his granddaddy. By this time Hamilton could no longer continue his work duties and was forced to stay at home with his daughter Louise. Reginald and Harry took over the job of lighting the lamps.

Just after the New Year in 1877, Hamilton Waters became ill, complaining of pain in his chest. By February, he could not even get out of bed and had difficulty speaking. Louise stayed with Hamilton in the smaller house to tend to his needs so that the others could continue working.

<hr />

One cold Sunday morning, as the family prepared to go to church, young Harry asked if he could stay with his granddaddy. Elizabeth was reluctant, as she liked the family to be together for church. But after the boy implored her to let him remain with Hamilton, she finally gave in. "All right Harry, you can stay as long as it's OK with your Aunt Louise, and if you promise to have a service with your grandfather."

"I promise, Mama. We can sing his favorite spirituals."

Louise was delighted to have the youngster sit with Hamilton while the family was at church. Elizabeth walked Harry up the stairs to where the elderly blind man was lying in his tiny bedroom.

"We're going to church now, Daddy," she whispered into Hamilton's ear, waking him from sleep. "Harry's gonna stay with you while we're gone."

"OK den, I'll be seein' ya'," he replied in a whisper, barely opening his eyes.

She smiled and kissed her father on the forehead. "Good-bye, Daddy." She placed Harry in the chair next to the bed. At ten years old, his feet did not quite reach the floor yet. "Be a good boy, Harry. Take care of your grandfather." She kissed the lad on the cheek and walked to the door.

Before she left, Elizabeth lingered for a moment, smiling at the two friends. Then she turned and walked down the stairs. Her husband had already loaded the rest of the children into the carriage. He helped Elizabeth climb up onto the front seat, and they made their way to the church.

A few minutes later, Louise walked up the staircase carrying a tray of breakfast. "Here you are, Daddy, time to eat." Hamilton again was roused from sleep. "Harry's gonna join us while the family's at church."

"Harry's a good boy," the old man replied in a weak voice.

"He sure is," she answered with a wink to the lad. "Harry, do you want some breakfast?"

"No thank you," he replied. "I already had some pancakes."

"Pancakes? That sounds delicious. All right then, I guess you'll have to eat this whole plate by yourself, Daddy."

"I's not hungry right now," he replied. "I jest wants to talk wid Harry for a while."

"OK, I'll just leave the tray over here if you change your mind. Harry, if your granddaddy gets hungry, could you give this to him?"

"Yes, Aunt Louise," Harry replied.

Louise placed the tray on the chest at the foot of the bed and picked up the room a little bit before leaving the two alone.

Harry smiled at his granddaddy for a moment. "Mama told me we needed to have our own service, Grandpa, since we won't be going to church today."

"Dat sounds like yo' mother," Hamilton replied with a slight smile, straining to open one eye. "I sho' would love to have you take me to de Mission. No one 'round here sings de spirituals like dey do."

"I told Mama that we could sing together, like we do at church and when we light the lamps."

"I's too weak to sing today," Hamilton whispered. "But you has such a pretty voice. You sing a song to me."

"What do you want me to sing?"

Hamilton paused for a moment, breathing heavily. He loved Harry very much. A special bond had formed between them, and he wanted to share with him all that was in his heart. He turned toward the boy, though he could not see him. "Harry, I's about to be free. I's going to de land where der ain't no slave. Nobody's sick and der ain't no cryin'." He smiled as he continued. "Der's a ship comin' fo' to get me, Harry. De good Lawd done sent it, and it should be here soon. I has my trunk packed—been packed a good while—and am waitin' for de boat to round de curve."

Harry remembered the story that his grandfather used to tell of the angels and the chariot coming from heaven to get God's people. His eyes began to well up with tears. "Grandpa, is the fiery chariot coming to pick you up?" the boy sobbed.

"Now Harry, you be strong. Dis ain't a bad ting. I hasn't seen good fo' a long, long time. Pretty soon, I's gonna see jest fine." The old man smiled and turned his eyes toward the ceiling as if he were looking into heaven. "I's gonna see yo' grandma and my mama." He paused and turned back to look at the boy, his voice filled with wonder. "And Harry, wid my own eyes, I's gonna see Jesus."

The child burst into tears.

"My boy, my boy, don't be cryin'." Hamilton gestured for him to climb up onto the bed. Harry rushed to his side and gave his grandfather a big hug. Hamilton gently stroked his grandson's hair and smiled. "It's gonna be OK chile. I's gonna be free."

After a moment Hamilton patted the boy's leg and said, "I has an idea, Harry. Why don't you sing 'Swing Low' for yo' granddaddy." The boy continued to sob, burying his face in Hamilton's side. After a few moments the old man said in a quiet voice, "Harry, what would yo' mama say if she heard you didn't sing to me?"

Harry took several deep breaths and then sat up and wiped his eyes, gathering himself for a moment. Hamilton lay very still as Harry began to sing.

> Swing low, sweet chariot, comin' for to carry me home.
> I looked over Jordan and what did I see,
> Comin' for to carry me home.
> A band of angels comin' after me,
> Comin' for to carry me home.

As Harry continued the song, Hamilton fell back to sleep, his chest rising and falling peacefully. The boy looked out the window as he sang softly.

> If you get there before I do,
> Comin' for to carry me home.
> Please, tell my friends I'm comin' too,
> Comin' for to carry me home.
> Swing low, sweet chariot, comin' for to carry me home.

Tears streamed down the youngster's face as he finished the song. Harry didn't want to wake his grandfather, but he wanted to hug him again. He snuggled up next to the old man, laying his head on the pillow next to his. Harry whispered into Hamilton's ear, "I love you, Grandpa." Hamilton did not rouse from his slumber with the words. The sorrow of the moment overtook him, and the young boy cried himself to sleep.

It seemed like only moments before Harry was awakened by the sound of weeping. As he looked up, he saw that the room was filled with family members hugging one another and crying. The child lifted his head from the pillow and rubbed the sleep from his eyes. He looked at his mother and then at his granddaddy. "What is it, Mama?" he asked, knowing the answer before she gave it.

Elizabeth walked over and wrapped her arms around the boy. Wiping her eyes with a handkerchief, she smiled at her son and said, "Honey, the angels have come to take your granddaddy to be with Jesus."

Harry shook his head no and turned away from his mother, laying his head on the now-motionless chest of his old friend. He joined the family as they wept. Hamilton's body was still warm, and Harry didn't want to leave his side.

After several moments, young Harry thought of his mother's pain. He rose from the bed and buried his face in her bosom. They held each other tightly, their tears mingling in Elizabeth's apron.

After several moments, Harry wiped his eyes with his sleeves and looked up to comfort his mother. "It's OK, Mama," he explained, "Grandpa told me there was a ship comin' to get him."

"That's right, honey, the Lord sent a ship for him."

The boy smiled at his mother. "He's free, Mama." She smiled back through her tears. He wiped his eyes again with his shirtsleeves and looked at his grandfather's body. "He's finally free."

1893–NEW YORK CITY

As Harry sang the sweet strains of "Swing Low," he imagined the seraphim swooping down in a fiery chariot, leading his grandfather by the hand and carrying him up to heaven. A tear flowed from beneath one closed eyelid and down his brown cheek. Burleigh pulled a handkerchief from his pocket and dried his eyes. He looked over at the master, who had not said a word. Dvorak sat on the couch next to the thrushes, his eyes closed tightly. Tears flowed down his cheeks as well, soaking into his thick gray beard. The vocalist sat quietly on the piano bench. They remained silent for several moments.

Finally Dvorak said quietly. "You are a rich man, Harry T. Barley."

Burleigh drank the comment in, savoring it for a moment. He thought of his mother cleaning the public school. He remembered the early mornings extinguishing the gas lamps and delivering newspapers in all kinds of weather. He recalled the years learning the slave songs as he worked in the stables and on the lake steamers. He remembered the frustration of working as a stenographer when his desire was to be a concert singer. Finally his thoughts came to his current situation, toiling at school and working odd jobs to pay the rent and put food on the table.

"Yes, sir, Dr. Dvorak. I surely am a rich man."

"I have something to show you, Harry." The master stood and sifted through a stack of manuscripts on the edge of the piano. He pulled out a dog-eared piece, his own distinctive, sloppy handwriting smudged over the page. "May I sit?"

"Of course." Burleigh moved from the bench and Dvorak sat, placing the manuscript on the music stand. Harry recognized the music as part of the new symphony, since he had already copied a large portion of the piece.

"I have worked on the largo movement."

"Ah, splendid," Burleigh responded. "Then the work is finished?"

"Nearly complete, yes," Dvorak answered. "After reading Longfellow's 'Hiawatha' I decided this should be a wholly American theme, reflecting the music and spirit of this country. But I struggled with this movement, Harry. There was something deep inside of me that I wanted to express, but I just couldn't bring it forth. Then I thought of what you told me of the American slave plantations. I thought of your grandfather, Harry. Then it came to me, like a message from heaven, a simple melody.

"It shall begin with the *cor anglais*, the English horn set against the strings. As I listened to you sing I recognized that the English horn closely resembles the sound of your voice, Barley." Harry was caught off guard by the comment and felt a tingle run up the sides of his face. He could hardly believe what he was hearing and stepped back so that his teacher would not notice his expression.

Dvorak began to play. The sound of the second movement was not grand and elegant like the first, but simple yet profound in its beauty. He spoke as he played. "As I composed I heard your voice, Harry, singing those wonderful songs to me. I saw the look that comes over your face when you sing them. Sometimes you look like you are the one who is in slavery, with no hope of freedom. I felt the sorrow and the longing of your grandfather to be free.

"I saw your grandfather's plight unfolding in my mind and I heard your voice in my head, Harry. And that is what I have written."

Burleigh had been standing behind the composer, but now his knees began to feel weak. He worked his way over to the couch and slowly sat down. He was in shock. He didn't know whether to laugh or cry. As Dvorak played the piece, Burleigh's thoughts raced.

Here is the greatest musician in the world. He has welcomed me into his home. He has listened to the songs and stories of my people. And now he honors my race and my grandfather.

It was profoundly moving. The composer finished the movement and turned to the young singer. Burleigh stared straight ahead, his eyes glazed.

"Well," the Bohemian declared, "what is it that you are thinking?"

The young man blinked twice as tears ran down his face. He slowly raised his gaze to meet Dvorak's. "It is perfection," he replied.

Dvorak smiled in appreciation. He picked up the manuscript and carried it over to Burleigh, who rose to receive it. "Here you are, Harry T. Copy this for me please, and make the notes as big as my head so that I can see them."

Harry looked down at the manuscript. In the top corner of the final page Dvorak had scribbled, "Praise God! Finished on 24 May, 1893."

The composer led the young man to the door. Darkness had fallen on Manhattan, and light from the streetlamps shone through the window. Burleigh turned to Dvorak and patted the manuscript that he clutched to his chest. "You don't know what this means to me." He looked down to the ground and then back up at the master. "Thank you."

A smile stretched across Dvorak's face. He placed his large hand on Burleigh's shoulder. "Thank you, Barley, for letting me know your family and your people."

12

Heav'n, Heav'n

1893–NEW YORK CITY

The highlight of the year for the New York musical community came on December 16, 1893, when Antonin Dvorak's Symphony no. 9 in E Minor, nicknamed "From the New World" by the composer at the last moment, made its world debut at Carnegie Hall. Seated in the second-tier balcony, at the personal invitation of the composer, was Harry T. Burleigh. Though he could barely afford it, he had rented a tuxedo for the occasion.

The cultural elite of New York were in attendance for the gala affair. Musicians, politicians, educators, industrialists, and financiers were on hand for the festivities. The symphony's premier by the New York Philharmonic was conducted under the wand of Dvorak's friend Anton Seidl.

Word of the symphony's African American and Native American themes had spread through Harlem, and many leaders of the black community arrived at Carnegie Hall with great anticipation, matching their fellow attendees in elegance.

The leading ladies of New York knew this would be the social event of the year, perhaps even the decade. Robed in the finest of

European fashions, accented with necklaces of diamonds and every other imaginable precious stone, they gracefully entered Carnegie Hall.

Harry T. Burleigh was so excited about the symphony that he was one of the first to arrive, nearly an hour before the doors opened. As people slowly made their way to their seats, he glanced over the program. Dvorak's comments brought a satisfied smile to his face.

"I tried only to write in the spirit of those national American melodies," Dvorak wrote. "These beautiful and varied themes are products of the soil. They are American. They are the folk songs of America, and your composers must turn to them. All great musicians have borrowed from the songs of the common people. In the Negro melodies of America I discover all that is needed for a great and noble school of music."

Looking up from his program Burleigh noticed a stir in the audience as people turned and looked to the box seats. Suddenly, Dvorak and his wife appeared in the front box on the first-tier balcony. The audience rose to its feet and broke into excited applause. He was dressed elegantly in a black suit, white silk shirt, black tie, and his trademark emerald-green vest. His beard was neatly trimmed for the occasion, but as long as ever. The composer graciously waved to the audience and took his seat.

After the orchestra was brought into tune by the concertmaster, Maestro Seidl strode onstage to enthusiastic applause. Everyone understood this was a great moment for American music, and for the United States as a nation. A world-class composer had written a symphony from American themes on American soil, and it would premier under the foremost American symphony. The atmosphere was electrified.

As the audience grew quiet and Seidl raised his baton, Burleigh felt the goose bumps rise on his arms. He grasped the brass railing at the edge of the balcony and felt his grip tighten in anticipation of the first note. Seidl slowly lowered his baton and the adagio movement began with a quiet, mellow introduction, evoking images of a misty sunrise over the Atlantic.

The tone changed abruptly after the initial opening theme. The intensity quickly heightened as the symphony continued to build on itself through the opening movement.

A highlight for Burleigh occurred as the trombones began to carry, note for note, "Swing Low, Sweet Chariot." The joy felt by Burleigh was echoed through the hall as people turned to one another, acknowledging familiarity with the spiritual. The movement ended with a climax so closely resembling the plantation melody that it was unmistakable.

Burleigh had copied many of the orchestral parts of the "New World Symphony" from the master's original music. He knew the work inside out, but this was the first time he had heard it with a full orchestra. His heart raced, and again he grasped the railing to steady himself in anticipation of the largo movement. Try as he might to control his emotions, as the sweet melody of the second movement floated over the audience Burleigh once again felt hot tears course down his face. The influence of his people's music was unmistakable.

He listened with his eyes closed and saw his grandfather in chains, teaching himself to read. He heard the songs of the workers in his stepfather's stables and voices of the stevedores working the docks near his home. He remembered days sailing on Great Lakes steamers, listening to the sailors singing through the night.

"Your spirit lives on, Granddaddy," Harry said under his breath.

As the symphony came to its grand conclusion, Burleigh joined the audience on their feet in thunderous applause. Maestro Seidl turned, bowed deeply, and then waved his hand toward Dvorak's box seat. The composer stood to receive the admiration of the audience. The deafening ovation continued with whoops and whistles from the American crowd.

Chants of "Encore, encore," and "Dvorak, Dvorak," were heard above the applause. The master stood again, bowed graciously, and waved to the crowd below.

"Encore, encore," the shouts continued from the enthusiastic American audience. Maestro Seidl remained on the platform, looking toward the master. Dvorak gestured in his direction, encouraging him to continue.

To Burleigh's delight, the orchestra encored the largo movement, once again filling the hall with the smooth tones of the English horn. At the majestic climax, the audience rose again to its feet in admiration. The symphony had appealed to American nationalism as a product of Dvorak's experience in this relatively new nation. The usually tranquil American audience was enthusiastic to the point of frenzy. People hugged each other and even jumped in the aisles. Several threw their programs in the air.

The composer stood again and took a grand bow. He waved once again in the direction of the audience and extended his arm to his wife. Anna Dvorak had stood at her husband's side during the ovations. She was extremely proud of her husband, though her proper European training rarely allowed her to express it. She cherished this special moment and for the first time came to appreciate the freedom with which Americans expressed their admiration for the composer.

Dvorak later wrote to his publisher:

The papers say that no composer ever celebrated such a triumph. Carnegie Hall was crowded with the best people of New York, and the audience applauded so that, like visiting royalty, I had to take my bows repeatedly from the box like a king! (Don't laugh.) You know how glad I am if I can avoid such ovations, but there was no getting out of it, and I had to show myself willy-nilly.

Burleigh lingered as the audience slowly drifted out of the concert hall. The significance of the event was overwhelming. It was the first time in the history of classical music that an African American folk song had served as the major theme in a great symphonic work. It was a tribute to the spirit of the slaves: a cry for freedom—the longing for home.

Finally, the young musician stood and took one last look around the grand auditorium, drinking in the moment. Exiting the balcony, he descended the staircase slowly and made his way out of the hall, the melody of "Swing Low" echoing in his heart.

In the months to come some critics commented that the symphony was just European music with an American title. In Dvorak's mind it was both. The composer was a Czech, and he had only been in America a little less than a year when the piece was completed. Any music written by such a man would have a European flavor and would employ classical composition techniques. But there was no escaping the fact that Dvorak purposefully set out to write an American symphony. He announced to the musical world his intention to do just that. At the time other composers and music critics said it could not be done. But Dvorak refused to believe them.

He wrote to a friend in Czechoslovakia:

I have not much work at school so that I have enough time for my own work and am now finishing my new symphony in E minor. I take great pleasure in it and it will differ very considerably from my others. Well, the influence of America must be felt by everyone who has a nose at all.

The ostentatious Bohemian tweaked the noses of American composers with a controversial interview published in the February 1895 issue of *Harper's New Monthly Magazine.*

In the Negro melodies of America I find all that is needed for a great and noble school of music. . . . There is nothing in the whole range of composition which cannot be supplied from this source. . . . I am satisfied that the future of music in this country must be founded on what are called Negro melodies.

Many leading American composers, such as Chadwick, Parke, Paine, and MacDowell, chose to ignore Dvorak's advice. Some were actually offended by the famous European's views. But not everyone rejected his ideas. Within the decade white and black composers alike were incorporating African American, Native American, and other ethnic folk music into their compositions. Harry T. Burleigh and fellow conservatory student Will Marion Cook were two of the most gifted composers to adopt Dvorak's theories, creating music that would contribute to the foundation of a distinctly American musical style.

In an interview published before he departed for Europe in 1895, Dvorak made reference to his special relationship with Harry T. Burleigh. He told how he had discovered a young black man of talent upon whom he was building strong expectation. Dvorak openly acknowledged Burleigh's influence on the composition, and the Czech composer told many people how he deeply appreciated their relationship.

Even though he loved America, not long after his symphony debuted Antonin Dvorak found himself longing for his homeland. He was torn between the excitement and promise of this new land and the traditions, simplicity, and elegance of his home. The melancholy feel of the musical works he created in America during this time reflected his increasing homesickness.

At the same time America was suffering through a dismal financial depression. Due to the difficulties plaguing her husband's business, Mrs. Thurber was consistently late with payments on Dvorak's salary, and Anna Dvorak's patience had long since run out. She was the more practical of the two and knew her husband would have no trouble arranging a comfortable and consistent income in Europe. The master himself was much less businesslike, but eventually the reality of the situation became apparent to the composer, and he finally relented, making plans to return to Bohemia.

Before he sailed for Europe, Dvorak invited young Burleigh to his home for one final dinner. As they sat at the table, Dvorak reminisced over all that was accomplished during his stay in America. Harry did not want the moment to pass before satisfying a long-held curiosity. "Master, which movement of the New World Symphony do you like the best?" he asked.

Dvorak's eyes sparkled and he replied with a wry smile, "I love them all alike. Are they not all my children?"

Harry nodded his head with a smile. "Yes, sir. They truly are."

Once again the family retired to the sitting room, where the young soloist sang one of the master's favorite spirituals, "Nobody Knows the Trouble I've Seen." When he finished, Dvorak stood and called Burleigh over to stand in front of him. Placing his hands on the young man's shoulders, he looked intently into Harry's eyes.

"God has called you to take the music of your people and combine it with the music of my people to give the world something entirely new from this great nation that he has raised up. Through slavery these songs were given by God as a gift to your people. Now you must take your grandfather's legacy and share it with the world. Harry," Dvorak repeated, "give these melodies to the world."

In April of 1895, Antonin Dvorak returned to his home in Bohemia. In 1901, he became the director of the Prague Conservatoire. For the last three years of his life he devoted his creativity to symphonic poems and operas. He died in 1904, less than ten years after leaving America.

Burleigh's life and musical philosophy were forever altered by his interaction with this great European composer. In their relationship the Old World met the New, the classical met the common, and the world of music was changed forever.

Whenever asked of his relationship with the great composer, Burleigh always answered, "Dvorak, a Czech with a great love for the common people of all lands, pointed the way."

13

Hard Trials

In his first few years after arriving in New York, Burleigh filled his schedule with as many paid musical opportunities as he could, including singing in the choir of St. Phillip's Colored Episcopal Church, teaching individual students, and coaching several church choirs. He did all this while still maintaining his janitorial and clerical work at the conservatory—all the while looking for the open door to becoming a full-time musician.

One day, as he worked in Mrs. MacDowell's office, Jeanette Thurber burst into the room. "Harry," she said, "I just received a letter from the rector of St. George's Episcopal Church announcing an opening for a baritone soloist." She waited for his reaction. Harry sat behind the large oak desk, waiting for the punch line. When he didn't respond, she continued. "After much consideration, I have come to the conclusion that you would be the best candidate for the job. I want to encourage you to apply!"

Harry chuckled and then sat speechless for a moment. A puzzled expression came over his face as he searched for a diplomatic response.

154

"With all due respect, ma'am, why in the world would you think of me? There are several other qualified candidates."

Mrs. Thurber put her hands on her hips in exasperation. "Harry, this would be a wonderful opportunity for you, and what a great stride forward for the conservatory, to have one of our black students occupy such a prestigious post. This is what we've worked toward these many years."

Again she waited for his response, and again none came. She continued, "Of course, you're aware that this is the home church of the Knickerbockers, the Vanderbilts, and the J. P. Morgans?"

"Yes, I am," Harry finally replied. "And that is why I'm not sure I want to subject myself to that kind of audition." He stood up from the desk and carried a stack of files to a nearby cabinet.

Mrs. Thurber followed closely behind him. "And why not?"

He put the stack on top of the cabinet and turned to look her in the eye. "Begging your pardon, but as a black man, I don't think I would have a snowball's chance in hell in such an upper-crust parish."

This kind of response always threw Jeanette Thurber into a tizzy. She shot back, "Harry T. Burleigh, we did not accept you into this conservatory to allow you to shrink back from a challenge!"

"But Mrs. Thurber, this is not just a challenge." He paused, searching for the right words. "The highest members of New York society attend this church. To many of them, as you well know, colored people are merely servants. They will most likely laugh in my face and with their white gloves throw me right into the street."

"Not if you give the rector this letter." She handed him an envelope containing a card on which she had already written a note of recommendation. "Dr. Rainsford is a fair and sympathetic man. He is aware of what we are trying to do here at the conservatory, both artistically and socially. I'm confident he will allow you to audition."

Harry reluctantly took the envelope, looked down at it for a moment, then back up at Mrs. Thurber. "I'll do it for you."

Her eyes sparkled at his reply, and she hugged the young singer, who was still shaking his head in disbelief. "And you will succeed, Harry." She laughed joyfully. "You will succeed."

The following Sunday, Burleigh attended the service at the gothic St. George's Episcopal Church. Founded in 1749 as the first chapel of

Trinity Parish, over the years it had become one of the best-known churches in America. Since 1812, St. George's had stood as a Manhattan landmark, rising majestically above Stuyvesant Square. The front of the church was carved with ornamental marble, and a statue of St. George slaying a dragon stood perched above the arch of the doorway. Bell towers stood to the right and left of the entranceway, supporting two large clocks that stood like sentries over the neighborhood, though the modern skyscrapers of Manhattan now dwarfed the elegant brownstone church.

The twin parks of Stuyvesant Square included four acres with a fountain, ornamental landscaping, quaint iron benches, and a wrought iron gate. The park had been one of New York City's most fashionable spots since the mid-nineteenth century, when it was designed.

Burleigh entered through the heavy wooden doors of the church, carrying the letter from Mrs. Thurber in his pocket. An usher dressed in a red velvet coat and clean white gloves greeted him in the lobby and led him to a seat not quite halfway down the aisle.

The young musician examined the massive sanctuary as he waited for the service to begin. He had worked with church choirs throughout New York City, but no sanctuary was as grand as this one. A tall, graceful arch stood at the center of the platform and three colorful stained-glass windows perched high above the altar. In the center window, a large, red cross stood behind the heroic figure of St. George. In the window to the right the saint sat mounted on his horse in combat. The third, to the left, pictured him bowed in a devotional pose, a coat of arms at his side. Far below, choir risers stood to the right and left of the altar.

Suddenly the organ rang out with the processional melody as the eighty-voice choir slowly walked down the aisle, singing. The young singer sat enraptured by the sweet sound of this masterful chorus. When the opening hymns were concluded, Dr. Rainsford rose and climbed the few stairs to the pulpit. Standing more than six feet tall, he was an imposing figure in his white vestments. Harry decided it was a mistake to think he could be a part of such an aristocratic church.

What is a short black man from a small midwestern town doing in this grand cathedral, before this equally grand man?

He prepared to quietly sneak out the side entrance. But as he started to stand, Dr. Rainsford began his sermon. "The church must speak against the evils plaguing our society. We must play the role of mediator between groups and classes. It is our Christian duty to care for the poor, the unemployed, our brothers in bonds, and those tormented by social vices.

"Some would argue that these have nothing to do with the gospel. I tell you, the gospel affects each and all of these areas of human need. Jesus came not only to teach, but also to bring release to the captives. How can we save men's souls if we have not yet filled their bellies?"

His voice was soothing, gentle, and sincere. He spoke of God's love for man, of his grace, and of the need for social justice among all men. These were themes that were familiar to Harry, who had spent untold hours in church services in his twenty-eight years. His spirits lifted, and he sat enthralled through the rest of the sermon.

The service ended with a triumphant recessional by the choir. As the organist played the joyous music, Burleigh slipped out of his pew and approached an usher to ask whom he should speak to about the soloist position. The aged man, dressed in a handsome blazer, looked down on Harry with an uncertain expression. After a moment of thought, he finally directed Burleigh to speak directly with Dr. Rainsford.

The usher's reaction renewed Harry's fears. He turned to approach the rector and was suddenly overcome with timidity. Joining the choir of this great church would take enormous courage for any musician, but especially for a black man. The farther he walked down the aisle, the greater his anxiety grew. He approached the man whose words had seemed so helpful and sincere but a moment before. Now the rector seemed as fearsome as Goliath himself.

The greatest obstacle for Harry, and for most black people in 1894, was the ever-present feeling of despair—a result of years of discrimination. It was a heaviness so terribly present whenever one was about to make a stand against inherited weakness. The young vocalist summoned courage to continue. He ignored the looks of surprise in the faces of those he walked by and waited in line behind other parishioners gathered to speak with the rector. When he finally reached the front of the line, Harry cleared his throat and greeted the robed cleric.

"Hello. My name is Harry T. Burleigh, and I'm a student at the National Conservatory of Music."

Dr. Rainsford smiled and extended his hand to the young man. "Welcome to St. George's, Mr. Burleigh. It is a pleasure to have you today."

Harry enthusiastically shook the rector's hand. "Thank you, sir. I enjoyed your sermon very much—very much indeed."

"Thank you. I'm glad it encouraged you."

Harry paused for a moment, searching for the right words. Suddenly he remembered the letter of recommendation. "Oh, I have something for you." He reached into his pocket, pulled out the envelope, and handed it to the minister. "This is a letter from Mrs. Jeanette Thurber of the conservatory."

"Ah, Mrs. Thurber, yes, she is a dear lady."

"She has encouraged me to seek an audition for the baritone soloist position that is available here at St. George's."

Dr. Rainsford was momentarily taken aback, and he quickly looked up from the letter with a puzzled expression. His reaction once again shook Harry's confidence.

"Ah, I, um—that is, if the position is still available," Harry added.

A stern look came over the rector's face. He squared his jaw and looked as if he were debating the question in his head. He looked down again at the card in his hand. For a moment the two men stood silently as the minister read the letter. Finally, he looked back up at the young singer as a smile returned to his face. "I will tell our choir director, William Chester, of your application. Thank you very much for allowing us to consider you for the position. We will contact you when the time comes for your audition." The rector once again grasped the young man's hand and shook it warmly.

Something in his tone and simple manner set Harry completely at ease, and a feeling of hope welled up inside him. He smiled and replied, "Thank you, Dr. Rainsford. I will look forward to hearing from you." Burleigh turned and walked down the aisle, smiling and greeting those he passed along the way with a nod.

Surely a man who is so big and yet so simple will not allow color to prejudice him. Maybe this will finally be my chance, he thought.

International financier J. P. Morgan was senior warden of the church and served as chairman of the selection committee for the soloist position. Each applicant was required to audition before the committee and the choir director. In all, sixty men auditioned for the baritone soloist position. Burleigh was not only the lone black man to audition for the position, but he was the first colored person to apply for any position in the history of St. George's.

⬥————— ⬦ —————⬥

After what seemed an eternity, the day of the audition finally arrived. The singers were reviewed ten at a time, in alphabetical order. Burleigh was one of the first applicants to sing for the committee.

How will they view me? he wondered. *Can they look past my skin and hear my voice? Will I be able to maintain my poise?* The thoughts swirled in his head as he waited for his turn. *But I have sung for the great Dvorak himself. I've excelled in my studies. People look to me for musical direction. And I know God is with me, so I do not have to fear.* As he reassured himself, a feeling of peace and confidence swept over him. *If they don't want me, there will be other auditions.*

When Burleigh's name was called he entered the choir room, where a group of men were seated behind a long row of tables. The setting reminded him of his audition at the conservatory. The choir director smiled politely as Harry handed his musical selection to him. After a brief introduction, Burleigh began singing. His velvet, rich baritone filled the chamber with a glorious sound. The astonished choirmaster looked up from the piano for a moment, studying the man. Harry noticed this and fumbled the melody momentarily. He quickly looked back to the page and found his place.

Within seconds of hearing the first golden notes emanating from Burleigh's throat, J. P. Morgan exclaimed, "This is my man." He said it so loudly the entire committee—and Burleigh too—heard it clearly.

When the group met to decide who would be the next baritone soloist at St. George's Episcopal Church, J. P. Morgan, choir director William Chester, and Rector Rainsford all agreed that Burleigh was the person for the job. After his years of study at the conservatory Harry's voice was beautiful, rich, full, and musical to the last vibration. Burleigh accepted the position and began his career at St. George's on a salary of eight hundred dollars per year.

Harry arrived at his first choir rehearsal the following Thursday at the appointed hour, and Dr. Rainsford was there to introduce him. "We are truly blessed to have for our baritone soloist position an esteemed student of the New York Conservatory of Music—soon to be a graduate—Harry Burleigh. He comes with the highest recommendation, but the clincher for all of us was his beautiful voice. When you hear him sing, I'm sure you will all agree God has graced St. George's with a special gift. Please join me in welcoming Mr. Harry T. Burleigh." Dr. Rainsford finished his introduction and vigorously shook Burleigh's hand as the choir gave him a polite if somewhat tepid ovation. Harry took the soloist position in front of the choir, and the rector left the sanctuary through the chancellery door.

Amid the hushed murmuring of the choir, a middle-aged Wall Street trader named Conrad Miller left his place and followed the pastor into the chancellery.

"Dr. Rainsford," the man called out as he entered the room, his jaw set and his face bright crimson.

The rector was prepared for this and turned to face the man. "Yes, Mr. Miller, what can I do for you?"

"Sir, I am completely put out by your rash decision in this matter. Up to this point you have shown yourself to be a balanced and thoughtful individual. But this, sir . . ." Miller paused to take a deep breath, and then let out his fury. "To have a Negro in the choir of St. George's, of all places? Well, if the church is to become a minstrel house, then I will have no choice but to resign."

Both men stood nose to nose. The rector's jaw tightened, and he never lost eye contact with the man. Undaunted, he smiled and responded, "Thank you for expressing your opinion, Mr. Miller, but the decision has been made. Mr. Burleigh will be our soloist." With that the rector turned and walked out of the church, leaving the exasperated man fuming in his wake.

Burleigh's first service with St. George's was the final Sunday in February, 1894. Tension filled the air as the choir walked in single file from the chancellery. Conrad Miller strode to his place with a stone-faced expression. His lips remained pursed and his chin slightly raised as he glared at Dr. Rainsford as he entered the sanctuary dressed in his elegant vestments. The rector took his place, then smiled and nodded to the choir and the choirmaster. With that the service began, the choir singing the first number in full voice as the congregation followed in their hymnals.

For the second selection, the soloists stood forward. When it came time for Harry to sing his part, Miller led the way as nearly half of the choir walked out of their places and down the center aisle. A group of parishioners who had strategically placed themselves in the front pew stood to their feet and filed out of their seats, following Miller and his cohorts.

As the remaining choir members continued singing, row after row of parishioners stood and left the building. Harry tried to control the embarrassment and anger rising within him, fighting back the hot tears gathering in the corners of his eyes. He resisted the overwhelming urge to run out of the sanctuary. These people were leaving without even giving him a chance. That familiar, ugly, hopeless feeling returned, gnawing at him in the pit of his stomach.

By the time the choir finished the opening hymns, two-thirds of the congregation had left the building. His face now stern, Dr. Rainsford stood to give the homily. He climbed the stairs to the pulpit and looked out for a moment over the flock that remained. Finally, he smiled and said, "You are the courageous ones. I applaud and admire you all. God bless you for your stand with me today."

He paused and shook his head, staring down at the floor for several moments. Harry felt as though every eye but the rector's was on him. As he looked over the congregation he realized that not only was he the first black soloist, but he was the first black person to be a member of St. George's. Harry clenched his teeth to fight his anxiety. He waited with anticipation for the pastor to speak, hoping they would be words of peace.

The rector finally looked out on what was left of his congregation. "Our Lord Jesus dealt with similar persecutions on earth. In fact, he promised that if we follow after him we would face rejection. In John 15:18 our Lord said, 'If the world hate you, ye know that it hated me before it hated you.' My friends, we must ask ourselves this question, 'If Jesus were here today, what would he do in this situation?'" He paused and scanned the congregation. He looked at the choirmaster and then fixed his gaze for a moment on Harry Burleigh. "I think I have an idea what he would do."

Dr. Rainsford opened the large Bible in front of him and turned the pages with purpose as he spoke. "I was going to give another sermon today, but it can wait. You see, there were people in Jesus's time who were filled with all sorts of hatred, prejudice, and pride, just like today." He looked up from the Scriptures. "It's a familiar passage that I choose today, found in the Gospel of Luke, chapter 10, verses 25 through 37.

"Behold, a certain lawyer stood up, and tempted him, saying, 'Master, what shall I do to inherit eternal life?' He said unto him, 'What is written in the law? How readest thou?' And he answering said, 'Thou shalt love the Lord thy God with all thy heart, and with all thy soul, and with all thy strength, and with all thy mind; and thy neighbor as thyself.' And he said unto him, 'Thou has answered right; this do, and thou shalt live.'

"If we ended there we would have a wonderful truth to contemplate. But the story continues with the lawyer's response.

"But he, willing to justify himself, said unto Jesus, 'And who is my neighbor?' And Jesus answering said, 'A certain man went down from Jerusalem to Jericho, and fell among thieves, which stripped him of his raiment, and wounded him, and departed, leaving him half dead. And by chance there came down a certain priest that way: and when he saw him, he passed by on the other side. And likewise a Levite, when he was at the place, came and looked on him, and passed by on the other side.'"

Again Rainsford looked up at the congregation. "And here is where the story gets interesting. You see, his own countrymen, religious leaders no less, left the traveler bleeding on the side of the road. But along comes a Samaritan, a hated enemy of the Jewish people."

He continued reading. "But a certain Samaritan, as he journeyed, came where he was: and when he saw him, he had compassion on him, and went to him, and bound up his wounds, pouring in oil and wine, and set him on his own beast, and brought him to an inn, and took care of him.

"And on the morrow when he departed, he took out two pence, and gave them to the host, and said unto him, 'Take care of him;

and whatsoever thou spendest more, when I come again, I will repay thee.'

"Jesus looked around at the religious leaders who stood before him, and he said to them, 'Which now of these three, thinkest thou, was neighbor unto him that fell among the thieves?' And he said, 'He that shewed mercy on him.' Then said Jesus unto him, 'Go, and do thou likewise.'"

The sanctuary was silent as the rector looked around the congregation. "I believe this is God's call to us today. 'What is pure religion?' the apostle James asked. Is it not to visit the fatherless and widows in their affliction and to keep himself unspotted from the world?" He paused and let the words echo off the stone walls. "Let's be about the business of this kind of religion and leave the other to the Pharisees.

"As this bloody century comes to a close we often think of ourselves as having evolved to a higher state of being. We have magnificent ships that have conquered the seas and iron trains that have traversed continents. We have horseless carriages. We have every type of technological wonder, and yet perhaps we are not as advanced as we think we might be."

He pulled a piece of paper out of his pocket, unfolded it, and laid it on the lectern in front of him. "I read this quote while I was in the seminary and kept a copy of it in my files ever since. I suspected it would be appropriate today. A black man named David Walker penned this in 1829.

"He writes, 'Treat us like men, and there is no danger but we will all live in peace and happiness together. For we are not like you, hard-hearted, unmerciful, and unforgiving. What a happy country this will be, if the whites will listen.'"

The rector looked up from the paper. "Perhaps the day has come for us to listen to Mr. Walker." Dr. Rainsford turned and stared for a moment at Harry T. Burleigh. The young singer looked back. Without saying a word, a bond of trust and respect was forged between them at that instant. The rector smiled and stepped down from the pulpit.

The choir concluded the service and filed out of the sanctuary. In the choir room, well-wishers flocked around Harry, urging him to remain. "You are now a member of this group," stressed the choirmaster, "and your place is here with us." He thanked them, but in his heart Harry did not want to be responsible for tearing apart an important New York City church. And he was not at all interested in becoming the symbol of racial discord. He planned to turn in his resignation the following morning.

Of course, Dr. Rainsford would not hear of it. "Harry, if you do that, then those people will have won the day. We're not talking about the entire church here. One thing I've learned from my years in the ministry is that there are a few leaders and many followers. What we saw here was a small group of people who were thrown from the status quo and tried to make a loud statement. Mark my words, Harry, the followers will be back, and most of the leaders as well."

The members of the choir who left on Sunday were not present at rehearsal on Thursday evening. Choirmaster William Chester assured Harry they would return. He was a young man and an enthusiastic director with a genius for music. From the beginning there was mutual respect between the two musicians.

To honor the requests of Rev. Rainsford, Chester, and even J. P. Morgan himself, who had all asked him to stay, Harry arrived at St. George's on Sunday morning dressed in his white vestments. In the basement rehearsal hall, he joined the other choir members as they made preparations for the service. Conrad Miller and a few of the others who had left the week before were noticeably absent, but the majority of the choir had returned. Harry wasn't sure what kind of reception he would receive when he walked into the sanctuary.

As the choir gathered in the chancellery, the organ filled the church with its grand tones, signaling the beginning of the service. Harry walked in the single file line, following the others into the sanctuary. As he entered through the door, he had difficulty raising his eyes to look at the congregation. Finally he could no longer avoid it and slowly raised his gaze to look into the cavernous sanctuary. To his astonishment, every pew was filled to capacity. The congregation was dressed in their finest Sunday clothes, and they stood to greet the choir.

Tears filled Harry's eyes, and once again he fought to hold back his emotion. Those around him patted him on the back and whispered congratulations in his ear. After the initial shock, Harry was able to compose himself and joined the choir in the hymn. Following the opening prayer, Burleigh and the other soloists stepped forward to sing their parts. As Harry's beautiful voice filled the room, parishioners sat entranced. Tears came to the eyes of many who just the week before had walked out of the service. Dr. Rainsford sat with his eyes tightly shut and a bright smile on his face.

When the choir concluded, the rector rose and stepped to the pulpit. With a loud voice he said, "I think you can now see why we chose Mr. Burleigh as our new baritone soloist." He turned and nodded his head to Harry, who closed his eyes and slowly nodded back.

After the service Harry stopped at the telegraph office on his way home to send a wire to his mother.

Have been hired as soloist at St. George Episcopal, NYC. With love,

H.T.B.

"Praise God Almighty," she cried out after reading the telegram. She immediately walked over to her desk, pulled out some stationery and an inkwell, and wrote to her son, "The household rejoiceth. Now you'll be able to live in New York and prosecute your studies." This monumental event made an impact on the entire family. It was positively earth-shaking that a black man would achieve this kind of position in 1894.

Though Elizabeth never realized her lifelong dream of teaching, through her son all the years of struggle, heartbreak, and tears had culminated in triumph. Now Harry Burleigh would be the featured soloist in one of the most prestigious churches in the entire country. For Elizabeth, this was worth all of her toil.

This was only one of the many things that Dr. Rainsford did during his time as rector of St. George's to build an international reputation as a champion of social justice. In his autobiography, Rector Rainsford would later write:

I can only recall, in all those years, one serious commotion in my white-robed company. That was on the memorable occasion when, without warning—for this course I thought the wisest—I broke the news to them that I was going to have for soloist a Negro, Harry Burleigh. Then

165

division, consternation, confusion, and protest reigned for a time. I never knew how the troubled waters settled down.

Indeed, I carefully avoided knowing who was for and who against my revolutionary arrangement. Nothing like it had ever been known in the church's musical history. The thing was arranged and I gave no opportunity for its discussion.

Well, my choir held together! I don't think I lost a member of it, even if I forced into it a black brother. And oh! How glad I and the choir were afterward that I had acted as I did. St. George's is proud of him; proud of what he has accomplished as a musician, and loves and honors him for what he has proved himself to be as a Christian man.

14

The Trees Have Grown So

1898–NEW YORK CITY

When Harry was sure he would be successful at St. George's, he finally resigned from the janitorial staff of the conservatory. Jeanette Thurber rejoiced that he had received the position, as it was another step toward her dream of the conservatory becoming a world-class musical institution. "It's fitting that one of our graduates is in the choir of such an important church," she remarked.

The church position was a major turning point in his career. Suddenly, through the help of people like J. P. Morgan, Burleigh was in demand for concerts and recitals throughout New York City and beyond. The racial climate in the United States at the turn of the century made the climb to prominence nearly impossible for most Negro artists. Harry knew that he had to make the most of every engagement if he were going to rise in the musical world.

In the ensuing years, Morgan became a staunch supporter of Harry T. Burleigh. He arranged numerous performances in some of the wealthiest New Yorkers' homes and for visiting dignitaries. On one occasion, Morgan engaged Harry for a command performance before the governor of New York, Theodore Roosevelt. The governor's aide, Mr. Perkins, assured Morgan's people that all of Mr. Burleigh's accommodations would be taken care of.

Dressed in a fine tuxedo and standing in the ballroom of the governor's mansion, Harry was enthusiastically received by Roosevelt and his guests. Burleigh gave his standard concert, including classical numbers, popular songs, and the spirituals. The governor was visibly pleased with the young singer and applauded boisterously at the end of each number.

At the conclusion of the concert, Harry received a standing ovation and a warm and vigorous handshake from Governor Roosevelt. "Bully, my lad," the governor said. "Absolutely bully. We must have you back very soon."

Mr. Perkins rushed Burleigh to the train station so that he could catch the sleeper back to New York City. But long after the Roosevelts had retired to their private quarters, the governor's assistant returned with Burleigh in tow.

Roosevelt heard the commotion in the lobby and called for Perkins to ascend the stairs to give him a report. The young man joined Mr. Roosevelt in a room off of the hallway, speaking in a hushed tone. "Governor Roosevelt, I'm afraid we have found ourselves in a most uncomfortable position."

"What exactly do you mean?" Roosevelt asked in full voice.

"Well sir," he whispered, "we were not able to make it to the train station on time. I'm afraid Mr. Burleigh will have to spend the night in Albany."

"Splendid," Roosevelt retorted. "Perhaps we could engage him for a recital before he leaves tomorrow."

"But sir," the embarrassed aide interrupted, "we have been unsuccessful in finding a room for him at any local hotel."

Roosevelt's forehead furrowed as he began to understand what the secretary was unwilling to divulge in a straightforward manner.

"And you didn't arrange for lodging in advance?" the governor asked. "Are there no vacancies in Albany at this time of night?"

"We planned to send him back to New York on the late train, but the recital ran overtime with all of the encores. And . . ." He paused and looked down at the floor. "No sir. No one will take him."

Exasperated with the way the young man was trying to skirt the racial issue, Roosevelt clenched his teeth and barked at his assistant. "He will stay in the guest chambers at the governor's mansion. He will be given the finest accommodations with the same luxury afforded the most important of guests. You will personally see to it that any need he has will be addressed in an efficient manner. Do I make myself quite clear?"

The startled aide replied, "Ah, yes, sir. I'll take care of everything."

"Those ignoramuses," Roosevelt growled as he walked out the door. "This man is an American treasure. They are all fools." He turned back to Perkins. "Make sure he is well cared for."

The aide hurried down the stairs to deliver the governor's message to Burleigh and called for one of the butlers to follow him. The two men entered the side room where Burleigh sat, still dressed in his tuxedo. "Mr. Burleigh, I apologize for any inconvenience. The governor has instructed me that you are to stay in the guest chambers for the evening." Motioning to the servant behind him, he continued, "Mr. Seymore will assist you. If you have need of anything, don't hesitate to ask." He turned to the butler. "Mr. Seymore, will you carry Mr. Burleigh's bag?"

"Certainly, sir." The butler nodded and picked up Harry's suitcase. "If you will follow me, I will lead you to your room." Burleigh thanked Mr. Perkins and followed the other black man up the wide mahogany staircase. Mr. Seymore opened the door of the guest suite. It was decorated with the finest furniture and brass fixtures. A white ceramic-tiled bathroom stood off to the side. The butler followed Burleigh into the room and placed his suitcase onto a stand.

"Our staff is here to serve you, sir. The governor has breakfast at eight o'clock. He usually invites his guests to join him. Would you like me to wake you at any particular time?"

Harry could barely believe what he was hearing. Have breakfast with Teddy Roosevelt? He stood speechless for a moment. Finally, the butler made a suggestion. "Would seven o'clock be sufficient, sir?"

"Yes, seven would be fine. Thank you, Mr. Seymore, you are very kind."

"The pleasure is mine, Mr. Burleigh." The gentleman walked toward the door and then turned back. "The staff thoroughly enjoyed your performance tonight, sir."

Harry smiled and bowed his head. "Thank you, I appreciate that very much." The two men shared a satisfied smile.

"Good night, sir."

"Good night," he replied as the butler exited the room.

Harry walked across the room to look out the window. Watching the large white snowflakes fall to the ground, he caught his reflection in the pane and suddenly a realization struck him. This was the very home where his grandmother had served. "My grandmother most likely worked in this very room," he said aloud.

He remembered what his mother had told him of her grace and elegance, traits she learned in this mansion. He turned and surveyed the bedroom. The irony was overwhelming. "My Lord, if only Granddaddy was here to see this." Harry looked out again at the softly falling snow, seeing his reflection in the window. As his eyes filled with tears, the reflection slowly transformed into the image of his grandfather. Standing in his fine tuxedo among the elegant decorations and furniture, Harry mimicked his grandfather as he declared, "Hallelujah! Glory be!"

15

The Frolic

Harry T. Burleigh was one of the first black musicians to escape the wretched poverty that most African American artists struggled with at that time. His work at St. George's was keeping him fed. He used to gather with other black musicians and artists to compare war stories from time to time. Each one of them poured their souls into their work, neglecting many of the earthly necessities of life as they pursued their dreams.

The great black comedian Bert Williams often told the story of the gang hanging out after a long day of work. Their shabby apartment house on 53rd Street became a meeting place where artists like Will Accoe, Bob Cole, the Johnson brothers, Jesse Shipp, and Harry T. Burleigh could sit around in their shirtsleeves and talk, drink, and play endless hands of poker. Out of necessity nearly everybody was in one way or another associated with the minstrel shows—it was just about the only work a black artist could get in those days. Among themselves the common saying was, "All the best talent of that generation came down the same drain." The composers, the singers, the musicians, the speakers, the stage performers—the minstrel shows got them all.

The minstrel stage was the door of passage for black entertainers into the spotlight of American theater. For more than half a century, it was practically the only way a black performer could achieve any recognition in the United States. It was the farm league for musicians and entertainers. If it weren't for his mother, Harry may have given up singing in church choirs to become musical director for the Williams and Walker comedy extravaganza. In 1898 they were starring in a musical show known as *The Sennegambian Carnival.*

One night, the duo asked Harry to lead the orchestra when their conductor suddenly became ill.

A hush fell over the audience as the curtain rose in the Star Theatre at the corner of Broadway and 13th Street. A sellout crowd was on hand to see Williams and Walker's new comedy. The comedians were surrounded with a supporting cast of acrobats, impersonators, dancers, and singers. The footlights blazed, revealing an elaborately decorated set and a large, brightly costumed ensemble cast. At the podium in the orchestra pit was a noble-looking young Harry T. Burleigh, his hair greased back and his mustache neatly trimmed, impeccable in his tuxedo and tails.

Bert Williams and George Walker had organized the ensemble as an attempt to capitalize on the success of Cole and Johnson's *A Trip to Coontown*, and more recently Will Cook's *Clorindy*. The highlight of the evening was a "cake ballet"—a charming cakewalk in which Williams and Walker squared off in an elaborate dance competition. The cakewalk had been a common activity among slaves during harvest festivals on Southern plantations. Slaves competed for various prizes, and a decorated cake was a rare treat.

While banjos played, the slaves formed a circle, clapping along to the rhythm of the song. A couple would move to the center and dance in a frenzy, high-kicking to the music. Sometimes a slave would dance while balancing a bucket of water on his head. Another might imitate the aristocratic mannerisms of the master, eliciting hoots and laughter.

For the Williams and Walker show, a gigantic multicolored cake was placed on a low table at the foot of the stage and the competition began. One pair held the floor at a time. The comedians' mannerisms were in strong contrast. George Walker played the dandy, strutting confidently to meet his partner upstage. He bowed with exaggerated courtliness and she curtsied gracefully. They cakewalked downstage toward the prize, elbows squared, with intricate steps that would have seemed ridiculous if they were not in absolute harmony with the general attitude of airiness. The grand spectacle continued until the couple came to the footlights where the crowd showered them with applause. They acknowledged the praise with a royal nod, then gracefully walked to the side of the stage to observe the competition.

In distorted contrast, Bert Williams's grotesque paces were elaborate, practiced, and exactly timed. He walked like a rusty tin man, his joints stiff and jerky, closing his eyes as he sauntered like a drunken man across the stage where he met his equally large partner. In his clumsiness, he didn't even notice when he stepped on his partner's dress, causing her to land in a rumpled mess on the floor. He finally opened his eyes just in time to save himself from falling into the orchestra pit. Burleigh played along, covering his head as if to protect himself.

The audience roared in laughter as Williams wildly swung his arms, working to recover his balance. Relieved when he finally regained his composure, he pulled out a handkerchief and wiped the sweat from his forehead. He looked up in time to see that Walker had stolen his girl. With a woman on each arm, his competitor cakewalked again in a finely choreographed dance. The trio sashayed to the front of the stage where Walker picked up the cake and gracefully exited, to the cheers of the audience.

A befuddled Williams grimaced vengefully and marched to the back of the stage to sulk. After a moment of crying fake tears, he suddenly came up with a plan. Using pantomime, he created a voluptuous, imaginary woman. Once the image was clearly communicated to the audience he stood back to admire his goddess. He displayed her for the cheering crowd, again outlining her curves with his hands. Then he took the hand of his invisible partner and together they embarked on a second tour de grace. As clumsy as ever, Williams held tightly to the hand of his imaginary partner, frolicking gleefully across the front of the stage. Williams's huge blackface smile spread from ear to ear as he twirled and spun with his newfound love. The audience roared its approval as the curtain slowly fell.

The Williams and Walker cakewalk routine was so ingenious and entertaining that it catapulted the duo, and the dance, into nationwide popularity.

After most performances the cast and crew flocked to the Marshall Hotel in Harlem to dance. Williams invited Burleigh to come along. When they arrived at the Marshall, the popular comedian cheerfully made his way into the crowded hall. The ragtime band sat on wooden chairs on a small stage against one wall as couples swayed in rhythm to the music, dancing in a sweat-soaked frenzy at the center of the ballroom. Around the perimeter of the large room were dark green velvet booths. Five or six people sat shoulder-to-shoulder around the lit candles on each table.

Harry noticed Williams's partner, George Walker, over in a corner booth. Walker never cleaned up after a performance and so was always the first of the cast to arrive. He simply walked out the back door of the theater and caught a cab over to the Marshall, where he occupied the same darkened table every night. He was a well-dressed, sophisticated man who enjoyed having a woman on his arm—and it was rarely the same woman.

Walker noticed Burleigh looking his way and called to him from the darkness.

"Well, if it isn't the great Harry T.? What are you gawking at, boy?"

Burleigh laughed as he approached the table. "Forgive me for staring; I wondered if that was you."

"So, you decided to descend from the choir loft to mingle with the sinners?"

"We're all sinners, brother," Burleigh responded with a smile to the teasing.

"My mama told me that." The comedian untangled himself from his current young lady and extended his hand. "Some of us just do it better than others."

Burleigh shook his hand firmly and took a seat.

"What are you drinking?"

"I'll just have a club soda."

Walker scoffed and turned to his girlfriend. "What did I tell you, Valerie, he's a choirboy. Baby, go get me some gin, and get the reverend a club soda."

As he sat down, Harry surveyed the crowd and listened to the band for a while. He was not very impressed. As he would later feel about jazz, Burleigh believed ragtime occupied the basement of the musical palace. He was not terribly interested in the popular music of the day. His passion was for art songs, opera, and the symphonies of Dvorak, Brahms, and Beethoven.

After a while, as he looked around the room, his eyes suddenly met the gaze of a ravishing young lady who stood nearby with Bert Williams. She was the same pretty woman who had read her dialect poetry during the show. She smiled at him as their eyes locked for a moment. The noise of the room was somehow muffled, and the movement of the dancers seemed to slow as Harry's gaze lingered.

"Boy, you sure do know how to lead an orchestra." Walker's comment broke into Harry's thoughts.

"Pardon me?" Harry worked to refocus.

"We ain't never had someone that stepped up to the podium like you did without any rehearsal. It was sweet, my friend, sweet."

"Thank you, Mr. Walker."

"We sure could use someone with your talents leading our orchestra full-time. Your friend Will Cook has done a good job, but after the success of *Clorindy* he won't stay in one place for very long. Not that he ever did before." They both laughed. Will Marion Cook was known as a free spirit, and Burleigh agreed that his friend would not stay chained down for long.

Suddenly Williams approached the booth with the pretty young lady on his arm.

"Good evening, gentlemen," the tall comedian greeted them.

Walker spat out, "What are you doing with a beautiful woman like that at your side?"

"Only the most handsome man in New York deserves to have this princess on his arm," Williams responded.

Burleigh laughed and Walker rolled his eyes, retorting, "Then why is she with a gorilla like you?"

Everyone roared with laughter except Williams. "Move it over, Simple Simon," he said as he pushed his way into the booth.

"I'm movin', I'm movin'," Walker replied as he slid over to let them in. "Just leave room for Valerie. Harry, you remember Louise Alston from the show?" It was through the addition of more sophisticated performers like Louise that the comedians hoped to expand the appeal of their act. Her dialect poetry, they thought, would attract a more genteel audience.

"Of course, how could I forget? You gave a lovely presentation."

"Thank you, Mr. Burleigh. You are very kind."

Williams cut in. "Louise writes almost all of her own material."

"I am most impressed. You are very talented, Miss Alston."

"As are you, Mr. Burleigh. You did a wonderful job with the orchestra, especially at the last minute like that."

"I'm flattered. Thank you."

The band began to play a slow swing tune as Valerie arrived with the drinks. Walker gave Williams a knowing wink and slid out of the booth and onto the dance floor with his girl. Harry didn't want to miss the moment. He stood and extended his hand. "Miss Alston, would you care to dance?"

"Only if you promise to have me home by midnight."

Harry pulled out his pocket watch. "It's past midnight."

"I know. I meant midnight tomorrow." She smiled and looked over at Williams as if to ask his permission.

"What are you looking at me for? Get out there before the song is over."

She slid out of the booth and took Harry's hand, leaving Bert Williams to find conversation at another table. Burleigh smiled and led her onto the dance floor. He put his arm around her waist and they began to slowly dance.

After a moment, Louise spoke into his ear. "You know, I've heard you sing before."

"You did? Where was that?" Harry responded.

"At St. George's."

Burleigh pulled his head back. "Really? I don't remember seeing you."

Louise laughed. "Mr. Burleigh, St. George's is a very large church."

Harry looked into her eyes. "Yes it is, but I would have remembered this face."

She smiled and responded, "Harry T. Burleigh, are you calling me a liar?"

"No, of course not. I'm sure you were there." He paused for a moment. "I just wish I could have seen you."

Louise cocked her head and smiled. They danced and talked through the next couple of slow songs. But the crowd was getting restless and tired of the slow numbers. Several were calling for a coon song, while others wanted to hear a rag. The bandleader played the two sides against each other, whipping the crowd into a frenzy. He finally determined that more people were clamoring for the newly popular ragtime.

Amid the noise, Harry shouted, "How would you like to go outside for some air?"

"That would be lovely," she responded, yelling into his ear. Harry grabbed her hand and led her out of the ballroom, through the lobby, and out onto the street. It was June, and the streets of Harlem were still full of people.

"Where would you like to go?" Harry asked.

Louise closed her eyes and smiled, feeling the warm summer breeze on her face. "Anywhere, Harry. It's a beautiful night." Harry smiled and led her south toward midtown Manhattan. New York was bustling as always. Horse-drawn carriages carried passengers up and down the busy brick streets. A few of the new automobiles raced by, spooking the horses. The streetlights burned brightly, illuminating the sidewalk in front of the couple.

"Your reading was truly grand, Louise. I was very impressed," Harry began, after walking about half a block, searching for the right words to say.

"Thank you, Mr. Burleigh," Louise responded in a playful tone.

There was a spark in everything she said and Harry was invigorated by her. She was radiantly beautiful, with a caramel complexion and wavy hair that reached the middle of her back. Her dark brown eyes contrasted well with her fair complexion. She walked with a graceful air, as if she owned the streets. Though she carried herself in a confident manner, Harry supposed she couldn't be any older than nineteen or twenty.

"Are you from New York?" he inquired.

"No, I grew up in Washington, DC. My father was a house builder and a musician."

"Really, what did he play?"

"Violin," she responded. "He fought in the Civil War. But he was ill for most of his life after leaving the service. He died back in '93."

"Oh, I'm so sorry."

"Thank you. I stayed with my mother in Washington until earlier this year when I joined the show as a part of the chorus."

"You're a singer too?" They smiled at each other. "So, when did you start performing your poetry?"

"I had given many readings in Washington and somehow someone had seen me, and word spread through the cast until Mr. Walker gave me an audition."

"They are fortunate to have you." They walked for a while, watching passing buggies and nodding to others on the sidewalk.

"How about you, where are you from?" Louise finally broke the silence.

"Have you ever heard of Erie, Pennsylvania?" Harry answered.

"I've heard of Lake Erie."

Harry remembered a similar response when he met his friend Will Cook. He gave her his answer. "You know how the state of Pennsylvania looks like it has a smokestack on top and to the left?"

Louise looked into the sky as if imagining her geography lessons. When she had finally conjured up the image she laughed out loud. "All right, I see it now. A smokestack, yes. I never thought of it like that. Is that where Erie is?"

"Yes, at the very top of the smokestack, right on the lake." Louise laughed again, causing Harry to laugh as well. "My mother still lives there," he told her.

"What about your father?"

"My father was in the Civil War too. He died when I was young. My mother remarried, and my stepfather raised us as if we were his own."

"You're very lucky," Louise said, pursing her lips together. "My parents were divorced when I was very young. My mother remarried and had another baby girl, and I have another sister from her previous marriage. My father moved around quite often after he left us.

I visited him in the hospital a few times before he died, but I never really knew him."

"Did you live with your mother in Washington?"

Louise smiled brightly and skipped for a couple steps. "Until a few months ago. Now I live on the road with the Williams and Walker Minstrel Company." She said it in a singsong manner, as if she were a ringmaster announcing a new act in the circus.

Harry ran to keep up with her. "And what do you plan to do after the show closes?"

Louise didn't hesitate. With a wide smile and glimmering eyes she declared, "I plan to be a Broadway starlet!" Her enthusiasm was contagious, and Harry laughed out loud. "Are you laughing at me, Mr. Burleigh?" she said with a quizzical look.

"No, not at all, my dear. I'm sure you will achieve every dream you set your mind to." His response pleased her, and she curtsied in thanks. "Would you like a tour of Manhattan? I can hail a carriage."

She was filled with excitement. "Oh, that would be divine!"

Harry stepped into the street and flagged down a passing cabbie. The two climbed into the buggy and sat down. Louise wrapped her arm around Harry's as the carriage lurched forward.

"Take us to Broadway, Mr. Driver. We have a rising star in our presence." The driver tipped his top hat, and the couple rode off to discover New York after midnight.

The next day Williams and Walker offered Harry a huge sum of money to lead their orchestra. It was an outrageous amount for a black man at the turn of the century, but Williams and Walker were rising stars. No American comedian had ever reached the heights of Bert Williams. His facial expressions and pantomime were greater than anyone else's, by far. Hundreds of thousands of people paid big money to get into the Williams and Walker performances—money that the comedy team used to line their own pockets and to entice talented people like Harry T. Burleigh to make their shows even more professional.

As usual, Harry wired his mother and asked for her advice. She felt that the move would be unwise. She counseled him to stay with his

church job and develop other more sophisticated avenues of employment. And so, with his thanks, he turned down a proposal to earn
what was then considered to be a hefty salary by anyone's standard,
staying true to his art and to his mother's wise counsel.

Despite not becoming a member of the Williams and Walker team,
Harry Burleigh maintained his company with Louise Alston and soon
fell deeply in love. They were married that year after a whirlwind
romance. She was eighteen, and he was thirty-two.

16

King of Kings

1903–NEW YORK CITY

Burleigh's first great success as a composer came when people across America began playing his song "Jean" in their front parlors, at socials, and for piano recitals. The song was immensely popular and was the first of a string of hits that continued through the mid-1930s. Touring as a recitalist, composing, and singing at St. George's, Harry's daunting schedule left little time for interaction with his wife Louise, who was busy trying to build her own career.

Harry encouraged Louise to pursue her career as a singer, actress, and dancer, even as she enjoyed some continued success as a reader of her dialect poetry. Both Harry and their mutual friend, the great English composer Samuel Coleridge-Taylor, used some of her poems as lyrics in their songs.

Louise became pregnant soon after their marriage and gave birth to a son, Alston Waters Burleigh. Harry and Louise entrusted most of Alston's care to Louise's mother. The Burleighs lived in a flat on Park Avenue and focused on achieving success in their chosen fields. Soon the world began to take notice.

In a newspaper interview with Burleigh's good friend James Weldon Johnson, former ambassador to Nicaragua under President Roosevelt, Johnson declared, "Among us it was as a master that he was held. On all questions in the theory and science of music he was the final authority."

Later Johnson wrote, "If the twelve foremost classic songwriters of America were named, Mr. Burleigh would be included in the list."

Over the years, Harry had remained in touch with his dear mother, Elizabeth, and she continually urged him to remain faithful to the spirituals and to the church. But in March 1903, Harry was shocked by the devastating news that his mother had passed away after a short illness. Burleigh was overcome with grief. He and Louise traveled to Erie by train through a driving rain to attend the funeral service at Elizabeth's beloved St. Paul's Episcopal Church. It had pleased Elizabeth to no end that Harry had dedicated so much of his life in service to another Episcopal church. Her desire to see the family brought up in the ways of God had been fulfilled, and she had died a happy woman with many admirers.

Harry vowed to always give her credit for his success, and he remained true to his promise. As word spread of Harry and his talents, Elizabeth was remembered often as he adamantly tipped his hat to his mother's unceasing influence on his life. When he appeared as a soloist for a presentation of Coleridge-Taylor's "Hiawatha," a reviewer for the *Age* wrote, "New York's prize baritone, Mr. Harry T. Burleigh, made a profound impression. His splendid art and superb voice fairly overwhelmed the audience."

The newspapers were not as kind to Mrs. Burleigh, however. In a review of a minstrel performance, the *Age* critic wrote, "The writer knows that Harry Burleigh never bothers about coon songs, but Mrs. Louise Burleigh tried herself as a coon shouter when she sang, 'I've Got Good Common Sense.' Her rendition was above the ordinary. However, someone near me remarked when she was dancing that her feet hurt her. Of course we won't touch that—it's a live wire."

Comments like these wounded Louise, who dreamed of being a Broadway star. As the years passed, Harry was increasingly in demand, while Louise remained in his shadow. Though Louise maintained a respectable theatrical career, it paled in comparison to her husband's skyrocketing success. While Louise performed at society teas, college lectures, and church gatherings, Harry sang in the finest concert halls and before the eastern elite.

1903—BOSTON

In July 1903, Burleigh received an invitation from his friend Dr. Booker T. Washington, headmaster of the Tuskegee Institute, to travel with him to raise funds for the school. Washington enjoyed having Harry on the bill as a way to gather influential people—and to warm up the audience before he spoke.

Burleigh was a staunch supporter of Washington's philosophy of self-determination. Like Washington, Harry Burleigh believed African Americans should advance themselves through individual effort, in addition to political pressure. Burleigh's activism included touring the East Coast as time permitted, along with lecturing and performing at black colleges and universities, both on his own and with Washington.

Harry loved to tell acquaintances of the occasion in Atlantic City when he had accompanied Washington to a rally. In a hurry to catch a train, they asked a carriage driver to take them to the station. When the driver declined to do so because they were black, Washington exclaimed, "Well, you get down and ride, and let me drive the carriage!"

Washington had the highest regard for Burleigh, as well. Writing to Samuel Coleridge-Taylor about his upcoming visit to the United States, Washington said, "I shall lay the whole matter before Mr. Harry T. Burleigh, with whom I think you are already acquainted. Mr. Burleigh's judgment is sound and he is a man on whose word you can depend."

Burleigh, in turn, was always more than happy to lend his support to the institute.

⸺◇⸺

When Booker T. Washington arrived at Tuskegee in June of 1881, he found only a rundown plantation with a stable and a hen house. He was the only teacher, with thirty students. The school had been founded through the efforts of a white member of the Alabama legislature, Mr. Lewis Adams. At the prodding of Adams, the state appropriated two thousand dollars to fund a salary for a teacher. Mr. Adams's goal, it was said, was to create a strong Negro vote in his favor. But that didn't deter Washington. He was determined to make the school a success.

As difficult as conditions were, one of the things that irritated Washington most upon his arrival in Alabama was the attitude of many of his own people. Most of the black population in the Deep South looked on the race question and their own poverty-stricken condition as a problem to be solved by God alone. Washington raised the consternation of a noisy and largely illiterate black clergy by stressing the gospel of work along with a gospel of prayer.

"Sentimental Christianity, which banks everything in the future and nothing in the present, is the great curse of the race," Washington preached, much to the chagrin of the established ministers.

The greatest wrath came down upon him for his advocacy of agriculture, or as it was known at the time, tending the fields. Many African American ministers at that time believed that tilling the soil was part of the curse found in Genesis.

"Didn't the white upper class avoid labor and fatigue at all costs?" they protested. "Weren't poor white folks looked down on for laboring on the farms?"

"There is as much dignity in tilling a field as in writing a poem," Washington responded—and persevered, even when many of the white storekeepers refused to give him credit.

By the turn of the century, the black race in America had fallen into the deepest depression since emancipation. The rights that were won for blacks in the Civil War and reconstruction had been stripped away by Jim Crow. Southern blacks often lost their right to vote and found themselves segregated from society in nearly every way imaginable.

While much of the venom against the black man occurred in the South, Northern whites also adopted an attitude of supremacy in action and deed. Segregation occurred in the job market, in neighborhoods, in schools, and even in churches.

As a result, some former slaves barely thought of themselves as human. One poor man once told Washington, "There was five of us sold at the time, myself, my brother, and three mules."

The two thousand black inhabitants of the Tuskegee village were wretchedly poor and ignorant. Most farms were mortgaged to the fullest. Children grew up without proper adult supervision. Washington went to work, teaching the girls in town to cook, sew, and keep house. He taught trades to the boys and life skills to the adults. Washington's goal at Tuskegee was to educate his pupils from the ground up. He worked to impress on them the beauty and dignity of labor, as well as its practicality. He believed and taught that doing the common things of life in uncommon ways would bring fulfillment, purpose, and, in time, prosperity.

"No one cares for a man with an empty head and pocket," Washington told his students, "no matter what his color."

President Teddy Roosevelt caused a tumultuous stir when he invited Washington to dine with him at the White House in October of 1901. The Tuskegee educator became the first black American to dine in the White House at the invitation of the president. For weeks, southern newspapers decried the meeting. "Both men must pay for their sin," howled the editorials.

When the dust settled, however, it became clear that the White House dinner had not hurt Roosevelt among most white southerners, and that it had greatly strengthened his claim to leadership of blacks. Many also respected Washington's courage. He was well aware of the personal risks, yet he was willing to face the consequences to represent his race at the White House. In addition, Washington's cooperation with Teddy Roosevelt brought federal aid to the Tuskegee Institute.

Ironically, Booker T. Washington, the very black leader who had downplayed the role of politics in the black man's struggle, became the politician without peer among his race. Through his leadership and tireless promotion, Tuskegee became the leading vocational training institution for black people in America.

———◇———

The rally that Burleigh would attend was scheduled for late July 1903 in Boston, Massachusetts. One of Washington's archrivals, William Monroe Trotter, lived in Boston and had organized his cronies in an attempt to disrupt the meeting.

Trotter and his accomplices had previously been jeered and laughed down when they tried to confront Washington at the Afro-American Council at Louisville, Kentucky. Washington's message was entirely vindicated as a result of the violent, raucous behavior of these men. He had dismissed these opponents and later told a newspaper writer: "In reality, these men make such asses of themselves, and [everyone knows] that their object is to gratify a mere personal spite. The colored people in conventions do not take them seriously, and for that reason pay little attention to them in the way of opposing or giving notice to what they say."

From his summer home at South Weymouth in Boston's suburbs, Washington heard disturbing rumors of this new plot to embarrass him. The National Negro Business League had invited him to speak at the A.M.E. Zion Church. Trotter hoped that in a black church in his hometown he could count on a greater number of sympathetic listeners, and he planned to pack the hall with his supporters.

With word of possible trouble circulating throughout Boston, a squad of eleven policemen was dispatched to the church to maintain order. Nearly two thousand people gathered at the Columbus Avenue sanctuary, filling it beyond capacity. It became almost impossible to move as the aisles overflowed with people. The July night air was humid, and the crush of the crowd caused the temperature to climb ever higher.

The pastor of the church, Rev. James H. McMullen, opened the meeting with a word of prayer and introduced Mr. Thomas Fortune, the first speaker of the evening. He stood and spoke favorably about Mr. Washington, his words drawing hisses from the supporters of Trotter in the crowd.

"If there are any geese in the audience," he responded, "they are privileged to retire."

One of Trotter's associates, Granville Martin, dressed in his butler's uniform, tried to move toward the front of the hall to be heard. Ushers moved to his side through the thick crowd, attempting to keep him from approaching the stage. The man resisted, flailing his arms and shouting. Several policemen moved in, apprehended the man, and ejected him from the meeting.

When Mr. Fortune was finally able to quiet the crowd, he tried to speak, but immediately broke into a violent coughing spell. He reached for the pitcher of water that was normally placed at the podium for the speakers. During the confusion of the interruption, someone had emptied the water from the pitcher. His coughing became more violent, and suddenly others on the platform began to sneeze uncontrollably. It was later discovered that during Martin's disturbance someone had blown cayenne pepper onto the platform.

After several minutes, Mr. Fortune finally regained his composure and again tried to speak. From the back of the hall Martin, who had returned to the hall after being released by the police, once again began shouting, hissing, and stomping his feet. Several men on the platform stood and ordered the police to arrest the troublemaker. Once again the police surrounded Martin and carried him out the door.

Mr. Fortune completed his speech, but the crowd continued to murmur. The atmosphere was charged and tense.

At that moment Harry T. Burleigh rose and took the center of the stage. The strains of music floated over the audience like a cooling mist. As Burleigh sang the worshipful "King of Kings," a hush fell over the congregation. Suddenly, a different spirit entered the church as the gifted soloist lifted praise unto heaven.

The *Boston Globe*, reporting on the event the next morning, noted, "Harry Burleigh, a New York singer of some repute, arose and opportunely sang 'King of Kings.' The song had a quieting effect."

Burleigh finished the number and returned to his seat on the platform. But when the pastor stood to introduce Booker T. Washington, another ruckus ensued. Someone yelled, "We don't like you, and we don't believe you." Another taunted, "You're a traitor."

At that point scuffling and fistfights broke out all over the hall. One man was even stabbed and later carried out of the church. William Monroe Trotter stood on a chair and read off a list of questions, but could not be heard above the tumult. A crowd of screaming women surrounded the policemen but was dispersed when the officers threatened to use their clubs. After nearly a half hour of mayhem, the police were finally able to subdue Trotter and his cronies and shuffle them off to jail.

By the time order was restored in the church it was nearly ten o'clock. Washington finally stood and addressed the audience. He thanked them for their patience. "This disturbance was the work of only a few individuals who oppose free speech. Because their ideas are bankrupt, they feel they have to resort to such unbecoming tactics in order to be heard. Their actions betray their lack of credibility."

Speaking to reporters after the meeting, Washington observed, "Just as a few flies are able to spoil the purity of a large jar of cream, so three ill-mannered young men were able to disturb the good order of a large and otherwise successful meeting of our people in the city of Boston. They were unsuccessful, and we are united in our purpose."

Harry T. Burleigh was proud to be able to serve at the side of Booker T. Washington. He was proud of his heritage as a black man, and he was also proud to be an American. His humanitarian acts were mostly quiet and personal, helping numerous individuals to better their lot in life. He didn't march and protest to make his voice known, though he wasn't opposed to such action at the appropriate time. He merely stood and sang praises to the King of Kings, and the storm around him was quieted.

17

I Know de Lord's Laid His Hands on Me

1908–NEW YORK CITY

Harry's career reached even greater heights when J. P. Morgan arranged for him to sing for the king of England. Morgan's men made all the preparations for the trip, with help from the mayor of New York. Ambassador Whitelaw Reid, who was to introduce Burleigh to King Edward VII, organized the tour in Europe. Two weeks before they were to sail, the Burleighs received their itinerary from the ambassador's office in London.

"Harry, I'm not scheduled to perform at all?" Louise complained after reading the schedule. "I thought you were going to speak with Mr. Morgan's office to make sure I was on the itinerary!"

"Well, dear, I did make the request," Harry explained. While he was scheduled to perform several times, including a command performance for the king, Louise was only scheduled for social engagements.

"Perhaps you will be asked to read at one of these lunches?" Harry offered.

"Couldn't you speak with Mr. Morgan directly?"

"Louise, I'm just glad to be going at all. Mr. Morgan has been very gracious in organizing this tour. I already put in a request to have you perform. I don't want to impose further."

She flew into a rage. "So you choose to impose on your wife instead?"

"Louise, that's not fair. If you're not on the itinerary, there's nothing I can do about it at this point."

"Oh, I see," she responded. "So, it is to be another case of Harry receives the glory and Louise stands happily by his side applauding. Well, I didn't marry you to stay at home raising children and baking cookies." Louise stormed out of their Park Avenue apartment, slamming the door behind her.

Harry desperately loved Louise, but he also felt an obligation to J. P. Morgan. It was Morgan, along with Rector Rainsford, who had insisted Harry remain as the baritone soloist at St. George's in those controversial early days. Morgan had introduced Burleigh to all of New York society and to America's wealthy families from Boston to Norfolk. Through Morgan's good offices, Harry was being propelled into international fame—and now he would be singing for royalty.

Harry could not ask for any further favors.

As the date of their departure approached, Louise became less irritable and even grew excited about meeting the royalty of Europe. Though still angry over being excluded from the program, she planned to make the most of her journey. J. P. Morgan advanced a large check to the Burleighs to cover the cost of purchasing the necessary new wardrobe and luggage for the trip. Louise found a way to spend every penny, along with some of their own money, in preparation for the affair.

—————◇—————

On May 25, 1908, the Burleighs boarded the White Star steamship *Cedric*, bound for England. J. P. Morgan, who owned the White Star Line, had reserved his own luxury cabin for the couple. Morgan assigned one of his agents, Mr. Robert Becker, to accompany the Burleighs on board and ensure that everything was to their satisfaction.

The *Cedric* was one of the "Big Four" of the Liverpool/North Atlantic trade. Her sisters included White Star steamers *Adriatic*, *Baltic*, and *Celtic*. When she was launched in 1903, the *Cedric* joined the *Celtic* as the two largest ships in the world. And at a cruising speed of sixteen knots, she was also one of the fastest. Everything was abuzz at the 11th Street dock. Passengers and stewards wandered about the ship, loading luggage and exploring the vessel's amenities.

At 12:30 p.m. sharp the ship's whistle issued a terrific blast. Friends waved from the dock as the ship's crew began untying the mooring lines from the bollards. Above, people leaned out over the railings, waving handkerchiefs, throwing flowers, and shouting good-byes. Amid all the revelry, the band out on the front deck played a cheerful John Philip Sousa number. Below them, three large tugboats pulled and pushed the gigantic ship until she was midstream. Smoke billowed from her stacks as the *Cedric* came to life and steamed for the bay, the Narrows, and the open Atlantic.

When they were finally under way, Louise began the arduous task of hanging her dresses in the cedar-lined closet. One by one she lifted the elegant gowns from the garment trunk and placed them neatly on the rack. "Harry, would you be kind enough to ask Mr. Becker to remove my trunk to the baggage compartment?" Her husband didn't respond. He stood looking over the balcony as the ship slowly pulled away from the New York harbor.

"Harry, did you hear me?"

He didn't want to look away from the view of Manhattan. "Yes, dear, what is it?"

"Harry, will you come away from that balcony and help me, please?"

He finally turned to her. "Louise, we're under way. Don't you want to see the festivities?"

"No. I just want to unpack these dresses before they become wrinkled."

He rushed over to her and grabbed her from behind, his arms around her waist. "Why don't we go up on deck and wave to the people on the shoreline?"

She feigned a struggle. "I have too much to do to get ready for dinner."

Harry lifted her up in the air and she screamed in laughter. "Can't you get your mind off of your clothes for one moment?" he said playfully. "Here we are on one of the greatest ships in the world and all you want to do is work."

She turned and placed her hands on his shoulders. "And all you want to do is play." She smiled and they shared a long, tender kiss.

"On second thought, let's forget about the people on shore," Harry responded. "Since Mr. Morgan went to such great expense to reserve his stateroom for us, I think we should spend as much time in here as possible." He smiled and pulled his wife even closer to him.

"Harry, you are incorrigible," she giggled as they began to slowly dance, looking deeply into each other's eyes. The Burleighs enjoyed room service in their elegant suite that night, and the remaining dresses stayed packed until the following morning.

The second evening was to be one of the social highlights of the voyage. Mr. Becker met the Burleighs at their stateroom and escorted them to dinner. After the evening meal, the Burleighs would join the other first-class passengers at a ball.

As dinner got under way, the table stewards glided across the hall in perfect harmony—a minuet they had perfected in hundreds of Atlantic crossings.

Among those seated with them at the table were Mr. and Mrs. Donald Jordan, from Akron, Ohio. Mr. Jordan was in the rubber business and a friend of Mr. Morgan's.

"Mr. Burleigh, I understand you have done a good deal of work with Booker T. Washington?" Jordan inquired.

"Yes, Mr. Washington is a good friend."

"I find him to be a most sensible man," Jordan quickly replied. "There is so much back and forth between the races. I see him as a voice of reason amid the storm. Don't you agree?"

"Yes, I do," Harry responded. He chose his next words carefully, as the eyes of the entire table were now on him. "Mr. Washington often tells this story to illustrate his philosophy. A ship is lost at sea for many days, and suddenly it sights a friendly vessel. The captain cries out, 'Water, water; we die of thirst!' The answer from the friendly craft at once comes back, 'Cast down your bucket where you are.' A second time the signal appears, 'Water, water; send us water!' The friendly vessel answers again, 'Cast down your bucket where you are.' A third and fourth signal comes from the distressed boat and is answered, 'Cast down your bucket where you are.' The captain of the distressed vessel, at last heeding the injunction, casts down his bucket, and it comes up full of fresh, sparkling water from the mouth of the river."

Everyone at the table sat in silence, listening to the story. "Mr. Jordan," Burleigh continued, "we live in difficult times, to be sure. But if each one of us—white, black, Indian, Asian, and so on—would cast down our bucket wherever we are in life, by way of making friends in every way of the people of all races by whom we are surrounded, the progress would be inestimable."

Those around the table sat in silence for a moment, pondering Harry's words. Finally, Jordan replied, "Well said, sir. Well said."

Mrs. Jordan, who tired easily of politics, changed the direction of the conversation. "I understand that you are good friends with that talented Samuel Coleridge-Taylor. His 'Hiawatha' is just magnificent. Tell us about him, would you, Mr. Burleigh?"

Harry smiled and looked at Louise. "Mr. Coleridge-Taylor has become a dear friend of ours. We met him when he first conducted 'Hiawatha' in Washington, DC."

Mr. Becker interjected, "Mr. Burleigh has sung the baritone part in 'Hiawatha' many times across the nation."

"Really!" Mrs. Jordan excitedly exclaimed. "That is wonderful."

"Whenever Coleridge-Taylor comes to America," Becker continued, "he insists that Mr. Burleigh accompany him on his tours as a soloist."

"We hope to see him in England," Louise interjected.

"Samuel has used several of Louise's poems as lyrics for his songs," Harry said with pride, reaching over to clasp the gloved hand of his lovely wife.

"Did you bring any poems with you?" asked Mrs. Jordan.

"Yes, as a matter of fact I did."

"Then we must have you read them to the ladies at tea tomorrow."

"That would be lovely," Louise responded, and smiled at her husband.

Soon the stewards were collecting the dishes from the meal, and the orchestra began to play a waltz. Mr. Jordan looked at his wife. "Would you care to dance, my dear?"

"I have been waiting for you to ask. What took you so long?" The guests at the table laughed politely as the couple stood and walked onto the dance floor.

Harry turned to Louise. "May I have this dance?" he said softly.

"I've been waiting for you to ask," she responded gently with a smile. The two followed the Jordans out onto the dance floor as the others at the table looked on. Harry placed his arm around her waist and they gracefully glided across the floor. The portholes were open, allowing the cool night air to blow through the room. Harry looked into the eyes of his wife and smiled. "Mrs. Burleigh, are you enjoying yourself yet?"

She looked off into the air and responded with feigned weariness, "It has been so tedious, you can't imagine."

Harry played along. "And how are the other coal pitchers in the engine room holding up?" Louise smiled and placed her head on his shoulder. They danced in silence through the next few numbers, and then wished their acquaintances a good night.

On June 1, New York's African American newspaper, the *Age*, carried Harry's photo along with an article entitled "Mr. Burleigh Sails for Europe."

> Mr. and Mrs. H. T. Burleigh sailed on the White Star steamship "Cedric" on Thursday morning for London and Paris. Mr. Burleigh has a number of letters of introduction to the best people of London for whom he hopes to sing.

When the *Cedric* arrived in Liverpool several days later, Harry sent a telegram to the *Age*.

> All well. Had a fine trip over. Fooled the fish after all—H.T.B.

From the beginning, the trip was a smashing success. For Londoners, this was "the Season"—the short summer months crowded with activity. Every detail was arranged and the Burleighs merely followed the itinerary, escorted by Ambassador Whitelaw Reid and his entourage. At times Louise complained to her husband in private that Harry was receiving most of the attention. Once she was in the public eye, though, she became the model wife and supporter.

<hr />

On the evening of the royal recital, the Burleighs arrived at Buckingham Palace through the grand entrance, escorted by Ambassador and Mrs. Reid. The group was directed by the lords-in-waiting, who were dressed in scarlet and gold with white breeches, their heads powdered. They were escorted through the Picture Gallery into the Music Room, where Harry would sing for the king. The oval-shaped hall included a domed ceiling decorated in grand carvings and supported by eighteen deep blue columns. The towering windows overlooking the gardens were curtained in red and gold silk. Two magnificent chandeliers filled the hall with sparkling light.

In the audience was the Lord Chancellor, the British Prime Minister, the Archbishop of Canterbury, the Speaker of the House of Commons, the Leader of the Opposition, the Governor of the Bank of England, and various Service Chiefs, Field Marshals, and other dignitaries. The men wore tuxedos draped with stars, sashes, and various medallions. The women were decorated in grand gowns, with glistening tiaras, necklaces, and shimmering earrings.

A small platform stood at the end of the hall where Harry would sing. Burleigh's accompanist was seated at the grand, brass-inlaid walnut piano. The instrument was specially designed for the virtuosi who were invited to the palace. Mr. and Mrs. Reid joined the Burleighs in the front row.

Once the guests were assembled, the string orchestra played "God Save the King." As the guests stood in respect, King Edward and Queen Alexandra made their stately entrance. After an elegant procession, the king and queen were seated and their guests followed suit.

Ambassador Reid stood and approached the podium. "Your Royal Highnesses King Edward and Queen Alexandra, his holiness the Archbishop of Canterbury, Lord Chancellor, Mr. Prime Minister, Mr. Speaker, and honored guests. It is my distinct pleasure to present to you tonight a man who has delighted audiences throughout the United States of America. He gives something distinctively his own, a reading of the melodious folk songs of his people in the light of their whole colorful history. Everyone agrees that he is a splendid singer and also an accomplished musician. I am honored to present the renowned baritone soloist from America, Mr. Harry T. Burleigh."

The audience applauded as the singer approached the podium. Harry stood silent for a time, drinking in the experience. Before him were the king and queen of England, the royal court, and the leading lights of British society. He wanted to savor the moment. This was beyond any goal or aspiration he had ever dreamed of. Then, with a nod to the accompanist, Burleigh opened the recital with "The Wanderer" by Schubert. As he easily made the transition from one song to the next, the audience did not hesitate to express their approval.

A delightful point in the repertoire came when Burleigh sang "Adam Never Had a Mammy." Harry feigned nakedness, holding an imaginary fig leaf in front of himself. As he sang, from time to time he would allow the fig leaf to drop then sheepishly cover himself again. Burleigh gestured dramatically during the piece, much to the amusement of the king.

The baritone sang four groups of songs: German and Russian composers including Brahms and Tchaikovsky; plantation songs; American composers; and a final group featuring British composers. The grand finale was Burleigh's rendition of Coleridge-Taylor's "A Corn Song." Burleigh sang the popular work with dramatic effect. The number brought the entire audience to its feet, including the king and queen. Harry T. Burleigh had sung himself into the hearts of European royalty. The young baritone bowed graciously to the king and queen and then to the rest of the audience. The applause continued. He turned and gestured to his accompanist, who gently smiled and nodded his head. Burleigh turned back to the audience and took another bow.

With that the orchestra once again began to play. King Edward, still smiling, turned and led the royal procession through the Blue Drawing Room into the State Dining Room, where he would entertain a small number of honored guests. When the king and his entourage had exited the hall, well-wishers surrounded Burleigh, shaking his hand and congratulating him. The ambassador was approached by the steward of the household, who gave him a message from the king. Mr. Reid thanked the servant and then joined Burleigh in greeting the throng of admirers.

Later, during the carriage ride to the ambassador's mansion, Whitelaw Reid passed the king's message along to the Burleighs. "The king was delighted with your performance. He wanted me to tell you that he enjoyed your selections and greatly admired your voice."

Harry smiled and expanded his chest with pride. He turned to Louise, who praised him with a kiss. "You were wonderful, Harry."

"Here, here," the ambassador agreed. "This is only the beginning, my dear fellow. When word of your performance hits the press, you will be the toast of England. I hope you are full of energy, because we are about to embark on a whirlwind tour of London and beyond."

In New York, word of Burleigh's explosive success reached the editors of the *Age*:

> Since his arrival here a little over a month ago, Harry T. Burleigh has appeared before many of the crowned heads of Europe. To sing before a Duke or a Duchess is an everyday happening with him. Even the King and Queen of England have heard his folklore songs. They agree with the rest of the nobility that the New Yorker is a singer of no little merit.
>
> So successful has he been in private recitals that arrangements have been completed whereby he is to return to England next summer and will appear in a large public concert. As royalty has put its stamp of approval on his singing there is little doubt that the public recital will be a flattering success.

The trip was a rousing success, opening doors to Burleigh that were beyond his imagination. One of these blessings was an opportunity to enroll their son, Alston, in a prestigious private English school. Alston spent the next several years in England while his father's career exploded.

King Edward invited Burleigh back on several occasions to sing for him, and Harry ended up making several trips to Europe, visiting Alston and performing in England and on the Continent. Harry was now singing in front of the most prestigious audiences in America and in Europe. But Louise still struggled, and the disparity between their careers began taking a toll.

18

Hear de Lambs a-Cryin'

1910–New York City

Harry Burleigh was blowing open the barriers that had kept other black performers from being recognized by society. In addition to performances attended by King Edward, Burleigh sang for some of the most notable people of the day—including Anton Seidl, Madame Terina, the Duke and Duchess of Manchester, the Dowager Countess of Dudley, the Earl and Countess of Dudley, and the Archbishop of Canterbury. He sang for Darius Milhaud and Enrico Caruso during their stays in the United States. On one occasion, he even sang a composition of Ignace Jan Paderewski while the distinguished Polish pianist himself accompanied him on the piano.

When the Burleighs returned from England, they moved from their flat on Park Avenue to a charming brownstone townhouse at 823 East 166th Street in the Bronx. The Burleighs wrote several songs together, which they often performed in joint recitals.

By this time Louise was also beginning to receive some well-deserved recognition. Her photo appeared in the *Age*, accompanied by an article describing how literary critics had praised her poems, kudos resulting from a number of successful recitals given during the summer. At

Green Acre in Eliot, Maine, she was highly complimented by professors from Harvard, Cornell, and Yale.

In October of 1910, Louise performed at the American Academy of Music in Philadelphia with renowned violinist Clarence Cameron White. She was invited to read her own southern poems. Her recitation of "Marie Brown" caused uproarious applause, and the newspaper reported, "The occasion marked the most important musical event of the year."

In March of the following year, the Burleighs performed a joint recital for the benefit of St. Monica's Home for Sick Colored Women. The program included plantation spirituals, readings of dialect poems, and American art songs. The grand finale was the Burleighs' collaborative effort, "Dreamland."

Favorable press began to pour in upon Louise, and it appeared that her star was at last beginning to rise. Another article was published in the *Age* in April when she appeared in New York.

> Mrs. Burleigh in her readings gives promise of succeeding Paul Laurence Dunbar in carrying on the songs of the Negro. Her poems are true to nature and give evidence of much thought as well as genuine talent. Mrs. Burleigh's interpretation of her words is beyond criticism as she has set her own standard for them. Others rightfully should follow, and yet Mrs. Burleigh may not have been at her best, due to the large auditorium and the small crowd (which would have helped the performance greatly had they been ushered nearer to the footlights). Had Mrs. Burleigh been before an audience in a smaller music chamber many of her most artistic points, which were lost in the echo of the large hall, would have been more enthusiastically received.

In September 1911, the *Age* ran another photo of Louise, accompanied by an article stating that literary critics praised her poems after several successful recent recitals. The story mentioned a joint recital at Lake Mohony, New York, before an exclusive audience—including a "titled lady" from Scotland who was charmed with the poet and planned to have her come to Scotland the following year.

The article went on to list Mrs. Burleigh's spring engagements, including a tour of the South and her plans to publish her volume of poems, *Echoes from the Southland*. "She has a magnetic and charming personality and deserves much credit for her splendid work," the writer declared.

Despite all of the glowing press, however, there was growing friction between the Burleighs. Louise's jealousy of her husband consumed her, and as a result she wasted many of the opportunities that came her way. Harry and Louise were often asked to perform together, but as the years went by she was more often relegated to the role of an opening act for her husband.

On October 12, the *Age* reported a joint recital by Harry and Louise at New York's Mt. Olivet Baptist Church, for a YMCA benefit.

> At this artistic success, Mrs. Burleigh's readings were well received and delivered in characteristic style. This was her first appearance before a large audience in New York. Mr. Burleigh sang in his usual fine voice and pleasing style and was greatly enjoyed.

This was to be their last joint appearance as husband and wife.

OCTOBER 12, 1911–NEW YORK CITY

The Mistress of Ceremonies stood before the crowded recital hall and welcomed the guests. "To begin our evening, ladies and gentlemen, Louise Burleigh will read a selection of her poetry."

Louise stood and nodded her thanks for the introduction, then approached the center of the stage amid polite applause from the audience. Dressed in an elegant red velvet dress, Louise stood in the traditional dramatic pose of the day—erect, chin out, the left foot forward, turned slightly inward. In her hands she held a leatherbound portfolio in which she kept her readings. The audience sat hushed and attentive. On this night her repertoire included the three poems set to music by Samuel Coleridge-Taylor, "A June Rose Bloomed," "If I Could Love Thee," and "A Vision." When she finished, the audience responded with generous applause. Louise bowed gracefully and walked to her seat.

The Mistress of Ceremonies stood and walked to center stage. "Well, that was very nice, Louise. Thank you." Turning to the Burleighs, who sat at the rear of the wooden stage, she added, "We always enjoy your musings." Louise forced a half smile at the comment.

Already she felt as though the audience did not fully appreciate, or perhaps comprehend, her poems.

Turning back around to the audience, the Mistress of Ceremonies clasped her hands together and pulled them up to her heart as she exclaimed, "And now, the moment we've all been waiting for. Fresh from his tour of Europe, where he performed before royalty, including King Edward of England, I present to you the incomparable Harry T. Burleigh."

Amid a thunderous ovation, Harry rose and strode confidently to center stage.

Dressed in a white bow tie and black tails, he stood and bowed his head as the applause continued. He nodded to his accompanist and opened the program with "Thine Alone" by Victor Herbert. His repertoire included classical numbers by Schumann, Brahms, and Tchaikovsky, mixed with plantation songs like "Joshua Fit de Battle of Jericho" and "Nobody Knows the Trouble I've Seen."

Burleigh's rich baritone voice thundered through the hall, and as he concluded the program the audience rose to their feet. The atmosphere was electrified.

As the soloist bowed gracefully, the Mistress of Ceremonies walked to him and clasped his hands. "Oh my, that was thrilling, wasn't it?" she said when the applause finally subsided. "Please, Mr. Burleigh. Would you honor us with an encore?"

Harry looked back to his wife, standing in front of her chair at the back of the stage. With her lips pursed together, she smiled slightly and nodded that it would be all right. Burleigh turned back to the audience. "This is a song which I wrote along with my lovely wife, entitled 'Dreamland.'" Louise clenched her teeth and sat down as her husband began once again to entertain the audience.

Later that evening, as the couple's limousine made its way to their home through the thick Manhattan traffic, Harry smiled as he looked out the window at the bright city lights. Louise noticed her husband's satisfied expression.

"I suppose you think this night was a smashing success, don't you?"

The musician was startled as his wife's comment broke the silence of the ride home. "Yes, dear. I was quite pleased with the evening. I believe the audience thoroughly enjoyed the performance, don't you?"

"Well after the buildup you were given, how else would they respond?"

"What do you mean?" Harry turned and looked at her, his eyebrows furrowed.

"I mean that woman made a fool of herself in your introduction. You would think you were a vaudeville idol or something."

"Louise!" her husband responded sharply. "I'm surprised at you. I thought it was a proper introduction. After all, we did just arrive from a triumphant tour of Europe."

"That is exactly my point, Harry. *We* toured Europe, not just you." She turned and glared out the opposite window.

"Yes, of course we toured Europe."

Turning toward her husband she shot back, "But that is not what she said. She merely introduced me, but for you she made a terrific oration. *We* perform before the crowned heads of Europe, but my poems are 'musings.' *We* give a command performance before the king and queen of England, but it's your picture that makes the front page of the New York *Age*."

Harry was taken aback. The two sat in silence as the limo pulled up in front of their brownstone. The driver got out of the front seat, walked around to Louise's door, and opened it for her. As she turned to get out of the car, Harry leaned over and grabbed his wife's hand. "Louise, you were wonderful tonight. I am very proud to share the stage with such a distinguished actress and poet."

Her eyes filled with tears. She looked away to hide her emotion. Gaining her composure, she looked back at her husband. "Don't patronize me, Harry. After tonight, we will never work together again." She got out of the limousine and nodded to the driver. Harry sat stunned for a moment in the limousine as the driver came around to his side and opened the door.

From that point on Louise was looking for a way out of the marriage. She was true to her word. The couple never performed together again after that night. For the next several years, they were rarely seen in the same place at the same time. In 1915, Louise finally left Harry for good.

The terrible irony is that after years of struggle, Louise was finally reaping the rewards of her labor. This period marked her peak as a performer in the New York area. But she left because she couldn't bear to live in Harry's shadow.

When Louise took Alston back to his private school in England, she stayed for a while doing shows depicting herself as an Indian princess. Louise always said that she was part Indian on her father's side, though this wasn't true. She was born and raised in the black community, but her complexion allowed her to pass as a Native American, and this gave her something that set her apart.

She had established herself as a reader of Negro dialect poetry in America—a career that was relatively successful. And she was known as the wife of Harry T. Burleigh, the eminent African American baritone. But Louise wanted to carve out a niche that was exclusively hers. Her dream was to be a star on Broadway, but she believed that was impossible living in Harry's shadow.

Her opportunity to escape came when she met and began performing with a Winnebago Indian named Albert Lowe from a little town in Wisconsin. He was working as a New York subway employee when they met. He promised to take her back to Wisconsin and make her the star of his traveling Wild West show. This was the era of Annie Oakley and Buffalo Bill, and these Indian shows were quite popular at the time.

After she left Harry, Louise started performing across America as Princess Red Feather. Soon she learned that there actually was a real Princess Red Feather, and so changed her name to Princess Nadonis Shawa.

Her advertisements declared,

Princess Nadonis Shawa is a half breed Indian of the Ojibway Tribe. She was raised and educated among white people, and is a woman of charm, intelligence, and wonderful personality. She knows the original American, and brings to the platform a real interpretation of Indian life, story and song. Giving Indian interpretations and reading her own poems, she is dramatic and effective. In America, she starred in her own company, the "Princess Nadonis Indians" in Lyceum and Chautauqua, and has recently compiled a book of Indian Legendary Lore.

Of course, all of this was pure fiction.

It seemed as though she loved Albert Lowe very much. They lived together until 1930, when he left her for someone else. Louise never accepted the fact that there was another woman involved and maintained that his family had kidnapped Albert. After he left her, she started to exhibit even more bizarre behavior.

A story ran in the local Wisconsin newspaper:

Nadonis Shawa, half-breed Ojibway princess, has come to Madison from her log-cabin home near Mirror Lake to read fortunes at Hommel's Heidelberg Hofbrau. She reads from tealeaves, palms, or cards. This entertainment is without charge to guests of the Hofbrau.

Princess Shawa gives little outward appearance of the colorful and unusual experiences that have marked her existence since she was taken out of her native environment by a family of Pennsylvania Quakers to be educated. Her talent for writing poetry and reading won the attention of Ella Wheeler Wilcox and Sarah Bernhardt who, with Theodore Roosevelt, gave her assistance in receiving the artistic education she desired.

She has made seven trips abroad, and on her last voyage appeared before the King of England in a recital with Caruso and Nazimova at Kensington Palace. She recently compiled a book of Indian legendary lore, including accounts of "how the four lakes were formed around Madison."

Louise lived out the remainder of her years in Wisconsin. Neither she nor Harry ever filed for divorce. As a devout Episcopalian, Harry T. Burleigh was fundamentally opposed to divorce. Harry never saw her again. He loved Louise, but she hurt him terribly and he never fully recovered from it.

19

Deep River

1913–NEW YORK CITY

The years after he and Louise began to have trouble were busy, though somewhat unproductive for Harry. Louise's betrayal had devastated him. For a few years he did not publish anything of substance. One of the things that saved him in this dark time was his new role as a music editor. Because of his genius for musical composition, Burleigh was asked to join the staff of Ricordi and Company, one of the world's foremost music publishers. This promotion ushered in one of the most significant and far-reaching periods in Burleigh's life. He quickly became one of the most influential editors in the company and often traveled to the Ricordi offices in Italy. Soon he was looked upon as such an important member of the staff that no piece of music was submitted that did not pass through his hands. The fate of hundreds of songs rested on his judgment.

George Maxwell, the managing director of Ricordi, became a good friend and helped Burleigh return to composition. Maxwell urged Burleigh to pull himself out of the doldrums and to get back to the important work of creating arrangements of the spirituals.

And he gave him complete freedom to publish those compositions.

The embers of Harry's lifelong fascination with the spirituals were fanned into flame through the encouragement of Maxwell and other Ricordi staff. Soon Burleigh was scheduling tours to many of the black colleges across the country in an effort to find spirituals and plantation songs that had been lost to the general public. When he discovered what he believed was an authentic folk song, he would quickly write out the words and melody. Then he would return to New York, where he would work tirelessly on an artistic arrangement. When he was satisfied that the song was worthy of public performance, he would publish it under the Ricordi name. As a result of these tours, spirituals that had been previously unknown were saved from obscurity.

At the same time, Ricordi was responsible for publishing many of Burleigh's art songs, making them known worldwide. Once again, Harry T. Burleigh was rising to prominence.

In an effort to forget the pain caused by Louise leaving him, Harry threw himself into his career. He often worked at his small desk at home, arranging, making notations, and composing. Burleigh continued to sing on the weekends at St. George's and Temple Emanu-El. He also worked as a voice teacher and coach, conductor, accompanist, music editor, and lecturer.

It was a full life, which helped to fill the void of being alone. But he began to worry about being away from his son, Alston, who was still at boarding school in England. Burleigh visited him whenever he went to Europe. He thought about bringing his son home but was convinced that the boarding school was giving the lad the best possible education available.

In the spring of 1913, Burleigh lost another friend and supporter, the great financier J. P. Morgan, who passed away while vacationing in Italy. His body was returned to New York for the funeral, which was held at his beloved St. George's Church. Before his death, Morgan had asked that Harry sing at his funeral. Burleigh performed the requested "Calvary" by Paul Rodney.

By this point in his life other special honors began to come to Burleigh. In February 1914, through Victor Herbert's invitation, Burleigh became a charter member of the American Society of Composers, Authors, and Publishers. Herbert, James Weldon Johnson, and others organized ASCAP in 1914 as an agency of musical copyright protection. Burleigh joined along with fellow black composers Will Marion Cook, James Weldon and Rosamond Johnson, Europe's co-director William Tyers, and ragtime songwriter Cecil Mack. There were similar groups throughout the world, but the American society quickly grew into the richest and most powerful organization of its kind.

That same year the world was plunged into chaos as war broke out in Europe.

1914–THE GREAT WAR

Burleigh was in England during the summer of 1914, making preparations to bring his son, Alston, home. The winds of war were howling in the air, and Harry wanted to take Alston to safety before they whipped across the British Isles. In August of that year, Great Britain declared war on Germany. By early October, fifteen-year-old Alston was attending school in the United States. Harry had high expectations for Alston and hoped he would enter a prestigious university within the next two years.

Harry's responsibilities as a father were often overshadowed by his burgeoning career. This often caused friction in their relationship, which was strained for many years. Throughout his college career and early adulthood, Alston remained distant from his father.

Harry remained alone in New York, and he pressed forward with his musical endeavors to fill the loneliness he often felt. It was as a composer of songs that Burleigh first attracted the attention of noted American critics and performers. By the late 1910s, reviews and publications of concert programs of Burleigh's music were being found in such journals as *Musical America*, *Musical Courier*, and *Musical Opinion*. Burleigh's art songs ranked among the most highly regarded works of the era. With such praise, Burleigh's songs became increasingly popular and were being used by some of the finest soloists in concerts throughout the United States and Europe.

A music critic for *Musical America* named Burleigh as a worthy contemporary of any great American composer of the day—and this was a period when African Americans were rarely taken seriously in artistic fields. Such high praise was a true honor for Burleigh, and it opened doors for other black musicians and artists. Gradually, an appreciation grew for the place of African American music in the world—and, in time, a true love for it.

But the war in Europe diverted America's attention from music and art as it became increasingly clear that the country could be roped into the affair. In one of history's great ironies, Woodrow Wilson, the peace candidate, finally came to the conclusion that America could not avoid war. With the help of the federal government's mighty propaganda apparatus, Wilson forged a nation of immigrants into a fighting whole. Like other Americans, Burleigh did his part to keep the home fires burning. But he was concerned for Alston, who had graduated from Dunbar High School in Washington, DC, and immediately volunteered for service in the United States Army.

Despite the earth-shaking events around him, Harry T. Burleigh remained immersed in the musical world.

1916–Martha's Vineyard

Like other fashionable Boston and New York blacks in the 1910s, Burleigh adopted the practice of spending his summer vacations in Oak Bluffs, Massachusetts, a fashionable resort area on Martha's Vineyard. It was the most popular vacation spot in the country for African Americans. Oak Bluffs was a windswept cape dotted with summer cottages. It was a haven of beach play, elegant parties, evening band concerts, and a constant flow of boats bringing new visitors from the mainland. For thirty years, Burleigh stayed at the quaint Shearer Cottage, a guesthouse in the Highland section of the resort village. His studio bedroom overlooked the beautiful Baptist Temple Park. It was only minutes from the ocean and he could hear the low roar of the waves as they would roll along the nearby beach.

But Harry T. Burleigh was not a person who could merely lounge by the sea. He spent much of his vacations doing the work he loved—composition, singing, and even directing a local Episcopal choir. On many a steamy summer's day, Burleigh could be found hunched over a piano in a small corner room of the Grace Episcopal Parish house.

One evening, Harry arose from his bed after midnight when he couldn't sleep. Life seemed to be humming along smoothly, and he was on top of his profession. It was true that his soloist career had slowed in recent years, but this was compensated by the success he had achieved as a composer and editor. Besides, he had grown tired of exhausting tour schedules.

The night air blowing in off the ocean was cool enough for him to sleep, but something inside was gnawing at him. He donned his cotton bathrobe and stepped out onto the large front porch. For all of his success, he couldn't escape the fact that he was sad.

Something was missing.

Was it a need for companionship? It had been more than a year since Louise had left him. The pain had subsided somewhat, but he had not completely adjusted to the loneliness.

No, it was more than that. There was emptiness—or was it anger, or both? He couldn't quite put his finger on it.

I blame Louise. Now the anger began to rise within him. "What kind of woman would abandon her husband and child without cause?" He spoke aloud into the darkness. "And for what? To run around pretending to be an Indian and making a fool of herself?"

The frogs and crickets answered his outburst with their monotone evening chant. The anger built for a moment, then yielded to frustration. *She's gone, and there is nothing I can do about it. Face it, Harry, she's never coming back.*

He had held on to the hope of reconciliation, but now any illusions of a reunion had vanished. Many of his friends counseled him to file for a divorce, meet someone else, and get on with his life. But the notion went against Harry's religious principles. Harry leaned over the railing and gazed up at the stars that glistened in the pitch-black sky. It was only here at Oak Bluffs that he could see them so clearly. The lights of the city hid their brilliance, but out on the dunes of Cape Cod they radiated in full glory.

Oh, God, I know you hear me. I see you in these stars.

He closed his eyes and took a deep breath, trying unsuccessfully to hold back the tears. As they poured out over his cheeks, he prayed silently, *Lord, what is your purpose for me? Why am I so troubled? I must have peace. Please, God, show me the way.*

No matter how many songs he penned or how many he sang on the concert stage, when things grew quiet and he was alone in prayer, the melodies that bubbled up from the inside were his granddaddy's plantation songs, the spirituals. They were a part of his very being—his link to God.

He peered out into space, the great expanse. The stars shone magnificently, giving contrast to the dark night sky.

It is so dark, he thought. *And yet, it is so bright. How deep is the darkness?* A Bible verse his mother taught him, Psalm 8:3–4, came to his memory.

When I consider thy heavens, the work of thy fingers, the moon and the stars, which thou hast ordained; What is man, that thou art mindful of him? and the son of man, that thou visitest him?

Granddaddy's out there, and Mama too. Maybe the emptiness inside came from missing them. Though he'd stayed at St. George's at his mother's counsel, he felt a separation somehow from his roots. The church melodies he sang now were mostly Anglican. The music he wrote was mostly artistic, played in recitals and in the parlors of families across America. This was all good, but it was not complete.

"I miss you, Mama," he spoke into the night air. "And I miss you too, Grandpa." His voice shot out into the vacuum of space and then grew silent. The sound of the crickets and the surf rose once again to take its place.

A song taught to him by his grandfather and sung often in his home began to flood his soul, the melody welling up inside of him like an artesian spring. As the warm summer wind whipped up from the cape, the spiritual poured out of him like cool water.

> Deep river—my home is over Jordan.
> Oh, deep river, Lord, I want to cross over into campground.

He sang it again, drawing on all of the mixed emotions churning within him.

> Deep river—my home is over Jordan.
> Oh, deep river, Lord, I want to cross over into campground.

His rich baritone floated out into space and was quickly swallowed by the darkness. But somewhere out in that expanse, he wondered, perhaps his mama and granddaddy were singing along. The song built to its crescendo.

Don't you want to go to that gospel feast?
That promised land where all is peace.

He meditated on the line for a moment. *That promised land where all is peace.* Then slowly, gently, he finished the song.

Oh, deep river, Lord, I want to cross over into campground.

He stood in silence for several moments, hearing only the crickets and the low pounding of the waves in the distance. Suddenly another dear friend came to mind. *Where would I be today had Dr. Dvorak stayed in America—or even if he had lived to see my success?*

"My success," he said aloud, and scoffed. It had left him alone in a big, empty world. The vast expanse of space before him mocked his feelings of loneliness and isolation.

But even as the echo of his voice faded, the words of Dvorak echoed in his ears, as if the bombastic genius were standing before him. "These melodies are of the soil—of your people. Give these songs to the world, Harry. This is your destiny. It will be your legacy."

With all of the busyness that filled his life since leaving the conservatory, he had forgotten the charge given to him by the great Bohemian. Burleigh had made attempts at publishing the plantation songs, but they met with only minimal success. Not long after Dvorak's departure, Harry had published a collection of seven songs titled *Plantation Melodies Old and New*. In the years between the turn of the century and the outbreak of the Great War, however, Harry had only published a handful of spirituals.

Suddenly the thought dawned on him—he had not fully honored the memory of his grandfather and his mother. He had not heeded the charge of the great Antonin Dvorak. To his dismay, he realized that in all of his success he had not worked as diligently as he ought to give these plantation songs to the world as his mentor had charged him.

Now, with the success of Harry's own compositions such as the very popular "Little Mother of Mine" and the Italian fight song "The Young Warrior," he was now in a position to publish whatever songs he wanted. In addition, through his position at Ricordi he could forcefully promote the spirituals.

How vast is the sky? He heard the waves of the ocean break before him, though in the darkness he could not see them. *How deep is the ocean?*

Inspired by the memory of the great master, Burleigh rushed into his cottage to find staff paper and ink. Harry had arranged a version of "Deep River" before, but in his heart he heard a new melody—a choral arrangement. Sitting down at the dining room table, he started to furiously scribble notes on the staff. It was now three o'clock in the morning and he didn't want to wake the nearby Shearer family, but he needed a piano to hear the melody that was flowing onto the staff before him. He dressed, collected his music, and walked out the door in the direction of Grace Episcopal Church.

It was as if the many streams of his life had simultaneously poured out into a vast ocean of understanding. Remembering Dvorak's prophetic charge, he exclaimed to the night air, "I have my mission. I must make this music known."

20

In Christ There Is No East or West

Harry T. Burleigh kept his word to make the spirituals accessible to the world, and in time he became known as "The Dean of the Negro Spirituals." Of those who championed Burleigh's songs, one of his closest personal friends and most enthusiastic supporters was the wildly popular Irish tenor John McCormack. He was a bright star in the music world, and wherever he went, McCormack attracted a following. By 1914, nearly every concert hall where he performed was sold out in a matter of hours.

Even New York's Hippodrome, which seated more than five thousand people, was filled to capacity for every one of McCormack's concert appearances. The crowds adored him. In his ten or more encores, the Irish tenor usually included at least one Burleigh song.

The press loved McCormack too and printed favorable reviews of nearly everything he did. An adoring promoter ran an ad in the April 1914 issue of the *Courier*, reading:

Why are the McCormack concerts like Christmas?

CHRISTMAS is a matter of PRESENTS
and MCCORMACK CONCERTS are a matter of PRESENCE

213

Burleigh's "Little Mother of Mine" became one of McCormack's standards after its publication early in 1917. The tenor performed the song at the Hippodrome before the largest audience ever seen in America's largest playhouse—more than seven thousand people. There weren't enough seats in the house, so a thousand people were given chairs on the stage behind the singer. In the front row of these stage seats was a group of McCormack's New York friends, including Harry T. Burleigh.

It was a spectacular evening. The mammoth audience cheered every number, but especially the final group of songs, all written in English. The Irish tenor was an imposing figure, tall and barrel-chested. His boyish face and dark wavy hair elicited sighs from the many young ladies who flocked to his performances. On this night, McCormack was at his very best. The electricity that permeated the musical palace charged him with energy, and he sang with passion and sensitivity.

He saved the very popular "Little Mother of Mine" for the grand finale. When the applause from the previous number finally subsided, he turned sideways to look back at Burleigh.

"Ladies and gentlemen," he began, "I would like to dedicate my final selection of the evening to my good friend, and one of America's greatest composers, Mr. Harry T. Burleigh." The audience broke forth into hearty applause. "Mr. Burleigh is a fine gentleman and a gifted composer."

He addressed Harry personally. "I am honored, sir, that you have graced us with your presence here tonight." Harry closed his eyes and humbly bowed his head to the singer. McCormack turned back to the audience. "And now I give you Mr. Burleigh's exquisite piece, 'Little Mother of Mine.'"

The Hippodrome was rocked with thunderous applause for the song, which had swept America like a storm. McCormick stood erect, peering out into the darkness beyond the floodlights as the song's delicate introduction was played. Then gently he sang the tender words.

> Sometimes in the hush of the evening hour
> When shadows creep from the west
> I think of the twilight songs you sang
> And the boy you lulled to rest

> The wee little lad with the tousled head
> That long, long ago was thine
> I wonder if sometimes you long for that boy
> Oh little mother of mine

Burleigh was a man who was not afraid to weep. He told friends that he inherited the trait from his mother. As he listened to this sentimental melody, in this grand hall, being sung by the greatest singer of the time, he thought of his own dear mother. She had sacrificed so much to make sure that her children were raised properly. He saw himself as that wee little lad, rushing down the staircase, begging his mother to let him go to the Russell mansion to listen to the great musicians while she worked. He remembered the delightful evenings years later when they would work side by side and listen to the master musicians. He saw her sitting before more than a hundred parishioners, teaching the Bible directly from the Greek Bible.

The tears welled up in his eyes. *Mama, this is for you.*

> And now he has come to man's estate
> Grew stalwart in body and soul
> You'd hardly know that he was the lad
> You lulled with your somber song
> The years have altered the form and the life
> But the heart isn't changed by time
> And still he is only a boy as a man
> Oh little mother of mine
> Oh little mother of mine

With McCormack's glorious crescendo, the audience rose in a thunderous ovation. The great tenor turned to Burleigh and insisted that he come forward to acknowledge the applause. Burleigh, smiling modestly, declined the honor. Later someone asked him why he didn't join McCormack for the ovation. He shook his head, saying, "I couldn't. I couldn't. But he sang it wonderfully."

The more lyrical and sentimental the song in these concerts, the greater the roar of approval from the audience. For this reason, John McCormack frequently used Burleigh's "Little Mother of Mine" and "In the Great Somewhere" at many of his engagements in those years.

One crisp morning in the fall of 1917, McCormack invited Burleigh to visit him at New York's famous Ritz-Carlton Hotel. Harry was dressed in his usual impeccable style, sporting a three-piece suit, spats, and a felt homburg, which sat somewhat inclined on his head. As he entered the glorious lobby, bellhops breezed in and out of the front doors, pushing large brass luggage carts loaded down with suitcases. Harry had neglected to write down the room number when he spoke to the singer on the phone, so he stopped to inquire at the large marble registration desk.

The attendant looked up from his paperwork. "May I help you, sir?" His polite demeanor quickly dissipated when he saw that Burleigh was black, and his courteous smile melted into a scowl. Though he was somewhat taken aback by the attendant's expression, Harry proceeded with confidence. "Yes, could you give me the room number for Mr. John McCormack, please."

The clerk tilted his head. "May I ask what kind of business you have with Mr. McCormack?"

Now Harry tilted his head somewhat, but continued to smile. "Mr. McCormack is a personal friend of mine and a professional associate. He just telephoned and asked me to visit him at this hotel. May I have his room number, please?"

"Sir, Mr. McCormack receives hundreds of inquiries every day. Now, if you will excuse me, I must confirm with him that you are welcome. What is your name?"

"Harry T. Burleigh," he responded in an understanding manner. The request made perfect sense. After all, McCormack was an international star.

The attendant jotted down Harry's name, picked up the telephone, and rang the McCormack suite. "Mr. McCormack, this is the lobby attendant," he spoke in a smooth, egalitarian tone. "Are you expecting a visitor, sir? There is a . . ." he looked down at the scribbled note, ". . . a Mr. Burleigh who claims to have an appointment with you." The attendant looked down at the desk as he spoke. Harry turned around to examine the lobby. "Very well, sir. I will send him up." Burleigh turned back around as the man hung up the phone.

The attendant wrote the room number on a piece of paper as he spoke. "Mr. McCormack is on the tenth floor; here is his room number. You will be required to use the freight elevator which is loc—"

Burleigh interrupted him, "I'm sorry, what did you say?"

"The freight elevator," the attendant continued, pointing toward the rear of the hotel. "It's just down the hall, through the galley."

Burleigh could hardly believe what he was hearing. He had lived in New York for most of his adult life, and though he had experienced discrimination in various quarters, most New Yorkers in 1917 were somewhat fair-minded in their views on race. He pressed the issue, pointing his walking stick at the bank of fully functional elevators just behind him. "I don't understand. Your regular elevators seem to be working fine."

The attendant looked to make sure he was not bothering any other hotel patrons, then addressed Burleigh in a hushed tone. "Sir, it is the policy of this hotel that Negro persons be required to use the freight elevator. Now would you like one of the bellhops to escort you?"

Burleigh was dumbfounded. He would have expected this kind of behavior in Atlanta or Mobile, but in New York? "No, thank you," he replied. "I'm sure I can find it myself." He turned in disgust and walked down the hall toward the galley.

"They did what?" McCormack couldn't believe what Burleigh was saying. "Let's go," he declared and bounded for the door.

Harry was on his feet and nearly running to keep up with the taller man.

"We're going to the lobby to straighten out this bloody mess," McCormack continued. "If they don't fix this then they will hear from this Irishman, and that's the truth, boy-o."

Together they walked to the regular passenger elevators. The lift attendant was flabbergasted as the pair entered the elevator. "Uh, sir, there are no coloreds allowed on this—"

"Oh, shut up and take us to the lobby." McCormack was positively irate by now. Harry was stern-faced, but inside he felt like a schoolboy whose older brother was about to deal with the local bully. When they reached the lobby, McCormack made a beeline for the front desk. The same attendant was bent over the counter. He looked up with a smile. A quizzical expression quickly overcame him as he saw the giant singer and the short black man walking confidently toward him.

"I demand to speak with the manager," McCormack declared.

The man was caught off guard. "Um, uh—I can, uh, yes sir, um—I will get him right away. Would you like to follow me?"

McCormack wanted to take full advantage of the crowded lobby. "No, I will wait here for him."

"Sir, I'm sure we can clear up any problem, if you will just follow me to his office."

"No sir," McCormack's response was so loud that even Burleigh jumped. "I demand to see him right here, right now." His outburst caught the attention of everyone in the lobby, most who knew that this was the great soloist John McCormack. The lobby grew quiet and every person within earshot turned to watch the confrontation.

The clerk looked around nervously. "Yes sir, I'll get him immediately."

"Now we will get to the bottom of this," McCormack exclaimed. Curiously, no one approached him for an autograph while they waited. The manager emerged from his office and walked coolly over to the pair, while the clerk attended to others waiting in line. His face was like stone, without a hint of a smile.

"I understand there is some sort of problem?" he inquired.

His aristocratic demeanor inflamed McCormack's passions even further. "You're bloody right there's a problem. Mr. Burleigh here was denied access to your passenger elevators. He is an internationally known and respected composer, vocalist, and music editor. He has sung before kings and presidents, and today, in your hotel, sir, he was humiliated by being forced to use the freight elevator to visit my room. Now can you give me anything resembling a civilized explanation for such treatment?" His face was bright red. A large vein bulged from his neck.

The manager looked down and cocked his jaw. He was clearly angered by the public spectacle. "It is the policy of this hotel," he said, looking up at McCormack's steadfast gaze, "that colored persons are not to use the regular passenger elevators."

"What kind of barbaric policy is that? It's bloody 1917, not 1860." McCormack was shouting now. Burleigh stood calmly next to him, like a defendant in the shadow of his lawyer.

The manager looked puzzled. "Mr. McCormack, we do not forbid Negroes to visit the guest rooms. We merely prohibit them from using the main elevators. The freight elevator works perfectly fine, and I assure you, it is nearly as luxurious as the main elevators in many other New York hotels."

McCormack was furious. "I demand an apology. And furthermore, I insist that this backward policy be changed immediately. I would like to see that in writing. If I do not see such action by the end of this day, I will take my business elsewhere and encourage my colleagues to do the same." Every person in the lobby silently awaited the manager's reply.

"Mr. McCormack, I can assure you," the manager quickly said, with a smug expression, "you will not see a change in this policy, written or otherwise. As far as an apology is concerned, as I said, our freight elevators are better than the main elevators in most hotels. There is no need for any further explanation." Both men stared at each other for a tense moment. "Is there anything else I can do for you?"

The Irishman looked over at his black friend, and then back to the manager. He cocked his head and replied, "Yes sir, you can check me out of this bloody hotel. From this day on, I will never step foot in this backwater establishment again. And furthermore, I will use every ounce of persuasion in my power to encourage others to boycott your hotel until you decide to join the rest of us in the twentieth century."

McCormack turned to Burleigh. "Come, Mr. Burleigh, I must pack." The pair boarded the passenger elevators and ordered the attendant to take them to the proper floor. McCormack's entire entourage was instructed to gather their belongings and quickly prepare to move to another hotel.

John McCormack was true to his word. It was the last time the Irish tenor ever patronized the Ritz-Carlton.

21

I Don't Feel No Ways Tired

1924–NEW YORK CITY

Harry T. Burleigh was in his prime.

Of course, like all great artists Harry had an ability to re-create himself. When his popularity as a concert singer waned, he became a great songwriter. Then he became a world-renowned editor. And now he was revered as the master of the Negro spirituals.

After World War I, Harry continued his ritualistic existence. He kept a finely tuned schedule that consisted of work at Ricordi, rehearsals and services at St. George's and Temple Emanu-El, and travel to Martha's Vineyard and Europe.

Harry's son, Alston, returned from Europe after the war and enrolled at Howard University in Washington, DC. He inherited his parents' artistic abilities and completed his studies in music. Living through a war had mellowed Alston somewhat, and he began corresponding with his father more often and would visit when he was in the New York area.

It was the Roaring Twenties, and Harry T. Burleigh's pace could exhaust someone only half his age. His arrangement of "Deep River" brought him the public prominence that he had long deserved. It had been nearly twenty years since the publication of his first songs and now mainstream music critics who had ignored him for years because he was black could no longer brush him aside. By the 1920s, Ricordi and Company had released more than three dozen of his compositions. Honors were beginning to descend on him from around the world.

On June 11, 1920, an honorary Doctor of Music degree was conferred upon Burleigh at Howard University.

To celebrate Burleigh's thirtieth anniversary with the choir at St. George's in 1924, choirmaster George Kemmer inaugurated an annual service featuring Burleigh's arrangements of the spirituals. These concerts continued until long after Burleigh's retirement from the St. George's choir.

One of the modern inventions that Burleigh resisted was the phonograph recording. Though many companies approached the legendary singer and asked him to record his now-mellowing voice, Harry always refused. He had grown comfortable in his role as editor, arranger, and composer, and he wasn't interested in venturing into uncharted territory. Burleigh was not one to take risks, and recording a voice that was no longer as robust as it had once been was an imprudent gamble.

But Harry T. did fall in love with another one of the new technical marvels that swept across America like a firestorm—radio!

In 1926, Burleigh was invited to be a regular guest on WEAF's "Edison Hour." He was given fifteen minutes each week to lecture and sing his beloved spirituals. Instead of a single congregation of a few hundred people, Harry was suddenly sharing the spirituals with all of New York City.

On February 28, 1928, "The Frigidaire Hour," a gala broadcast from NBC sponsored by General Motors, featured both Harry and Alston Burleigh singing a collection of spirituals with the Hall Johnson Jubilee Singers. This was the first of many concerts the father and son duo would give over the next decade. Harry sang "Deep River" with the chorus, and the orchestra performed part of Dvorak's New World Symphony. Harry and Alston had not performed together often, so this broadcast was a special opportunity for father and son to display their musical gifts to the nation—and to spend some precious time together.

———◇———

Because of the friction between Harry and Louise, Alston was sometimes caught in the middle, causing uncomfortable tension between them at times. But Alston loved both his mother and father. He was devoted to each of them and worked to make them proud. There was much of each of his parents in him.

Like his father, Alston became a composer, arranger, and teacher of music. He was also an actor and played important roles in the Broadway plays *Run Little Children* and *Green Pastures*. He did professional theater off-Broadway as well, including a role in *Meek Mose* in 1928. That same year, Alston joined the touring company of the smash hit *In Abraham's Bosom*. In 1935, NBC broadcast a concert that was directed by Alston, in which Harry performed as baritone soloist.

When the Second World War broke out, Alston was called up from the reserves. He eventually attained the rank of Major in the United States Army. Despite all the strain of his parents' separation, his time away at boarding school, and his father's tendency to be a perfectionist, in the end, Alston was proud to be Harry T. Burleigh's son. And Harry was extremely proud of his favorite protégé.

1934–NEW YORK CITY

In the mid-1930s, a reporter asked Harry T. Burleigh if he took more pride in being a singer or a composer. Harry didn't hesitate in his answer. "I hope my greatest reputation will be as an arranger of Negro spirituals. They are the pure gold of the black race."

This was his calling—his life's work. Harry T. Burleigh took the folk music that was inaccessible to most people and brought it onto the concert stage and into people's parlors through his artistic arrangements. Like Antonin Dvorak, Burleigh recognized the spirituals as true American music and as a distinctive gift to the rest of the world. He worked tirelessly to popularize the spirituals and showcase their great power and beauty.

Fearing that some of the spirituals might be lost forever, Harry wrote arrangements for more than one hundred of the haunting melodies. As a skilled musicologist, he traced the history of the spirituals as far back as he possibly could to document their authenticity.

Other than the arranging of spirituals, Burleigh's creative output was waning, though many of his protégés, like Marian Anderson and Paul Robeson, were being recognized as some of the finest artists of the era. One of Harry's most promising protégés was a Juilliard student named Josephine Herrald, whom he met in 1933 at the home of their mutual friend Charlotte Murray. Harry loved the opera, and he would often take a student with him. The hall was always packed, so he would always stand at the back of the concert hall while students such as Josephine sat in his seat. Afterward, Burleigh would often take a young musician with him to his favorite restaurant, the Oyster Bar in Grand Central Station.

Every summer, Burleigh sailed to Italy to relax, see the sights, and work out of Ricordi's offices in Milan. Vacationing abroad was the fashionable thing for those with the means in those days—and with his many publications, along with his salary at St. George's and Ricordi, Harry T. Burleigh now had the means. Soon after his journey he wrote to his young friend Josephine Herrald:

My Dear Josephine,

Thank you so much for your letter. I was beginning to feel that with the many things you must do now as Head of the Music at Bennett you will have little time left to keep in touch with your friends in remote places.

Had a wonderfully revealing summer in Italy—Naples (Capri, Sorrento, etc.), Rome, Florence (best beloved city in Italy), Milan, Venice, etc., etc. Came back in September refreshed in mind, body, and spirit.

With intense wishes for your success and assurances of my personal regard, I beg to remain, as ever

Faithfully yours,
H. T. Burleigh

In the years that Josephine was a student at Juilliard in New York, the talented pianist had become a great admirer of Harry T. Burleigh. Her uncle, Lucien White, well-known music critic for the New York

Age, was vocal in his praise of Burleigh's abilities. At the urging of Miss Herrald, the Juilliard Student Club invited Dr. Burleigh to speak on the history and significance of the spirituals.

As he approached seventy years of age, Burleigh was still in demand on the speaking circuit. So when Josephine asked him to share his thoughts on the spirituals at Juilliard, he gladly accepted the invitation.

1934–THE JUILLIARD SCHOOL, NEW YORK CITY

The Juilliard School was originally founded in 1905, only a few years after Jeanette Thurber's husband went bankrupt in the 1890s depression. As Thurber was the largest donor to the National Conservatory of Music, the failure of his chain of grocery stores sounded the death knell for the institution. The founders of the Juilliard School took up the cause where Jeanette Thurber left off. Originally called the Institute of Musical Art, Juilliard was established to rival European conservatories. Like Jeanette Thurber before them, the founders of Juilliard believed that gifted Americans should receive the training they needed in the United States without having to travel abroad. Since the release of Dvorak's groundbreaking New World Symphony, there was strong opinion among the eastern establishment that America's concert stages should now feature great American musicians side by side with their European counterparts.

In 1919, a wealthy textile merchant by the name of Augustus Juilliard died, leaving in his will a bequest of twenty million dollars for the advancement of music. It was the largest single academic endowment of its kind up until that time. The Institute of Musical Art became the Juilliard Musical Foundation in 1920 and was dedicated to the development of music in the United States. In 1924, the trustees of the foundation created the Juilliard Graduate School in the old Vanderbilt guesthouse at 49 East 52nd Street to help worthy students acquire a complete musical education, tuition-free.

In 1931, the Juilliard Graduate School moved into a new Claremont Avenue building adjacent to the institute. It was here that Burleigh addressed the student body on May 10, 1934. The floors of the elegant hall were made of stone, as were the walls. The chairs were made of wood, and the tall ceilings were covered in lightly swirled plaster, which gave the room a robust acoustical feeling with just the right amount of echo. Burleigh sat in an oak chair on the stage next to Josephine Herrald and Charlotte Murray.

By the time the lecture was scheduled to begin, all of the seats in the auditorium were full. Students, faculty, and other onlookers stood lining the walls and even poured out into the vestibule. The program distributed at the door included the title of Burleigh's lecture: "The Negro in Music."

The evening began with a rendition of the spiritual "Keep Me from Sinking Down," masterfully played on the organ by Carlette Thomas. Soprano Anne Wiggins Brown followed with two of Burleigh's original compositions, "You Ask Me If I Love You" and "Tide." This was followed by a piano version of "Juba Dance" by R. Nathaniel Dett. The capacity crowd applauded enthusiastically for these introductory numbers, setting the tone for the evening.

The Harlem Renaissance had spawned a renewed interest in the spirituals, and on this night, young and old had come to the Student Club filled with anticipation of hearing from the "Dean of the Spirituals," Harry T. Burleigh. The atmosphere was charged with energy.

When the applause for the music finally subsided, Josephine Herrald stood and walked to the podium. The amplifier carried her voice clearly to the rear of the hall. The talented young pianist stood confidently before her peers as she read from the notes in front of her.

"Good evening and thank you for joining us for this special meeting of the Juilliard Student Club. There are certain people that come into one's life through the providence of God who make such a distinct impression that by being in their presence, you are changed forever. Harry T. Burleigh is just such a man.

"As a boy, Harry accompanied his grandfather, Hamilton Waters, as he lit the gas lamps every night in Erie, Pennsylvania. As they went from lamp to lamp, Hamilton, a former slave, taught young Harry the spirituals and plantation songs that sustained him in a life of cruel slavery—songs like 'Wade in de Water,' 'Joshua Fit de Battle of Jericho,' 'Sometimes I Feel Like a Motherless Child,' and 'Swing Low, Sweet Chariot.'

"From an early age, music burned in Harry's heart and he determined that he would pursue the life of a professional musician.

225

"But in those difficult years of reconstruction after the Civil War, there were not many opportunities for young colored men in the world of music, other than the degrading minstrel show. Harry did whatever he could to remain connected to the world of music. He sang at weddings and funerals. He sang in the Episcopal choir, at the mission church for former slaves, and in the Jewish temple choir in Erie. He toured for a year with a traveling band of black singers and nearly starved to death."

Josephine looked back at Harry and chuckled along with the audience. Many of these musicians could identify with Burleigh's early struggles.

"Discouraged by those hard times," Josephine continued, "Harry surrendered to the reality that the life of a full-time musician was beyond the grasp of any black man who wasn't willing to wear blackface greasepaint. But Harry's God-fearing mother forbade him from going near the minstrel house. With the help of friends who raised money for his train fare, Harry traveled to New York and won the scholarship to the former National Conservatory of Music.

"Harry tells the story of how during the course of his duties as janitor for the school, he was mopping the hallway and singing one of the spirituals when the great Czech composer Antonin Dvorak came bounding into the hall crying out, 'What is this sound?'"

The audience chuckled at Josephine's attempt at an eastern European accent.

"Taking young Harry Burleigh under his wing, Dvorak asked him to sing every Negro spiritual and plantation melody that he knew. Over the course of nine months, Dvorak drank in the themes of these haunting melodies. From this inspiration he wrote his masterpiece, 'Symphony no. 9: From the New World.'"

At the mention of the wildly popular symphony, the audience broke into enthusiastic applause.

"Since that time, Harry T. Burleigh has fulfilled his promise to Antonin Dvorak and has given the spirituals to the world, first as a world-class vocalist, handpicked by J. P. Morgan to be the baritone soloist at St. George's Episcopal Church in Manhattan, then later singing for Teddy Roosevelt when he was governor of New York, and King Edward of England in Buckingham Palace. Dr. Burleigh then began his life's work of publishing artistic arrangements of the spirituals, taking these beloved melodies beyond the colored community and transporting them to opera houses, churches, and family parlors around the world.

"Ambassador James Weldon Johnson, who worked to found the NAACP, wrote of him, 'Burleigh's concert performance arrangements of the spirituals are today recognized as the single greatest factor in the awakening of American interest in this now highly honored art form. To this day, these are still considered the standard against which all other spiritual arrangements must be judged. Dr. Burleigh is regarded as one of the greatest of all arrangers of spirituals.'"

Josephine looked up at her fellow students and smiled. Bursting with pride, she declared, "Ladies and gentlemen, it is my privilege to introduce to you a friend, mentor, teacher, and musical pioneer, Dr. Harry T. Burleigh."

The distinguished gentleman rose to his feet, and much to his surprise, the entire audience also stood to welcome him. Miss Herrald warmly shook Harry's hand as he walked to the podium. Now in his late sixties, the silver-haired musician stood behind the podium and smiled shyly as the applause continued for several minutes. He nodded his head in thanks for the ovation, motioning for the audience to be seated. After another minute the applause finally died down as people took their seats.

"The story of the Negro can be told in his music," he began with a slight smile and a twinkle in his eye. "From beginning to end, his life is attuned to song.

"The history of Negro melody in America is comparatively short. No successful attempt was made to collect it before 1830, and few letters or articles describing it have been preserved. Best known to the world are the plantation songs, known as spirituals, which, on account of their great number, lovely melodies, compelling rhythms, and deeply emotional content, are unique examples of folk song."

The acoustics in the great hall carried his amplified voice so that even the overflow crowd in the vestibule could hear him clearly. In the seats below the stage, students took notes in hard-covered composition books.

"Who can tell? A beautiful melody sung by the Hebrews in those far-off days recorded in the Old Testament may have been overheard by African Negroes and carried through the centuries of trials and countless mutations to flower on American soil!

"No songs in the world have a greater or more deserved popularity than those spirituals that tell of the universal striving and weariness of all men, not alone of the Negro race. Who can forget the tender 'Somebody's Knockin' at Yo' Door' and 'I Bin in de Storm So Long'; the imploring 'I Want to Be Ready' and 'Standin' in de Need of Prayer'—this latter song being used, with modifications, by Louis Gruenber, in his 'Emperor Jones'—and, of course, the truly exquisite 'Deep River.'

"In the narrative spirituals, the Negro has translated the marvelous stories of the Old Testament into simple home language. Each tale in its telling is colored by his own exaltation and understanding of the Scriptures. Here we find 'De Gospel Train,' 'Didn't It Rain,' 'Who Built de Ark,' and 'Ezekiel Saw de Wheel.' Many modern composers see in the unusual rhythms of Negro song, and its simple but expressive melodies, material to use in a thematic way in the writing of great artwork."

Burleigh smiled and paused for a moment, reliving a memory in his mind. He pulled his glasses off and paced the front of the stage as he told the story. "The week that Dvorak sailed back to Europe, a prominent journal commented that no sum of money was large enough to keep Antonin Dvorak in America. The reporter noted, 'He left us his New World Symphony and his American Quartet, but he took himself away.'"

The old man stopped, looked out at the audience, and pointed his finger demonstratively. "But he also left behind a deeper appreciation of the beauties of Negro song—its peculiar flavor, its sometimes mystical atmosphere, its whimsical piquancy, and its individual idiom, from which many other splendid artists have already drawn inspiration."

Smiling, the musician spoke of his advancing years. "Of course, I don't feel no ways tired," he said, eliciting laughter from the assembly. "My good friend Booker T. Washington often whistled the spiritual, 'I Don't Feel No Ways Tired,' to rest himself after a strenuous day." Harry looked off into the distance for a long moment, as if surveying another realm.

Finally he continued, "The spirituals were a needed safety valve through which pent-up energies escaped and emotions were expressed. These songs represent America's only original and distinctive style of music. I am confident the spirituals are destined to be appreciated by more and more people of various backgrounds as the years go by."

He shook his head and smiled. Looking at some of the faculty seated in the front row, he declared, "These songs are set to music that is beyond my powers of explanation." The teachers smiled and nodded their heads in agreement. Burleigh turned back to his notes. "Previously, southerners regarded Negro songs as a joke, and laughed over them until Negroes themselves grew half ashamed of their wonderful melodies. For a while, our people were even reluctant to sing them in public gatherings."

Once again, Burleigh took off his glasses and spoke in slow, almost sorrowful tones. "Until recently the use of the old plantation melodies has been repugnant to many people of African descent. Not having felt nor undergone the hardships of vassalage, they were too far removed in freedom of spirit and not far enough separated by duration of time to welcome the allusion to slavery. Many felt that the plantation hymns were but a reminder of the misfortunes of a race.

"They resented, too, the attitude of many Caucasians in their wish to restrict Negro singers to folk songs and in their expressed desire to hear students in Negro schools sing plantation hymns to the exclusion of other music."

The musician paused for a moment to allow the thoughts to sink into the minds of the students before him. He placed his glasses back on his face and smiling, continued his lecture. "But despite the desire of some to forget these precious melodies, we must not ever allow that to happen. The spirituals are a part of who we were, who we are, and who we will be. They owe their origins to religious impulse, and their dignity expresses both tragedy and sadness. There is no anger, malice, or retaliation in the songs—only hope."

Burleigh looked out at the students and smiled. "I have done my part to preserve this legacy, now it is in your hands to keep the spirit of these songs alive. Sing them loud. Sing them often. Sing them well. Sing them not from the mind, but from the soul. Thank you, and God bless you."

Again the students stood to their feet in raucous applause, and as they did, Burleigh bowed and nodded his head in thanks. When the applause subsided, Harry looked back at the others on the stage. "Josephine Herrald will now present some more spirituals, and one of my original songs."

The comment brought cheers from the audience. Miss Herrald and Charlotte Murray stood and walked to the front of the stage as Harry returned to his seat to enjoy the performance. Josephine took her place behind the piano, while a trio of Juilliard student vocalists stood side by side near the footlights. They sang Burleigh's arrangement of "Sinner, Please Doan Let This Harvest Pass" and the haunting "Were You There."

> Were you there when they crucified my Lord?
> Sometimes it causes me to tremble, tremble, tremble.
> Were you there when they crucified my Lord?

The songs were greeted with more enthusiastic applause, along with cries of "Encore! Encore!" The response surprised Burleigh, and with great delight he encouraged the trio to repeat both numbers. When they finished, soprano Ruby Elzy rose from her seat and walked over to the piano. When the singer was in place, Josephine Herrald spoke into the microphone as she sat at the piano. "Ladies and gentlemen, we are proud to present to you Dr. Burleigh's latest composition—a song entitled 'Lovely Dark and Lonely One,' written to the lyrics of Langston Hughes from the book *The Dream Keeper.*"

> Lovely dark and lonely one,
> Bare your bosom to the golden sun.
> Do not be afraid of light,
> You who are a child of right.
> Open wide your arms to life.
> Whirl in the wind of pain and strife.

Suddenly, the song changed pace and the music heightened in intensity.

> Face the wall with the dark, closed gate.
> Beat with tireless hands and wait.

Just as quickly, the music mellowed, as if the singer understood the pain that must be endured in patience until the new day of tranquility dawns.

> Wait—wait.
> Lovely dark and lonely one,
> Bare your bosom to the sun.

As the final chord resonated in the hall there was a momentary silence, as if the students were drinking in the poignancy of the moment. Then, suddenly, the room erupted in applause and every person rose to their feet in admiration. Both the pianist and the soloist turned and stretched out their hands to deflect the praise to Burleigh. Harry stood and bowed one more time to the audience. He walked over and shook the hands of the performers, thanking them for their beautiful interpretation of the song.

As the students and faculty continued to applaud, the elderly man turned again to them and bowed his head in thanks. The generous ovation continued for several minutes as students whistled and cheered. This pioneer of the Negro folk songs—who had learned them from his grandfather, who had learned them from his mother—stood before the appreciative crowd in the most prestigious music school in the country with a full heart. He had accomplished his mission. He knew by the smiles on the faces, the tears in the eyes, and the enthusiastic applause that he had successfully passed on their spirit to yet another generation.

1940–NEW YORK CITY

Harry's final artistic arrangement was created for the hymn, "In Christ There Is No East or West" in 1940. The music was set to words written by William A. Dunkerley for the "Pageant of Darkness and Light" at the London Missionary Society's exhibition in 1908. In one final flourish, Harry T. Burleigh declared the message of his life's work to the world.

> In Christ there is no East or West,
> In him no South or North;

But one great fellowship of love
Throughout the whole wide earth.

In him shall true hearts everywhere
Their high communion find;
His service is the golden cord,
Close binding humankind.

Join hands, then, members of the faith,
Whatever your race may be!
Who serves my Father as his child
Is surely kin to me.

In Christ now meet both East and West,
In him meet North and South;
All Christly souls are one in him
Throughout the whole wide earth.

22

Goin' Home

As World War II drew to a close, Harry T. Burleigh was still as dapper as ever. At seventy-eight years of age, his grooming was still meticulous, and he sported a derby hat, morning coat, striped trousers, gray spats, silver-headed cane, and, always, a fresh gardenia in his buttonhole. His dark eyes, white brows, clipped white mustache, and gray hair were attributes to the simple dignity of an earlier age—one that was becoming a distant memory in the fast-paced world where America was now the most powerful nation. When the weather permitted, Harry still walked briskly through rush-hour sidewalk traffic in mid-Manhattan, swinging an umbrella or cane in his right hand. As he had for many years, he lived in his charming brownstone in the Bronx.

Mocked at one time because he sang what some considered "old songs," Burleigh was now recognized as one of the foremost musical pioneers of his people. It was said of Harry T., "Wherever folks heed God and own a piano, you will hear his arrangements of America's well-loved spirituals."

Looking back on Burleigh's illustrious career, his publisher at Ricordi told a reporter:

> He has done things which would have been remarkable in a man who began with everything in his favor and had no such fight to make as Burleigh had. But he has so much more in him. If only someone had the vision in Burleigh's youth to set him free from that long struggle for mere existence and make it possible for him to spend his strength in the work he was made for, he would rank with MacDowell himself. One must have time for symphonies, months and years; and they bring in no ready money. America, and the whole world of art, is the poorer because Burleigh had to fight for his daily bread so long.

When someone read this quote to Burleigh, he just smiled and looked down at his cane. "I had my living to make. I am like other people. I must do the best I can with what I have and not cry for what I can't get."

Harry Burleigh had also walked the road of discrimination and prejudice, yet he was not bitter. "We've all gone through those things," he remarked quietly to a student who inquired of his experience with racism. "It's how you respond to the storms of life that determines your character. You can complain when the storms blow and you will go around and around the mountain. Or you can put your head down and plow through life's difficulties by God's grace. If you will do that, you will take your Promised Land."

Burleigh still worked daily on composition and visited his editorial office at Ricordi almost every day. One day, while he was working in his Manhattan office, the telephone rang.

"Mr. Burleigh, this is Josephine Herrald."

"Hello, my dear, how are you?"

"Oh, I'm fine."

"How are your parents?"

"They are well, thank you. We're all just making preparations for my wedding."

"Yes, that is coming up quickly, isn't it?"

"Yes it is, next month to be exact. As a matter of fact, I'm on tour right now, and I'm in town for a couple of days to see friends and do some shopping. I was wondering if you wanted to meet me for lunch while I'm in New York."

"That would be wonderful. You say you're doing some shopping."

She hesitated, then responded, "Yes, Mr. Burleigh, but . . ."

"Where are you shopping? May I join you?"

She was embarrassed to say what she was shopping for, but finally blurted it out. "Actually, this morning I'm looking for a nightgown for my honeymoon, so I don't think you would be able to help me." She laughed politely. "Can I meet you somewhere for lunch at noon?"

The situation didn't faze the elderly musician. "I would imagine that you will need a man's opinion of your purchase then?"

Josephine tried, unsuccessfully, to hold in a giggle. She responded to his suggestion, "I imagine a man's opinion would be helpful. But if you're coming along, I will shop for a housecoat instead."

"That would be fine with me," Burleigh responded. "Where are you staying? I'll hail a taxi and be over to your place within the hour." They made arrangements and then hung up the telephone.

Burleigh was a father figure to the ladies he escorted to the opera or to a play. In all the years that Josephine knew him, there was never an occasion where he said or did anything discourteous. So while she was somewhat embarrassed, she ultimately had no problem with the elderly gentleman tagging along on her shopping trip.

Forty-five minutes later, Josephine met Dr. Burleigh on the street in front of her hotel. With a hug, he exclaimed, "My dear, are you ready to paint the town?"

Taking on an air of royalty, she grabbed his arm and responded, "What colors are you interested in, sir?"

"Anything but pink," he responded. They chuckled as they jumped into the taxi, on their way to a delightful day of shopping in midtown Manhattan. They made the traditional stops at Macy's and Bloomingdale's and then turned in to a lingerie boutique on Park Avenue. Burleigh entered the small women's store and immediately went to work.

"Good morning, dear," he said to the attendant. "We are in need of a housecoat. Could you bring us a selection of the latest fashions?"

"Of course," the woman replied. "Does madam have any preference as to color?"

Josephine winked at the old man and then turned to the attendant. "Anything but pink." The woman nodded and disappeared into a back room. Josephine and Harry perused the tiny shop and spoke of her career.

"You say that you are on tour?" he asked.

"Yes, it's a little grueling with the wedding only a month away, but this tour has been scheduled for some time, so I couldn't back out of it."

"I wanted to thank you for finding time to keep in touch with me," Harry said as he took a seat in a leather chair. "You are so kind to keep me up to date about your work and your family."

Josephine held Dr. Burleigh in the highest personal regard. He had always been available to talk to when she had to make important decisions about her career. "You have always been so good to me. I am the one who should be thanking you. How can I return the favor?"

"You can join me for lunch at the Oyster Bar after we're finished here," he replied.

"With pleasure," she responded. Suddenly the attendant reappeared from the rear of the store carrying an array of the most beautiful fashions. "Oh my," the young woman ran her hand over the satin, silk, and lace material. "Aren't these lovely?" She sorted through the selection and chose several to try on for size.

Harry lit a Cuban cigar, picked up a copy of the *New York Times*, and began to leaf through it. A few moments later Josephine emerged from the dressing room adorned in a fine satin housecoat. Delicate white lace trim highlighted the lapels and sleeves.

"What do you think of it, Mr. Burleigh?" she asked as she stood in front of the full-length mirror, modeling the garment.

"Marian, you look gorgeous," he replied enthusiastically.

Josephine looked puzzled by the comment. She turned to the elderly man and responded, "Marian? You mean Josephine, don't you?"

"Did I say Marian? I'm sorry, Josephine. You are just so ravishing I was confused for a moment."

Even though Harry was nearly three times her age, she was flattered and blushed at the comment. "Do you think he'll like it?"

"Only a fool would not like it. You are an image of loveliness, my dear."

"I'll take this one," she told the attendant and then went back to the dressing room. "One thing I know for sure," she said quietly to herself, placing the beautiful housecoat back on its padded silk hanger, "I'm not telling my fiancé that I modeled this first for another man." She laughed at the idea and finished getting dressed.

The pair walked the short distance to Grand Central Terminal and made their way toward the Oyster Bar below the grand lobby. As always, Burleigh stopped to chat with the redcaps who worked at the station. He loved to hear the latest stories making their way around the platforms. He introduced Josephine to the kindly men and then bid them farewell.

When they were a safe distance away, Burleigh spoke quietly to his friend. "It's a shame that men of such intelligence have had no chance to follow a more rewarding profession." As they entered the Oyster Bar he added, "We are both very fortunate, Josephine. Very fortunate indeed."

1946–NEW YORK CITY

By the following year, Burleigh's health and voice were rapidly failing. Time had caught up with the grand old man. It was plain to see and hear that Harry was growing weary. All his customary vitality had left him. His step was not as brisk and his hands shook uncontrollably. His rich, golden baritone had faded into memory. For several years his voice had been slowly faltering.

Yet he refused to retire.

Until the winter of 1946, he traveled the length of Manhattan from his brownstone in the Bronx on Tuesday and Friday nights for choir rehearsals. By spring he could no longer make the trip on his own. His driver, Mr. Sumner, took time from his normal cabbie route to pick him up and make sure he was safely delivered to his destinations.

Every year on Easter Sunday, Harry Burleigh sang "The Palms." It had become a New York tradition for well-to-do families to dress in their finest Easter apparel and make the trip to Stuyvesant Square to hear the famous baritone sing this moving hymn. The *New York Herald Tribune* recorded Harry's final singing of "The Palms" in April of 1946.

The mellow baritone of Harry Thacker Burleigh, Negro soloist and composer, filled St. George's Protestant Episcopal Church in Stuyvesant Square yesterday for the 52nd consecutive Palm Sunday. Standing in the midst of the red-cassocked adult choir, Mr. Burleigh sang Faure's *The Palms* at both the morning and vesper services.

Mr. Burleigh was surrounded by a large group of admirers in the church's basement choir room after the morning service. "Just think of that, going on eighty and I can sing *The Palms* the way I did," he said. "I think to be able to sing *The Palms* at my age is really something. I was seventy-nine last September—I think they ought to say, 'Burleigh take a rest.' I'd like to re-arrange some more Negro spirituals and work on another *Deep River*, but I just haven't got the time. I sing here every Sunday, you know. This morning I really do think I sang fairly well for a man my age, but I'll do it even better this afternoon."

Out of respect, the press gave him generous reviews, but it was obvious to everyone that the time had come for him to step down from the choir of St. George's.

Finally, sadly, Harry himself came to realize that there was no more that he could do. Peculiar visions were becoming more frequent now, and he could no longer ignore the visitations of his old friends. He had to speak with them, to spend time with them. He had to ask them of their world. He no longer had time for the mundane affairs of this life.

"Do you want me to go till I drop?" the singer asked the clergy and the choir when they feigned a protest of his retirement. "Think of it! Fifty-two years in one church!" St. George's was reluctant to relinquish its most precious legend, but it was clear the time had come. In the pews of the grand cathedral were older parishioners who had first heard Harry T. Burleigh sing in the choir when they were small children. On a cold day in November 1946, their grandchildren accompanied them as they listened to the great man sing as a soloist for the last time.

Early that morning, Reverend Miller, the new rector at St. George's, entered the cold sanctuary two hours before the service was to commence. He began his usual Sunday morning routine of turning on the lights and unlocking the doors. As usual, a solitary figure sat four rows back on the center aisle.

With a slight smile the youthful rector quietly walked up behind the singer and engaged in the now-familiar routine. "How are you feeling this morning, Mr. Burleigh?" The question echoed in the empty chamber.

"Fine, fine, and how are you Rector Miller?"

"I'm a wee bit chilly," he answered as he rubbed his arms with both hands. He asked the question three previous rectors had asked of the soloist. "What brings you here so early?"

The old man smiled and twisted his cane in front of him. He turned and looked up at the young rector. "I'm just getting the feel of the place," he said with a slight smile and a wink.

The pastor reached out and gently patted him on the back. After a long moment he inquired, "Are you at all sad that you will be leaving us?"

Burleigh thought about it for a moment then replied, "It's time I ease up a bit. Besides, I have a great deal of work to keep me busy. I'd like to write a communion service using the spirituals, what would you think of that?"

Miller laughed. "I think that you're not really interested in easing up." He paused and looked up at the stained-glass windows high above them. "I haven't known you like previous rectors, but in my short time here I have grown to admire you greatly, sir." He looked back at the man. "You will truly be missed."

Burleigh smiled and nodded his head in thanks. "And I shall miss this wonderful place. But not to worry, I have lots of friends to keep me company. Yes, my good rector, many dear friends."

The sanctuary was filled to capacity that Sunday morning. Looking down from the gallery in the grand sanctuary, it appeared that all of Burleigh's friends, old and new, had turned out to honor his retirement. The choir, many with tears in their eyes, sang Burleigh's rendition of "I Know de Lord's Laid His Hands on Me." Then Mr. Burleigh stepped forward, and in a wavering voice sang as baritone soloist with the choir for the final time.

All of the New York newspapers carried the story of Burleigh's retirement. The New York *Age* ran a handsome front-page portrait. George Kemmer, choirmaster and organist at the church, was quoted in the *New York Herald Tribune*: "We will miss him greatly, but we have known for some time that he wanted to retire and devote more time to writing music. He is a remarkable man, and we appreciate him too much to impose on him."

Mr. Burleigh was in excellent spirits after the service. To try and dispel any rumors that he might be in failing health or voice, he sang for reporters a few bars of "Go Down Moses." The reporters applauded the impromptu performance.

The elderly man attended church for the next few months, joining in the hymns from his regular pew, and Rector Miller saw to it that a pension was provided for him. But soon after Harry left the choir, his unusual visions intensified. One day his good friend Victor Herbert stopped by the brownstone and asked Harry to join him for a concert at Carnegie Hall.

"Victor, you look absolutely marvelous," Burleigh mumbled into the air. "I know that you are at least ten years older than me. Why is it that you look like you're in your prime and I'm an old man?" The vision laughed at the comment and encouraged the singer to step lively. After all, there would be a grand show at Carnegie Hall.

The two men strode confidently through the streets of New York, talking about music and bygone days. Though he asked several times, Burleigh couldn't get Victor to tell him about his current position. All that the apparition would discuss were events from long ago.

As he approached Carnegie Hall, Burleigh's good friend Josephine Herrald noticed him and came over to greet the elderly musician. "Dr. Burleigh, it is so good to see you."

This is rather forward. Who does this vixen think she is? Come Victor, let's get inside before we are mobbed by our admirers.

Josephine said hello again, trying to get the old man's attention, but Burleigh did not return her greeting. He walked by the young lady as if she were a stranger, all the while mumbling into the air. Josephine let him pass by and into Carnegie Hall. With tears in her eyes, she turned and watched the musical legend as he faded into the crowded lobby.

A month later Alston Burleigh found his father wandering dazed on the street several blocks from his townhouse, handing out money to strangers. Alston could no longer trust Harry to take care of himself, so he moved from Washington, DC, to New York to look after his ailing father. But after a few short weeks, he realized that Harry's condition was much worse than he was equipped to handle. With a heavy heart he admitted his father into the Oakes, a convalescent home on Long Island. Once in the care of the nursing home, Burleigh's health deteriorated even further.

Harry told his son of his many visitors at the home. "It is really the strangest thing, Alston. My friends have been coming by daily to visit with me. I mean people that I have not seen in years. If I knew I'd have this many friends over to see me I would have retired years ago. It's just too bad that I can't see them that well. My eyes are failing me, Alston, and these glasses just do not fit."

Alston suspected that his father was being overly medicated. He withdrew him from the Oakes and placed Harry in Stamford Hall, a private convalescent home in Stamford, Connecticut. However, Harry did not improve with the move—and the visitations continued.

1948–STAMFORD, CONNECTICUT

Even in his waning years, Harry T. Burleigh remained a beloved elder statesman in the music world. In March 1948, the Howard University Choir performed at the Stamford retirement home in his honor. More than three hundred residents watched the smartly dressed singers present a full-length concert. Alston and his wife, Erma, came to hear the choir and to share Easter Sunday with their beloved father.

The choir sang two of Burleigh's arrangements, "Were You There" and "My Lord, What a Morning." When they concluded, Harry slowly rose to thank them with the aid of his son. He was slightly stooped over, and his hand shook rapidly as he spoke. Alston stood at his side, holding on to his father's arm to steady him. Burleigh spoke to his son as if he were the only person in the room. "My heart is warmed to hear these young people singing so wonderfully the songs of our people. My grandfather was a slave when he learned these songs from his mother, and he taught them to me." Alston smiled and shook his head in agreement, as if this were the first time he had heard all of this.

"My mother sang them while she cleaned the public school—she was fluent in three languages and could have taught there, but they wouldn't hire a colored woman at that time, so she got a job cleaning the school instead," Harry continued. "I sang them with my brother when we sailed on the Great Lakes. I also sang them to the great Bohemian composer Antonin Dvorak, who wrote them into his New World Symphony. I sang them for President Teddy Roosevelt and J. P. Morgan. I even sang them for the King of England, himself."

Suddenly Burleigh looked up and around at the people in attendance as if he had just noticed that they were in the room. He turned to the choir. They were spellbound by the words of the great Harry T. Burleigh. He was a living legend and the students gave him their full attention despite his unusual behavior. He pointed a shaking finger at them, betraying the fact that he had been paying attention the entire time. "You have learned these songs well," he said with the forcefulness of a college professor. "But don't just sing the words without feeling the feelings. These songs have life because they represent the lives of millions of people—men and women who toiled in chains under the whip; sorrowful souls who labored under bitter poverty and cruel racism; families that stayed together and prospered because of faith in God, education, and hard work. These songs helped them endure it all. Keep singing these songs, my friends. Don't ever stop singing them."

He nodded his head, looked down at the ground, and smiled. "I will soon be free from this world, like my mother and granddaddy before me." He looked back up at the students. "But these songs are a part of the soil, and they won't ever die. So sing them well, because when you do, they make us all free."

His words brought tears to the eyes of many in the auditorium. Even some of the orderlies and nurses were wiping their eyes.

"The great master, Dvorak, once said this to me, and now I say it to you." He paused for a moment, as if he were listening to another voice. Finally, he finished the thought. "Give the spirituals to the world, young people. Give these songs to the world." He too had tears in his eyes as he turned back to the elderly patients gathered for the concert.

"Here I go, crying again. I get that from my mother." Around the room people chuckled at the comment. He smiled as he pulled out a handkerchief and wiped his eyes. Turning again to Alston, he declared, "My friends came by to honor me today." He surveyed the crowd and smiled as if he were talking to a room full of acquaintances. "All of my friends are here with me today. It is quite an honor. Thank you for being here for me."

When he finished, the students and residents stood to their feet and applauded the great musician as Alston helped him back to his seat. Burleigh sank into his chair and waved at the young singers as tears flowed down his cheeks.

Late in 1949, Harry began to have a peculiar vision, different from the ones he had seen before. He saw a ship coming from heaven. Somehow he knew that the Lord had sent it, and it would arrive for him soon. He felt an urge to have his things packed, though he had few belongings at the nursing home.

Every day Harry would shuffle around the small room pulling his clothes out of the drawers and closets, folding them, and placing them on the bed. As he worked he repeatedly announced to Alston and the nurses, "I've got to get my trunk ready. The ship is coming for me." As he searched for his steamer trunk, Alston quietly picked up the clothes and placed them back in the drawers. For more than a week this scenario was repeated dozens of times as Harry anxiously prepared for the arrival of the ship.

On September 12, 1949, Harry T. Burleigh was waiting for the ship to round the bend. From his bed he suddenly saw a grand white paddlewheel vessel come into view through the mist. Throwing off the covers, he stood and walked toward the vision. Harry easily slipped out of his room and onto a sloping hill leading to the riverbank. As he approached the river he could now see clearly his sweet mother leaning over the railing, smiling and waving her handkerchief. Harry could hardly believe what he was seeing, but it was there before him as plain as day.

A throng of people stood with her on the deck, clapping and cheering. Harry saw his father and his stepfather, his little sister Adah, his Aunt Louise—and his Aunt Jane, whom he had never met, but somehow he knew who she was. Next to them he noticed his good friends Booker T. Washington, John McCormack, Will Marion Cook, and Victor Herbert. Also at the railing was the great master, Dvorak himself, wearing his old familiar green vest.

At the front of the ship, dressed in a long black jacket with a black bow tie, and smiling proudly, was his granddaddy, Hamilton Waters. Harry cried out loudly, "Oh, my good Lord." His heart was bursting with joy as tears poured down his cheeks. With the sight of his grandfather he ran like a young man down the pier to meet the ship. "I knew you were coming," he hollered. "I've got my trunk packed, Grandpa, just like you told me to." Hamilton clapped his hands together and raised them above his head, shaking them triumphantly. The grand ship slowly pulled up to the pier as Harry's loved ones gathered near the gate to greet him. Before the vessel could come to a complete stop, Harry leapt from the pier and into the arms of his sweet mama.

At 6:15 a.m., the ship left the dock with Harry on board and drifted toward the middle of the river amid the cheers, hugs, and kisses from his loved ones. As Harry embraced his grandfather, the former slave began singing his favorite spiritual, "Swing Low, Sweet Chariot." One by one his family and friends joined in. Finally Harry wiped the tears from his eyes with his mother's handkerchief and joined in the song as the ship turned and moved upriver.

> Swing low, sweet chariot
> Comin' for to carry me home
> Swing low, sweet chariot
> Comin' for to carry me home

Harry T. Burleigh was free—he was finally free.

Acknowledgments

Many thanks to the late Charles Kennedy, founder of the Harry T. Burleigh Society, whose tireless efforts to keep Burleigh's legacy alive first inspired me to pursue this project. Thanks also to his wife, Cindy, who has been a friend and encourager over the years. I want to extend my sincere gratitude to my agent, David Van Diest, of the D. C. Jacobson Literary Agency, and his wife, Sarah, for your ongoing support and friendship. Thank you to my professors at Regent University, including Dr. Bob Schihl, Dr. Greg Stone, Dr. Corne' Bekker, Dr. Timothy Wright, Dr. Doug Tarpley, Professor John Lawing, and Dr. Kathleen Reid-Martinez. Thanks also to Dr. Terry Lindvall, Dr. George Selig, Dr. Gil Elvgren, and the members of the Shorehaven Group for their constructive criticism. Thanks to Georgia Shaffer and Linda Jewell for reading the manuscript and giving your generous input. My gratitude to Cecil Murphey for being a mentor and spiritual father, not only to me but to so many others. Thank you to Bob and Gloria Slosser for your friendship and vision.

Thanks to Josephine Herrald Love and Ada Lawrence for your personal memories of Harry T. Burleigh. Thanks to Anne Key Simpson for her biography, *Hard Trials: The Life and Music of Harry T. Burleigh*. Thanks to Dr. Jean Elizabeth Snyder for her excellent dissertation, "Harry T. Burleigh and the Creative Expression of Bi-Musicality."

Acknowledgments

Thanks to Harry T. Burleigh II and Harry T. Burleigh III for your encouragement. Thanks to Annita Andrick, archivist at the Erie County Historical Society. Thanks to Earleen Glaser of the Sister Mary Lawrence Franklin Archival Center at Mercyhurst College. Thanks to the staff of the Schomburg Center for Research in Black Culture in Harlem, New York.

I want to express my appreciation to my professional colleagues who have encouraged me in the writing of this book, including Christopher Sloan, Twila Belk, Torry Martin, Diana Flegal, James Scott Bell, Jeff Gerke, Gerry Wakeland, John Van Diest, David and Sheila Kudrick, Marita Noon, Florence Littauer, Gordon Robertson, Demetria Stallings, Joel Natalie, Chris Carpenter, Hannah Goodwyn, Beth Patch, Janet White, Marlene Bagnull, and Kenny Jackson. Thanks to my fellow scribes in the One Voice Christian Writers Group. Thanks to my parents, Clemens and Carol von Buseck, for inspiring me with your love of God and of the arts. Thanks to my brothers and sisters who are all artists and lovers of Jesus—Barbie, Jennie, Scott, Dawn, Sean, and Erin. Thank you to my children, Aaron, David, Margo, Victoria, Christen, and Kevin. Finally, thank you to my wife, Robin, for your ongoing love, support, and encouragement.

Bibliography

Aborn, Merton Robert. "The Influence on American Musical Culture of Dvorak's Sojourn in America." PhD diss., Indiana University, 1965.

Allen, William Francis, Charles Pickard War, and Lucy McKim Garrison. *Slave Songs of the United States*. New York: A. Simpson and Co., 1867.

Allison, Roland. *Classification of the Vocal Works of Harry T. Burleigh (1866–1949) and Some Suggestions for Their Use in Teaching Diction in Singing*. PhD diss., Indiana University, 1965. Ann Arbor: UMI, 1973.

America Online. "White Star Firsts." *Liners of the Olympic Class*. http://members.aol.com/Aravantis/olympicclass/firsts.htm.

Baker, Theodore. *Baker's Biographical Dictionary of Musicians*. 5th ed. New York: Schirmer, 1958. 382.

Ball, Sarah B. Private correspondence to Mr. J. W. Henderson of the New York Public Library. August 12, 1956.

Beckett, Henry. "A Mighty Voice at 77." *New York Post*. April 24, 1944.

Bohle, Bruce, ed. *The International Cyclopedia of Music and Musicians*. New York: Dodd, Mead and Company, 1975.

Bullock, Ralph W. *In Spite of Handicaps*. New York: Association Press, 1927.

Burleigh, Harry T. "Letter to the National Association for the Advancement of Colored People." Press release. November 10, 1922.

———. *The Spirituals of Harry T. Burleigh*. Melville, NY: Belwin-Mills Publishing Corporation, 1984.

Campbell, Bill. "Erie Composer Harry T. Burleigh Contributed Much." *Erie Biography*. September 13, 1949.

Carpenedo, Karen. "Harry T. Burleigh Buried in Erie." *Times-News* (May 29, 1994): A1.

Charlton, Mellville. "Harry T. Burleigh." *Dunbar News*. January 22, 1932.

Clapham, John. *Antonin Dvorak, Musician and Craftsman*. New York: St. Martin's Press, 1966.

Cuney-Hare, Maud. *Negro Musicians and Their Music*. Washington, DC: Associated Publishers, Inc., 1936. Repr. New York: Da Capo Press, 1974.

De Lerma, Dominique Rene. *Black Musicians in Our Culture*. Kent, OH: Kent State University Press, 1970.

———. "Classical Music in Black and White." *National Public Radio*. 1998.

Eaton, Eleanor. "Fiftieth Anniversary of Harry Thacker Burleigh's Membership in the Choir of St. George's Church." St. George's Episcopal Church press release. February 5, 1944.

Erie Daily Times. "An Inspiring Erie Story." March 4, 1981.

Erie Dispatch-Herald. "Great Revival of Music After War Seen by Harry T. Burleigh." 1944.

———. "Harry Burleigh Is Paid Tribute by New Yorker." March 21, 1937.

———. "In Memoriam: Harry T. Burleigh." September 13, 1949.

Erie Morning Gazette. Untitled article. December 2, 1888.

Erie Observer. Untitled obituary. February 27, 1873.

Finck, Henry. *My Adventures in the Golden Age of Music*. New York: Funk and Wagnalls, 1926. Repr. New York: Da Capo Press, 1971.

Forth. "Harry Burleigh, Singer-Composer and Churchman." April 1944, 18–19.

Hammond, Lily Hardy. *In the Vanguard of a Race*. New York: Council of Women for Home Missions and Missionary Education Movement of the United States and Canada, 1922.

Hampson, Thomas. "Henry Thacker Burleigh (1866–1949)." *I Hear America Singing*. http://www.pbs.org/wnet/ihas/composer/burleigh.html.

Hampton School Journal. Erie County Historical Society. Harry T. Burleigh Collection.

Handy, William Christopher. *Negro Authors and Composers of the United States*. New York: Handy Brothers Music, 1938. Repr. New York: AMS Press, 1976.

Hauser, Dorothy Drummon. "Man with a Glory." *Newark News*. November 1, 1970.

Hawley, Barbara. "Burleigh: He Attributes His Success to Three Sources." *Erie Biography*. March 11, 1928.

Hicks, James L. "Millionaires, Plain People Mourn at Burleigh's Rites." *Journal and Guide*. September 24, 1949.

Hughes, Edwin. "New York Church Pays Tribute to Burleigh." *Musical America* (April 12, 1924): 21–27.

Jablonski, Edward. *The Encyclopedia of American Music*. New York: Doubleday, 1981. 115.

Janifer, Ellsworth. "Harry T. Burleigh, Ten Years Later." *Phylon* 21 (1960): 144–54.

Johnson, James Weldon. *Black Manhattan*. New York: James Weldon Johnson, 1930. Repr. New York: Atheneum, 1977.

———. *Along This Way: The Autobiography of James Weldon Johnson*. New York: Viking Press, 1933. Repr. New York: Da Capo Press, 1961.

Jones, Randye L. "H. T. Burleigh (1866–1949)." *Afro-Centric Voices*. http://www.afrovoices.com/burleigh.html.

The Juilliard School. "The Juilliard School: A Brief History." http://www.juilliard.edu/about/brief-history.

Kennedy, Charles, Jr. "Second Look: Why Burleigh Is Important To Us." *Morning News* (February 16, 1994): A7.

Kramer, A. Walter. "H. T. Burleigh: Composer by Divine Right and 'The American Coleridge-Taylor.'" *Musical America* (April 29, 1916): 25.

Lee, Henry. "Swing Low, Sweet Chariot." *Coronet* 22 (July 1947): 54–60.

Locke, Alain LeRoy. *The Negro and His Music: Negro Art, Past and Present*. New York: Arno Press and *New York Times*, 1969. 106–7; 118–21.

Lowry, Raymond W. "Harry Burleigh: Singer Superb." *The Dallas Morning News*. September 3, 1970.

Marsh, John L. "Harry Thacker Burleigh: Hard Knocks and Triumphant Days." *Journal of Erie Studies*, 1980. 18–28.

McKee, Elmore M. "Burleigh: The Man, His Music, His Mission." Sermon at St. George's Episcopal Church, New York: May 4, 1980.

———. "Harry T. Burleigh Funeral Program." September 15, 1949.

———. "Harry T. Burleigh Obituary." St. George's Bulletin, October 2, 1949.

———. "The Spirituals—and Mr. Burleigh." St. George's Bulletin, May 21, 1939.

McNamara, Daniel. "Harry T. Burleigh: The Student That Inspired Dvorak." *New York Dispatch-Herald.* August 14, 1938.

Miller, John. "A twentieth century history of Erie County, Pennsylvania: a narrative account of its historic progress, its people, and its principal interests." Erie County Historical Society: 320. New York Public Library Online Archive. http://www.archive.org/details/twentiethcentury01mill.

Murray, Charlotte W. "The Story of Harry T. Burleigh." *The Hymn* 17:4 (October 1966): 101–11.

National Public Radio. "Interview with Dominique-Rene de Lerma." August 1997.

Nelson, S. B. *Nelson's Biographical Dictionary and Historical Reference Book of Erie County.* Erie, PA: S. B. Nelson, 1896.

The New Deal. "How Harry T. Burleigh Rose to Fame and Fortune." Erie Public Library Burleigh Collection.

———. Untitled article, 9. Repr. Jean Snyder. *Harry T. Burleigh and the Creative Expression of Bi-musicality.* PhD diss., University of Pittsburgh, 1992.

New York Age. "Burleigh Bier Seen By Many." September 17, 1949.

———. "Burleigh Sings Before King." July 16, 1908.

———. "Mr. Burleigh Sails for Europe." May 21, 1908.

New York Amsterdam News. "WCBS Pays Tribute to Harry Burleigh." n.d.

New York Evening Post. "Negro Singer Long at St. George's." March 22, 1924.

New York Herald Tribune. "Burleigh at 79 Sings 'Palms' at 52nd Service." April 15, 1946.

———. "Burleigh Sings 'Palms' on 46th Palm Sunday." March 18, 1940.

———. "Church Honors Harry Burleigh For 50 Years' Service in Choir." February 5, 1944.

———. "Harry Burleigh Leaves Choir at St. George's." November 19, 1946.

———. "Harry T. Burleigh Is Dead at 82; Sang for 52 Years at St. George's." September 13, 1949.

———. "'The Palms' Sung by Burleigh for 41st Year at St. George's." April 15, 1935.

———. Untitled article. April 15, 1935.

New York Sun. "St. George's Choir Sings." December 12, 1924.

New York World. "Harry T. Burleigh Honored To-Day at St. George's." March 30, 1924.

———. "Negro Baritone Is Paid Tribute in Old St. George's." March 31, 1924.

New York World Telegram. "'Sweet Chariot' Inspired Anton Dvorak to Immortalize Negro Spirituals." September 12, 1941.

The New Yorker. Untitled article. January 16, 1926.

Rainsford, William Stephen. *The Story of a Varied Life; An Autobiography*. New York: Doubleday, 1922. 266–67. New York Public Library Online Archive. http://www.archive.org/details/MN5045ucmf_2.

Reasons, George and Sam Patrick. "Burleigh—Saved Negro Spirituals." *Evening Star*. August 1, 1970.

Reed, Sarah. "Address by Miss Sarah Reed at the One-Hundredth Anniversary of the Founding of St. Paul's." St. Paul's Episcopal Church Archives, Erie, PA. March 15, 1927.

Riis, Thomas L. *Just Before Jazz: Black Musical Theater in New York, 1890–1915*. Washington, DC: Smithsonian Institution Press, 1989.

Roberts, Mili. "Erie Black Became Famed Composer." *Erie Daily Times*. September 19, 1970.

Sadie, Stanley, ed. *The New Grove Dictionary of Music and Musicians*. Washington, DC: Macmillan Publishers, 1980.

Sample, James. "Edward MacDowell—Harry T. Burleigh: An Analogy." Unpublished essay. Erie, PA. 1994.

Seifert, Berta. "Resolution on the Death of Our Beloved Member, Mrs. Elmendorf." Woman's Friendly Society of St. Paul's Church, Erie, PA. March 20, 1903.

Seton, Marie. *Paul Robeson*. London: Dennish Dobson, 1958.

Simpson, Anne K. "The Amateur Historian at Work: Norman Tyler Sobel and Harry T. Burleigh." *Journal of Erie Studies* 16 (Spring 1987): 63–69.

———. *Hard Trials: The Life and Music of Harry T. Burleigh*. Metuchen, NJ: Scarecrow Press, 1990.

———. *Norman Tyler Sobel's Unfinished Dream*. Erie County Historical Society, 1994.

Skvorecky, Josef. *Dvorak in Love*. Toronto: Lester and Orpen Dennys Limited, 1983.

Snyder, Jean E. "Review of *Hard Trials* by Anne K. Simpson." *American Music* 12.2 (Summer 1994): 197.

————. *Harry T. Burleigh and the Creative Expression of Bi-musicality: A Study of an African-American Composer and the American Art Song.* PhD diss., University of Pittsburgh, 1992. Ann Arbor: UMI, 1992. 9304259.

Sobel, Norman Tyler. *Biographical Sketch of Harry Thacker Burleigh, Including the Part Played by Isador Sobel and Norman Tyler Sobel.* Burleigh Collection: Erie County Historical Society. 1980.

Southall, Geneva. "Black Composers and Religious Music." *The Black Perspective in Music* 2:1 (1974): 80–84.

Southern, Eileen. *Biographical Dictionary of Afro-American and African Musicians.* Westport, CT: Greenwood Press, 1982.

————. *The Music of Black Americans: A History.* New York: W. W. Norton and Company, 1971.

State of Maryland. "Bill of Sale for Lovey Waters." Department of General Services. Hall of Records. Annapolis, MD, 1832. Burleigh Collection: Erie County Historical Society.

————. "Deed of Manumission for Hamilton Waters." Department of General Services. Hall of Records. Annapolis, MD, 1832. Burleigh Collection: Erie County Historical Society.

————. "Certificate of Freedom for Hamilton Waters and Lovey Waters." Department of General Services. Hall of Records. Annapolis, MD, 1832. Burleigh Collection: Erie County Historical Society.

Still, William Grant. "The Negro Musician in America." *Music Educators Journal* 56.5 (January 1970): 100–101, 157–61.

Tamplin, Lois M. "Composer Harry Burleigh Returns Home to Erie." *Music Clubs Magazine* (Spring 1995): 14.

Thompson, Sarah S. *Journey from Jerusalem: An Illustrated Introduction to Erie's African-American History, 1795–1995.* Erie, PA: Erie County Historical Society Publications, 1996.

Time. "Harry Burleigh's 50th." February 14, 1944.

Tortolano, William. *Samuel Coleridge-Taylor, Anglo-Black Composer, 1875–1912.* Metuchen, NJ: Scarecrow Press, 1977.

Turner, Patricia. *Dictionary of Afro-American Performers.* New York: Garland Publishing, 1990. 82–89, 116–17.

Walton, Lester A. "Harry T. Burleigh Honored Today at St. George's." *New York World.* March 30, 1924. Repr. *The Black Perspective in Music* 2.1 (1974): 80–84.

Washington, Booker T. *Booker T. Washington Papers*. Edited by Louis R. Harlan and Raymond W. Smock. Urbana: University of Illinois Press, 1977.

Washington Post. Untitled article. 1890. Repr. Jean E. Snyder. *Harry T. Burleigh and the Creative Expression of Bi-musicality*. 1992.

Washington Tribune. Untitled article. May 18, 1940.

Waters, Edward M. *Victor Herbert, A Life in Music*. New York: Macmillan, 1955.

Wellejus, Ed. "A Biography of One of Erie's Greatest." *Erie Daily Times*. January 21, 1991.

Whittlesey, Dr. Federal Lee. "A Service of Negro Spirituals Program." Church of the Covenant, Erie, PA. June 11, 1944.

Dr. Craig von Buseck is a published author, a contributing writer for CBN.com and Cindy Jacobs's Reformation Prayer Network, and the editor of ChurchWatch.co. He holds a Doctor of Ministry and an MA in religious journalism from Regent University in Virginia Beach, Virginia.

His books include *Praying the News: Your Prayers Are More Powerful Than You Know*, cowritten with *700 Club* news anchor Wendy Griffith; *NetCasters: Using the Internet to Make Fishers of Men*; and *Seven Keys to Hearing God's Voice*. His latest book is called *Yes, I Can*, which he cowrote with Dr. James Post, a quadriplegic medical doctor. Along with his work at CBN, he has written for *Charisma* magazine, the Israeli Bureau of Tourism, Nicky Cruz Ministries, the Christian Coalition, Regent University, and several other Christian magazines. He has taught as an adjunct professor in the Regent University schools of Divinity, Communication, Business, Government, and the College of Arts and Sciences.

Craig has extensive ministry and speaking experience. He travels often to speak at conferences, professional events, and writer events. For more than ten years, he served on the Executive Board of the Internet Evangelism Network (IEN). Craig has been a keynote speaker at the Write-to-Publish Conference at Wheaton College; the Blue Ridge Christian Writers Conference; the Colorado Christian Writers Conference; the Philadelphia Christian Writers Conference; the Florida Christian Writers Conference; the CLASS Christian Writers Conference; and the Indy Christian Writers Conference. He has also served as a faculty member at the Jerry Jenkins's "Writing for the

Soul" Christian Writers Conference and the Heart of America Christian Writers Conference.

Craig and his wife, Robin, live in Elizabeth City, North Carolina.

Contact: craigvonbuseck@gmail.com
P.O. Box 2714
Elizabeth City, NC 27909

www.vonbuseck.com
www.churchwatch.co
http://www.facebook.com/craigvonbuseck
http://twitter.com/craigvonbuseck

.